T0271236

Conversations with
Angela Davis

Literary Conversations Series
Monika Gehlawat
General Editor

Conversations with Angela Davis

Edited by Sharon Lynette Jones

University Press of Mississippi / Jackson

The University Press of Mississippi is the scholarly publishing agency of
the Mississippi Institutions of Higher Learning: Alcorn State University,
Delta State University, Jackson State University, Mississippi State University,
Mississippi University for Women, Mississippi Valley State University,
University of Mississippi, and University of Southern Mississippi.

www.upress.state.ms.us

The University Press of Mississippi is a member
of the Association of University Presses.

First printing 2021
∞

Library of Congress Cataloging-in-Publication Data

Names: Jones, Sharon L. (Sharon Lynette), editor.
Title: Conversations with Angela Davis / Sharon Lynette Jones.
Other titles: Literary conversations series.
Description: Jackson: University Press of Mississippi, 2021. | Series:
    Literary conversations series | Includes bibliographical references and index.
Identifiers: LCCN 2021013966 (print) | LCCN 2021013967 (ebook) |
    ISBN 978-1-4968-2957-3 (hardback) | ISBN 978-1-4968-2958-0 (trade paperback) |
    ISBN 978-1-4968-2959-7 (epub) | ISBN 978-1-4968-2960-3 (epub) |
    ISBN 978-1-4968-2961-0 (pdf) | ISBN 978-1-4968-2962-7 (pdf)
Subjects: LCSH: Davis, Angela Y. (Angela Yvonne), 1944—Interviews. | Black
    Panther Party. | African American women political activists—Interviews. |
    African American women—Interviews. | Women communists—United States—
    Interviews. | African Americans—Civil rights. | Civil rights workers—
    United States—Interviews.
Classification: LCC E185.97.D23 C66 2021 (print) | LCC E185.97.D23 (ebook) |
    DDC 322.4/2092 [B]—dc23
LC record available at https://lccn.loc.gov/2021013966
LC ebook record available at https://lccn.loc.gov/2021013967

British Library Cataloging-in-Publication Data available

Books by Angela Y. Davis

Angela Davis: An Autobiography. International, 2018. (Random House, 1974)
Women, Race & Class. Vintage Books, 1983. (Random House, 1981)
Women, Culture & Politics. Random House, 1989.
Blues Legacies and Black Feminisms: Gertrude "Ma" Rainey, Bessie Smith, and Billie Holiday. Vintage Books, 1998.
Are Prisons Obsolete? Seven Stories Press, 2003. (Angela Davis et al.)
The Meaning of Freedom: And Other Difficult Dialogues. City Lights Publishers, 2012.

Books Edited by Angela Y. Davis

Beyond the Frame: Women of Color and Visual Representation, edited by Neferti X. M. Tadiar and Angela Y. Davis. Palgrave Macmillan, 2005.
If They Come in the Morning: Voices of Resistance, edited by Angela Y. Davis et al. Third Press, 1971.

Contents

Introduction

Angela Davis has profoundly influenced the discourses on social justice in relationship to race, gender, and class nationally and internationally through her writings and her role in organizations such as the Communist Party and the Student Nonviolent Coordinating Committee (SNCC) in the past, and her more recent activism through the prison abolitionist organization Critical Resistance, along with being an honorary co-chair for the Women's March during 2017, which occurred in Washington, DC (Long). Additionally, her work being university professor for UCLA, San Francisco State University, and University of California, Santa Cruz (where she became professor emerita in 2008), provides an example of her commitment to education and raising awareness about the social, political, cultural, and/or economic issues related to social justice. Davis, who earned a bachelor's degree in French literature from Brandeis University in 1965, a master's degree in philosophy from University of California, San Diego, during 1968, and a PhD, awarded by Humboldt University in Germany, is a highly respected scholar and educator who has continued to travel nationally and internationally, speaking at colleges, universities, conferences, and elsewhere, providing both older and younger generations with her extensive knowledge about human rights, animal rights (Ta), and environmental rights (Ta; Rubio) in relation to the past, the present, and the future. She is a prolific writer. Her publications include *Angela Davis: An Autobiography* (1974), *Women, Race & Class* (1981/1983), *Women, Culture & Politics* (1989), *Blues Legacies and Black Feminisms: Gertrude "Ma" Rainey, Bessie Smith, and Billie Holiday* (1998), and *Are Prisons Obsolete?* (2003). She co-edited with Neferti X. M. Tadier *Beyond the Frame: Women of Color and Visual Representation* (2005), and she contributed to and was involved in the preparation of *If They Come in the Morning: Voices of Resistance* (1971). The recent acquisition of more than 150 boxes with Davis's archival materials by Harvard University's Schlesinger Library (Bruzek and Becker), the "Radical Commitments: The Life and Legacy of Angela Davis" Conference scheduled for October 28–29, 2019, at Harvard University, the inclusion of

Angela Davis in the National Women's Hall of Fame in 2019 (Pluviose), and a 2018 Fred L. Shuttlesworth Human Rights Award by the Birmingham Civil Rights Institute (Danielle) demonstrate the continued relevance and recognition of Davis as a scholar, educator, and activist. Despite a controversy that erupted in 2019 due to the Birmingham Civil Rights Institute rescinding that award, reportedly "because of her long support of the Boycott, Divestment, and Sanctions (BDS) movement in support of Palestine," there was an award reinstatement by the Birmingham Civil Rights Institute later that year (Johnson). This reinstatement occurred following "the resignation of several board members" (Johnson) for the Birmingham Civil Rights Institute, as well as responses and reactions by other people critical about the rescinding of the Fred A. Shuttleworth Award. In April 2019 Angela Davis participated in Birmingham, Alabama, events, including "Power to the People: Activism and Justice Forum," as well as "A Conversation with Dr. Angela Davis" (Johnson). By August 2019 it was reported that "Dr. Angela Davis has agreed to accept the 2019 Fred L. Shuttlesworth Award from the Birmingham Civil Rights Institute" (Johnson). In 2020 Angela Davis was the recipient of that aforementioned award in an online event (Wright). According to Erica Wright, "during the virtual ceremony held on Juneteenth, Davis was presented the award which honors outstanding individuals for significant contributions to human and civil rights."

Although interviews of Davis have appeared previously in other notable books, *Conversations with Angela Davis* differs from other texts due to the depth, scope, range, and number of interviews. For example, *The Angela Davis Reader* (1998), edited by Joy James, contains two interviews from 1994 and 1995; *Abolition Democracy: Beyond Empire, Prisons, and Torture: Interviews with Angela Davis* (2005) contains four interviews; *Freedom Is a Constant Struggle: Ferguson, Palestine, and the Foundations of a Movement* (2016), edited by Frank Barat, contains three interviews from 2014; and *African American Philosophers, 17 Conversations* (1998), edited by George Yancy, contains one interview of Angela Davis. These interviews in *Conversations with Angela Davis*, ranging from mass-circulation publications to highly specialized peer-reviewed academic journals, from 1972 to 2016, testify to Davis's commitment over several decades as a significant writer, philosopher, and social justice activist in relationship to social, economic, political, and cultural transformations for several decades nationally and globally. Thus, the reader is able to chart the growth, development, and evolution of Davis's intellectual thought and activism over a sustained and extended period of time in comparison to other previously published books containing interviews of Davis.

The earliest examples of interviews of Angela Davis at the national and international levels include interviews of Davis while she was jailed in 1972, which provided her an opportunity to shape, frame, control, and direct the social, historical, and cultural contexts of her captivity as a means of eliciting support for her defense in publications such as the *Black Scholar* in 1972. The *Black Scholar* is an academic peer-reviewed journal that targets a college-educated readership of undergraduate students, graduate students, scholars, and professors with an interest in Black studies and/or African American studies. Thus, the readership of this journal would have held comparable or similar academic credentials to Angela Davis and would have undoubtedly been a group of people among her peers in higher education, given her status as a former professor at UCLA and civil rights activist at the time. In "A Conversation with Angela," which appears in *Black Scholar* (March–April 1972), Rev. Cecil Williams interviews Angela Davis while she is incarcerated in Santa Clara Jail, prior to her bail and acquittal during 1972. The interview also occurs during the Free Angela Davis movement, an international campaign to raise money to fund her legal defense and highlight the plight of people imprisoned for political reasons. The questions and answers highlight her social, political, and economic viewpoints in relationship to civil rights activism, membership in the Communist Party, and her subsequent incarceration. This 1972 interview from jail in Santa Clara County is significant for revealing her attitudes and beliefs about the Black Panthers, the Soledad Brothers, communism, the Free Angela movement, gender, and the relationship between prisons and US culture. Also, historically it bears significance in illustrating her ideas when she was incarcerated and before acquittal. This interview humanizes Angela Davis because it presents her as a complex and nuanced individual whose plight can be understood alongside that of other people incarcerated in part due to their politics and resistance to repressive forces.

During the 1970s after her acquittal, Davis continued to engage in social justice activism related to criminal justice. In "Interview with Angela Davis," by Mike Hannigan and Tony Platt, which appears in *Crime & Social Justice* in Summer 1975, Davis speaks about the National Alliance Against Racist and Political Repression and the organization's activism surrounding race, gender, and/or class equity. This interview begins with information about National Alliance Against Racist and Political Repression, including its founding during 1973, Davis's role as cochair, and its commitment to social justice through an interracial and interethnic coalition of people. This interview reflects Davis's belief in coalition building with people from a variety of backgrounds and perspectives. It also reflects her continued concern about the relationship between the government and what she considers to be repressive practices and actions. Also, the interview demonstrates how Davis's own history as an incarcerated woman contributes to her ideas about social justice or civil rights, in *Crime and Social Justice*, a peer-reviewed journal appealing to undergraduates, graduate students, and professors in higher education interested in civil rights.

Angela Davis sought political office in 1980 and 1984 as a candidate in the vice-president slot (Communist Party). Throughout the 1980s she continued to be actively involved and engaged in social, political, and/or economic activism, which is revealed in the interview by Kum-Kum Bhavnani, "Complexity, Activism, Optimism: An Interview with Angela Y. Davis," published in 1989 in *Feminist Review*, a peer-reviewed scholarly journal with primary appeal to students, scholars, and professors within academic contexts in the discipline of women, gender, and sexuality studies. The interview took place in July of 1988 in Berkeley, California. Davis was still a Communist Party member, and she explores her connection with communism in the interview. She explains that she gravitated toward the Communist Party because she did not feel there was a space for her in the women's rights movement at the time, although she acknowledges the progress that has been made with the women's movement in terms of social justice, pointing out that white feminist Gloria Steinem served in a treasury position for her legal defense fund. Optimism is an attitude that Davis expresses in relationship to the future of social justice, citing Jesse Jackson's 1988 candidacy for president of the United States as an example because of his diverse group of supporters.

In addition to looking at the plight and status of Black women as a whole in the US, Davis also addresses how race and gender influenced her own history with incarceration. After recounting the circumstances related to her fugitive status and later incarceration from 1970 to 1972, she claims that her historical research on gender, race, and oppression enabled her to successfully defend herself while jailed. Looking at gender from a global or international perspective, Davis discusses her travels in Cuba in the 1960s and 1970s, and her interest in the National Black Women's Health Project, and showcases an awareness of how gender, class, and religion intersect in praising the work of feminist Jewish activists supporting workers' rights. Additionally, Davis also expresses support and solidarity for gay as well as lesbian rights in relationship to social justice. Davis concludes the interview by stressing the importance of continuing a tradition of activist activity.

By the late 1980s, Angela Davis continued to be viewed as an important contributor to the civil rights movement. Not surprisingly, she was interviewed for the *Eyes on the Prize II* documentary series, which chronicled people, places, and events vital to the civil rights movement in the United States. In this 1989 interview by Terry Rockefeller and Louis Massiah, Angela Davis comments on studying abroad in Europe, her role in the Communist Party, and student activism at UC San Diego, the controversial firings that happened to her while she was a faculty member at UCLA, her experience in jail, her commitment to prison abolition, her experience as an undergraduate attending Brandeis University, and her family's support of her campaign to free her when she was jailed during the 1970s. This transcript's importance lies in the fact that it contextualizes her role in the civil rights movement, and it also demonstrates how in the late 1980s, Angela Davis was still considered to be a voice and authority on social justice activism.

Angela Davis's interest as a scholar and activist centers around a variety of topics, including the relationship between music and identity in relation to social justice. The interview "Nappy Happy," which appears in *Transition* in 1992, is evidence of that interest and her willingness to debate and exchange ideas with rap artist Ice Cube. The introduction to the article highlights the relevance and significance of Ice Cube (ex-member of NWA, a successful rap group popular in the 1980s and 1990s) and acknowledges Ice Cube's successful post-NWA career with his recordings *Amerikkka's Most Wanted* and *Death Certificate*, as well as his appearance within movies and his role as a product endorser. Additionally, this section of the article indicates Davis's concerns about *Death Certificate*, noting that her lack of awareness about a song called "Black Korea," which she calls "problematic," would have influenced and affected the questioning within this interview.

In the interview, a variety of topics are discussed, including hip-hop, law enforcement, parent–child relationships, gender, reproductive rights, religion, politics, integration, higher education, and identity. In fact, the title of the article stems from when Ice Cube describes himself as being "nappy happy" because he no longer felt a need for processed hair. The interview also contains a discussion relevant to activism in the African diaspora in reference to anti-apartheid activism in South Africa. Davis and Ice Cube also discuss the role of politics in relation to being an artist, with Ice Cube stressing how his own education and knowledge development related with spreading messages toward his consumers. The interview with Ice Cube and Angela Davis in the early 1990s shows her viewpoints in the context of the rising popularity of hip-hop music in the 1990s, in the peer-reviewed academic journal, which focuses on social, political, economic, and cultural issues relevant to the African diaspora.

"An Interview with Angela Davis" by Nina Siegal, which was published in September/October 1998 of *Ms.* Magazine, reflects important social, economic, and cultural concerns relevant to the 1990s as individuals such as Angela Davis tried to continue the gains in civil rights as a result of activism in the 1960s and the 1970s. "An Interview with Angela Davis" also appeals to a feminist audience readership in a mass-market and mass-circulation publication. The interview emphasizes the relationships between race, class, motherhood, gender, and imprisonment within the United States and Cuba. The interview illustrates Davis's continued commitment to prison abolition.

In the twenty-first century, Angela Davis continues to be viewed as a source of knowledge about civil rights, and the interviews appearing post-2000 show her considerable knowledge of race, gender, class, politics, and incarceration in the past and the present. "Angela Davis" by David Barsamian, which appears in *The Progressive* in 2001, begins with a brief biographical overview, which also identifies Davis as a University of California Santa Cruz faculty member. In the interview Davis comments about herself in a historical context, emphasizing her attempts at personal growth as well as development, pointing out that she has changed and doesn't view herself as having the answer to everything. She says she belongs to the Green Party and is no longer a Communist Party member. This interview appearing in *The Progressive* is aimed at a more general but progressive-minded audience, in comparison to the readership of peer-review journals. Its value lies in how it reveals that Angela Davis continues to be an important symbol of socially progressive thought during the twenty-first century among readers in academic and nonacademic contexts.

In addition to her work as as an activist in behalf of social justice, Angela Davis is also a notable autobiographer (*Angela Davis: An Autobiography*, edited by Toni Morrison) and philosopher. The interview in *Radical Philosophy Review* by Angela Y. Davis and Eduardo Mendieta called "Politics and Prisons: An Interview with Angela Davis" in 2003 demonstrates her commitment to autobiography, philosophy, and prison reform in relationship to race, gender, and class. She discusses how the interview occurs thirty years since that autobiography was published. She claims that at the time of its publication, she was aware of her fame and the international support that helped to liberate her from prison. Her intention was writing an unconventional autobiographical text that reflected upon how social justice activism affected her. Davis acknowledges that her writing falls within traditions of literature about incarceration, and she mentions the influence of George Jackson (Soledad prisoner) upon her ideas, while also acknowledging the influence of Herbert Marcuse (her professor at Brandeis University and at University of California San Diego) on her political ideology.

As a notable activist on gender, race, and class issues and a symbol of social justice, Angela Davis's interviews have been included in documentary films such as *The House on Cocoa Road, Eyes on the Prize, 13th,* and *Free Angela & All Political Prisoners.* An interview that examines Angela Davis as the subject of a documentary appears in "Angela Davis on *Free Angela & All Political Prisoners*" by Livia Bloom Ingram in *Filmmaker Magazine* (September 15, 2012). The article begins with a quote from *Angela Davis: An Autobiography* about being apprehended in New York while a fugitive from the FBI as well as Davis's employment at UCLA being jeopardized in the 1960s due to her Communist Party membership. This brief introduction highlights Davis's dignified demeanor in spite of her challenging circumstances and how this is displayed within *Free Angela & All Political Prisoners,* directed by Shola Lynch. In the interview, Davis explains that she became connected with the movie *Free Angela & All Political Prisoners.* She is related to Eisa Davis, who portrays Angela Davis in some parts of this film. The interview's inclusion in *Filmmaker Magazine* demonstrates how during the twenty-first century Angela Davis continues to be a subject of interest among filmmakers and afficionados of cinema.

Although "Angela Davis" by Frank Barat, which appears in *New Internationalist* (March 2013), is a brief interview, its importance rests in the insights it provides about Angela Davis in her response to questions about the past, her age, politics, inspiration, fright, and "home." Davis discusses growing up in the racially segregated and sometimes violent southern USA. For Davis, the passage of time and age means she comprehends how being spiritually, physically, as well as mentally is important and the need for being in contact with younger individuals. Speaking politically, she examines the role of gender and violent activity, the plight of immigrants, and Palestinian rights. She admits being fearful that people won't recall the importance of individuals trying to transform societies, and she insists there needs to be more social justice activism. Davis states that her sense of feeling "at home" exists in being around individuals who are engaged in anticapitalist, antiracist, and antiheteropatriarchy work. The interview in *New Internationalist,* a magazine that includes articles about social, economic, and political issues, reveals that Davis continues to be a fierce advocate and promoter of civil rights domestically and globally in the second decade of the twenty-first century.

Davis's human rights activism is also highlighted in *Social Justice*'s "Interview with Angela Davis" by Tony Platt in 2014. This differs from the other interviews in this collection because of its context, which includes an audience present for the interview consisting of an international and national group of individuals as well as the presence of individuals studying a variety of subjects at institutions of higher learning. There is also a "Questions and Comments" portion of the interview, which promotes an interactive atmosphere. Davis comments on a variety of topics, including her teaching at and termination from UCLA in the late 1960s and early 1970s, her Communist past, her education at Elisabeth Irwin High School, Brandeis University, the Student Nonviolent Coordinating Committee, genders, the National Alliance Against Racist and Political Repression, the Black Women's Political Caucus, the Black Panthers, her incarceration during 1970–72, and prison abolition. In the "Questions and Comments" section, Angela Davis comments upon her work in spreading the use of "prison-industrial complex" terminology as a way of influencing how people perceive prisoners, as well as a conference by the organization Critical Resistance, which attracted thousands of individuals related to prison activism, drawing upon people nationally and internationally. She also expounds upon the gender inclusiveness of her prison abolitionist work and the role of the Quakers in the proliferation of prisons in the United States and in prison abolitionism.

In the article Davis also acknowledges the complexities of being politically engaged. She comments on how one can be both joyful and outraged as an activist. A person, according to Davis, must not be isolated. She mentions her practice of meditating as well as yoga in preparation for the interview in *Social Justice*. She also expresses the idea of being hopeful while yet also experiencing a nightmarish feeling, especially with concern about the then-impending election. She also warns people to be cautious about some people who are interested in prison reform when it is motivated by opposition to government's size. Davis feels there needs to be larger governmental role, with increases for education, helping people with psychological problems, and recreational opportunities. She also explains how Critical Resistance means thinking critically as well as resisting critically. The interview, which appears in a peer-reviewed academic journal appealing to a readership interested in civil rights movements, shows Davis to be a reflective, intelligent, and nuanced individual who avoids easy and facile responses to complicated topics of inquiry and discussion. Her commentary in *Social Justice* reveals a depth and complexity of thoughts, positions, and ideologies.

In "Angela Davis: 'There Is an Unbroken Line of Police Violence in the US That Takes Us All the Way Back to the Days of Slavery'" by Stuart Jeffries in *The Guardian* (December 14, 2014), Davis also comments on the relationship between the present and the past. In this interview she discusses race, law enforcement brutality, and oppression in the United States and in England. Davis addresses the death of Michael Brown, an African American man killed by a law enforcement officer in Ferguson, Missouri, and the lack of an indictment against the law enforcement officer by the grand jury in that case, placing it in a historical and social context in relation to race and justice. She also draws an analogy between George Zimmerman's shooting of Trayvon Martin, a Black youth in Florida, several years ago, with patrollers of enslaved people in the past. According to Davis, injustices and oppressions continue to exist, an example being a "prison industrial complex," which features a disproportionate number of racial minorities incarcerated who have no voting rights and few employment opportunities after they are freed from prisons within the United States. At the same time, Davis takes a globalist perspective, noting that Britain has more incarcerated Blacks than the USA, proportionally. Davis ties in a prison industrial complex to capitalism, pointing out that companies use incarcerated people as employees to earn profits. In this interview Davis resists holding then-president Barack Obama accountable for injustices or as the cause of societal inequities, suggesting that people must take responsibility for making the world better and not place the burden upon one person. The article also mentions how Angela Davis lectured on a Black woman named Marissa Alexander, who was sentenced to two decades when she fired "a warning shot over the head of her estranged, unharmed husband, who attacked and threatened to kill her," prior to Stuart Jeffries's (author of article) meeting with Davis. When Jeffries asks Davis why she mentioned Marissa Alexander at that lecture later, she states that women's incarceration experiences are not given enough attention. Jeffries also points out that following Davis's lecture during that previous day, Davis was asked by audience members about police who shot Black males not being incarcerated afterward, and about whether Beyoncé could be a terrorist. Davis responded to audience members, according to Jeffries, by expressing a positive reaction to Beyoncé's sampling a feminist address by the writer Chimamanda Ngozi Adichie. According to Jeffries, when asked about her comments about Beyoncé a day after the lecture, Davis said it is inappropriate to label Beyoncé as terroristic, because the language has been historically employed as a means of criminalizing liberatory activity.

Davis also comments on the plight of Ruchell Magee, a codefendant in 1972, in the *Guardian* interview. She points out that Magee was not acquitted and remains incarcerated, as do numerous people from the period of the Black Panthers. She does express happiness about Albert Woodfox of the Black Panthers being released following more than forty years' incarceration, but she questions the length of time he spent prior to being released. She also expresses dismay at the treatment of Black Panther Assata Shakur, "who was convicted as an accomplice to the murder forty years ago of a New Jersey state trooper" (according to the article) and concern about the potential for a mercenary individual capturing Shakur (exiled within Cuba) as a means of obtaining money from the FBI because she is on their list of fugitives. Davis also praises the Occupy social justice movements for their critique of capitalist enterprises. The interview in *The Guardian*, an international publication with a readership from a variety of backgrounds, demonstrates Davis's concern about the relationship between social and economic structures and race, class, and gender oppression.

The final interview featured in *Conversations with Angela Davis*, which is "The Radical Work of Healing: Fania and Angela Davis on a New Kind of Civil Rights Activism," in *Yes!* magazine (2016), by Sarah van Gelder, provides in-depth insight into the relationship between Angela Davis and her sister Fania Davis, and how their sisterhood has shaped their identities as activists. Both sisters comment on important issues related to identity and civil rights, including their childhood in Birmingham, Alabama, the bombing of the 16th Street Baptist Church in Birmingham, Alabama, and Fania Davis's role in the Free Angela movements during the 1970s. Most importantly, the interview between Fania Davis and Angela Davis shows the relevance of Angela Davis's family and kinship to her growth and development as a person in the past and in the present. This highly personal and engaging interview is aimed at a general audience. Unlike other interviews in *Conversations with Angela Davis*, it reveals a more personal side of Angela Davis as sister and daughter, while also demonstrating the shifts in her identity and purpose later in her life.

The interviews appearing in this volume of *Conversations with Angela Davis* present the interest in the life and views of Davis since the early 1970s up until now. The diversity of publications, ranging from mass-market and mass-circulation periodicals to peer-reviewed scholarly and specialized publications, reveals the broad range of readers interested in Davis's nuanced and complex perspectives. Although earlier published interviews of Davis tended to appear in the form of print publications, the popularity of the internet has led to some interviews appearing there. Collectively, these interviews in *Conversations with Angela Davis* show her engagement with political and civil rights organizations. The interviews chronicle her commitment to a host of issues, such as prison abolition, reproductive justice, gender equity, employment rights, Palestinian rights, antiracism advocacy, hip-hop, and anti-police-brutality activism. Angela Davis's views encompass local, regional, national, and global concerns within social, political, historical, cultural, literary, cinematic, musical, and/or philosophical contexts. Spanning 1972–2016, or approximately four decades, these interviews provide readers with an opportunity to better understand and comprehend the richness, vitality, and continued relevance of Davis as an activist, educator, intellectual, and author within national and global communities.

This volume would not have been possible without the support and encouragement of numerous people and institutions. I am grateful for the support of Katie Keene and Mary Heath at University Press of Mississippi. While working on this volume, I was the recipient of a professional development leave from Wright State University. I received a fellowship for archival research at the Stuart A. Rose Manuscript, Archives, and Rare Book Library at Emory University in Atlanta, Georgia. I am thankful to Dr. Pellom Mc-Daniels, Kathy Shoemaker, Courtney Chartier, and other staff of the Stuart A. Rose Manuscript, Archives, and Rare Book Library for their support, assistance, and guidance as I engaged in archival research. I was given the opportunity to present "Archives, Activisms, and Actions: Contextualizing the Interviews of Angela Davis" at the Stuart A. Rose Manuscript, Archives, and Rare Book Library at Emory University on October 29, 2018. I also wish to thank Dr. Letitia Campbell and Dr. Robert Franklin at Emory University's Candler School of Theology for the opportunity to present "Viewpoints about Angela Davis" to the class "Religion, Ethics and Civil Rights" on October 3, 2018. While at Emory University on October 10, 2018, I had the opportunity to attend a lecture by Angela Davis sponsored by the Candler School of Theology and talk to her afterward. I want to thank Dr. Catherine Frank at UNC Asheville, where I presented "Legacies of Engagement: Civil Rights Movements and Angela Davis" on October 17, 2018. I am thankful for the opportunity to speak about Angela Davis on October, 30, 2018 to the class "Global Influences and Major 20th Century African American Authors" at Spelman College, thanks to Dr. Donna Akiba Sullivan Harper. I also want to express gratitude to Dr. Leslie Carver, Dr. Amber Vlasnik, and

Autumn Monteforte at UC San Diego, where I spoke to students about Angela Davis and activism in "Constructing Past and Present Identities: Evaluating Depictions of Angela Davis in Popular Culture," as part of the Marshall College Lecture Series on November 8, 2018, at UC San Diego.

I also visited numerous archives in 2017 and 2018 as I engaged in research about Angela Davis. I am appreciative of the help and assistance of Chloe Morse-Harding and other staff at Brandeis University's Robert D. Farber University Archives & Special Collections, Bridget Whittle and other staff at McMaster University's William Ready Division of Archives and Research Collections, Jill Chancellor and other staff at Northeastern University's Archives and Special Collections, staff at the Schomburg Center for Research in Black Culture, Lynda Corey Claassen and other staff at UC San Diego Library's Special Collections and Archives, and Dunbar Library staff at Wright State University. I also appreciate the support of the following individuals: Dr. Emily Rutter; my colleagues in the Department of English Language and Literatures at Wright State University, the Women, Gender, and Sexuality Studies program at Wright State University, and the African and African American Studies program at Wright State University. Thanks to Dr. La Fleur Small, Dr. Tracy Snipe (whose class I lectured to about Angela Davis in Spring 2018 at Wright State University), Dr. Mary Beth Pringle, Dr. Linda Caron, Keith Jones, Emily Jones, Joe Jones, Rose Cuddy, Julie Snyder, William Loudermilk, Dr. Randall Burkett, Christine Alcosiba, Kathleen Cleaver, Dr. Barbara McCaskill, Dr. John Lowe, Dr. R. Baxter Miller, Jocelyn Robinson, Yemi Mahoney, Kari Kalve, Dr. Liesl Allingham, Dr. Dolan Hubbard, and countless others. Without the various types of support I received, this volume would not have been possible. Also, I wish to thank Angela Davis for her unwavering commitment to social justice, and for her graciousness when I spoke to her at Earlham College on April 3, 2019; Emory University on October 17, 2018; and September 22, 2017 at Ball State University. Also, I thank her for speaking at Wright State University on February 23, 2009, as part of the Presidential Lecture Series. Her work as a scholar, a writer, and an intellectual has been a guiding force and support through this project.

Bibliography

Bruzek, Alison, and Deborah Becker. "Angela Davis' Archive Finds a New Home at Harvard." Radcliffe Institute for Advanced Study Harvard University. Radio Boston WBUR.org, February 20, 2018, www.radcliffe.harvard.edu/news/in-news/angela-davis-archive-finds-new-home-harvard.

Danielle, Britni. "Angela Davis to Receive the Birmingham Civil Rights Institute's Highest Honor." *Essence*, October 22, 2018. www.essence.com/news/angela-davis-to-receive-the-birmingham-civil-rights-institutes-highest-honor/.

Davis, Angela Y. *Abolition Democracy: Beyond Empire, Prisons, and Torture.* Seven Stories Press, 2005.

Davis, Angela Y. *Freedom Is a Constant Struggle: Ferguson, Palestine, and the Foundations of a Movement.* Edited by Frank Barat. Haymarket Books, 2016.

James, Joy, ed. *The Angela Y. Davis Reader.* Blackwell, 1998.

Johnson, Roy S. "Dr. Angela Davis to Accept Once-Rescinded Fred L. Shuttlesworth Award." Al.com, August 29, 2019. https://www.al.com/news/birmingham/2019/08/dr-angela-davis-to-accept-once-rescinded-fred-l-shuttleworth-award.html.

Long, Stephanie. "In Case You Missed It: Must-See Highlights from the Women's March on Washington." *Newsone*, January 21, 2017. https://newsone.com/3646229/womens.

Pluviose, Davis. "Dr. Angela Davis among 2019 Women's Hall of Fame Inductees. *Diverse Issues in Higher Education*, July 12, 2019. https://diverseeducation.com/article/149627/.

Rubio, Carolina. "Angela Davis' Fight for Social Justice Continues." *The Sun Southwestern College*, April 13, 2017. www.theswcsun.com/angela-davis-fight-for-social-justice-continues/.

Ta, Linh. "Angela Davis: 'The Earth Is Being Poisoned for Generations to Come.'" *Des Moines Register*, September 29, 2016. www.desmoinesregister.com/story/news/politics/2016/09/29/angela-davis-earth-being-poisoned-generations-come/91271554/.

Wright, Erica. "Angela Davis Receives Birmingham's Top Civil Rights Award." *Birmingham Times*, June 20, 2020. https://www.birminghamtimes.com/2020/06/angela-davis-receives-birminghams-top-human-rights-award/.

Yancy, George, ed. *African-American Philosophers: 17 Conversations.* Routledge, 1998.

Chronology

1944   Angela Davis, who hails from Birmingham, Alabama, is born. Her
        mother is Sallye Davis, an educator. Her father is Frank C. Davis,
        a former educator who owns a gas station.

1959   She is a student at Elisabeth Irwin High School with American
        Friends Service Committee scholarship funding. While a student
        at New York City's Elisabeth Irwin High School, she resides with
        W. H. Melish (an Episcopal minister) and his family.

1961   Davis pursues an education at Brandeis University and majors
        in French literature, after earning a scholarship. During her first
        year, there are only three Black first-year students.

1962   Davis travels to Europe, participating in the Eighth World Festi-
        val for Youth and Students (Helsinki, Finland). When she arrives
        back in the United States, she is interrogated by FBI because of
        the festival's connection with Communism.

1963–1964 Davis goes to France as part of a study abroad program with
        Hamilton College on scholarship from Brandeis. While in Europe,
        she learns of Birmingham's 16th Street Baptist Church bombing.
        Her sister Fania had been friends with Carole Robertson, one of
        the girls killed.

1965   She graduates from Brandeis University with honors and returns
        to Europe. She becomes a student of philosophy attending Johann
        Wolfgang von Goethe University (Germany).

1967   She leaves Western Europe, heading to London. She arrives later
        to California, to begin studies at University of California San
        Diego as a graduate student of philosophy, with mentor Herbert
        Marcuse. Becomes involved with anti–Vietnam War activism and
        is briefly jailed. She also becomes involved with an attempt at cre-
        ating Black Student Union at UCSD.

1968   Davis is involved with Student Nonviolent Coordinating Com-
        mittee. She is also involved with activism related to combating
        violence against people by law enforcement officials, including

People's Tribunal Committee. Serves as director for SNCC's Liberation School. In July, Davis joins Che-Lumumba Chapter of Communist Party, and she later becomes involved with Black Panther Party of Los Angeles. In that same year, Davis earns master's degree at UCSD.

1969   Davis becomes involved with efforts demanding that "third college" at UCSD (later, Thurgood Marshall College) be named Lumumba-Zapata College and focus on activism and Black and Chicano and lower-income members of the student body. She travels to Mexico, Cuba, Haiti, and Santo Domingo, before arriving in Guadeloupe, where she and her companions are briefly detained due to accusations of trying to spread Communist ideology and materials.

1969   Davis becomes professor of philosophy for UCLA; however, California Board of Regents decides she should lose her position, due to Communist membership. She is fired in June a year later due to her advocacy around Soledad Brothers, incarcerated males facing homicide accusation.

1970   In August 1970 Jonathan Jackson (brother of Soledad Brother George Jackson) goes to court in San Rafael, California, where he gives some incarcerated men weapons while asking for Soledad Brothers to be freed. Individuals are taken hostage. Shooting occurs. Several individuals die, while others suffer injury. A warrant for Angela Davis is released August 15, 1970, because Jonathan Jackson was using weapons bought by Davis. She is among FBI's Ten Most Wanted. After fleeing California, she is arrested in New York City on October 13. She is jailed in Women's House of Detention (NY).

1970–1971   Davis is in Marin County Jail from December 22, 1970, to December 2, 1971, and then transfers to San Jose Jail on December 2. *If They Come in the Morning: Voices of Resistance* is published by The Third Press (1971).

1972   On February 23 she is freed on bail, in part due to Free Angela Davis activism. She was jailed for a sixteen-month period prior to being acquitted of all charges on June 4.

1973   Angela Davis is among founders of National Alliance Against Racist and Political Repression for liberating incarcerated people.

1974   *Angela Davis: An Autobiography* (Random House) is published. Toni Morrison is editor of the book.

1980   She is Communist Party's vice-presidential candidate.

1983   Her *Women, Race & Class* is published by Vintage Books. There is a 1981 Random House previous publication.

1984   She is again Communist vice-presidential candidate.

1989   *Women, Culture & Politics* is published by Random House.

1994   Angela Davis becomes presidential chair of African American and Feminist Studies for University of California Santa Cruz.

1998   *Blues Legacies and Black Feminisms: Gertrude "Ma" Rainey, Bessie Smith, and Billie Holiday* is published by Vintage Books.

2003   *Are Prisons Obsolete?* by Davis and others is published by Seven Stories Press.

2005   *Beyond the Frame: Women of Color and Visual Representation* is published by Palgrave Macmillan. Neferti X. M. Tadiar and Angela Y. Davis are editors of the book.

2008   Angela Davis becomes distinguished professor emerita at University of California Santa Cruz.

2014   Angela Davis works for UCLA again, teaching graduate-level course as well as lecturing publicly as Regent's Lecturer.

2016   *Freedom Is a Constant Struggle: Ferguson, Palestine, and the Foundations of a Movement* is published by Haymarket Books. Frank Barat is editor, and Cornel West contributes foreword. It includes interviews of and speeches by Angela Davis.

2017   January 21, Angela Davis speaks at Women's March (Washington, DC). She is also a cochair (honorarily) for the rally/demonstration.

2018   There is an announcement about Harvard University housing Davis archives. Some other institutions with archival materials on Angela Davis include Emory University, UCLA, Brandeis University, UC San Diego, McMaster University, Northeastern University, and the Schomburg Center for Research in Black Culture.

**Conversations with
Angela Davis**

A Conversation with Angela

The Reverend Cecil Williams / 1972

From *Black Scholar*, March–April 1972, pp. 36–48. © The Black World Foundation, reprinted by permission of Taylor & Francis Ltd, http://www.tandfoonline.com on behalf of The Black World Foundation.

A victory of the people, Angela Davis was released on $102,500 bail from the Santa Clara County Jail in Palo Alto, California, after eighteen months' incarceration. Miss Davis is on trial now in San Jose on charges of murder, kidnap, and conspiracy to commit both. The charges stem from an abortive escape by Black prisoners from the Marin County Court House, August 7, 1970. She has denied any involvement in the attempted escape. Prior to her arrest, Sister Davis was teaching in the Philosophy Department at the University of California in Los Angeles. She was fired twice by the University's Regents: once because she is a member of the Communist Party, and the second time for her speeches and other activities on behalf of the Soledad Brothers and all political prisoners. Her book *If They Come in the Morning: Voices of Resistance*, edited by Angela Davis and Bettina Aptheker, was published October 1971 by Third Press, New York.)

Cecil Williams: I guess one of the most important things that we can start off talking about is the fact that you have been called a revolutionary, a militant; much of the media has pictured you this way. That's talked about all over the world. What do you see as the meaning of the term "revolutionary"?

Angela Davis: There's no single, simple meaning for the term "revolutionary." A revolutionary is a man or a woman who is a lot of things, but basically the revolutionary wants to change the nature of society in a way, to create a world where the needs and interests of the people are responded to. A revolutionary realizes, however, that in order to create a world where human beings can live and love and be healthy and create, you have to completely revolutionize the entire fabric of society. You have to overturn the economic structure where a few individuals are in possession of the vast majority of the wealth of this country, a wealth that's been produced by the majority of the people; you have to destroy this political apparatus which, under the guise of revolutionary government, perpetuates the incredible misery on the masses of people.

Williams: One of the interesting things about the term revolutionary is the fact that people, so many people, see it in the context of violence, that revolutionary means violence, violence every day, every minute, at any given time, no matter what the circumstances. How do you view this in the context of violence?

Davis: Of course, that's part and parcel of the same attempt to separate and isolate revolutionaries from the people. Revolution does not mean violence in the sense that is its defining characteristic.

Williams: Yet there are those who see it that way.

Davis: Well, yes, and that's done in a very conscious manner to mislead people and to lead people, for instance, to equate a progressive socialist revolution with fascism. During the time that I was out in the streets and speaking throughout California, I found it incredible how many people define socialism or communism as if it were the Third Reich. Certainly, in the history of revolutions and not only socialist revolutions but bourgeois democratic revolutions such as the American Revolution, you have had the occurrence of violence as a means of seizing power from the oppressor, but why?

Because the oppressors have failed to acknowledge the fact that the people were right and that the people had the right to control their destiny. So the oppressors are the ones who always initiate the violence. If people are serious about moving ahead to create a better society, then of course they should not allow themselves to be deterred simply because of a few people at the top who are in possession, usually, of a monopoly on violence, who decide that they're going to unleash all of their forces of oppression to stop the forward movement of the people.

Williams: Angela, the interesting thing, I think, that's emerged is your struggle with the Soledad Brothers and your struggle with the Soledad trial. How did you get involved in this whole area of demonstrating, speaking, and organizing for the Soledad Brothers?

Davis: I was invited in the spring of 1970 to attend the meeting that had been organized by some of the attorneys involved in the Soledad Brothers case. The meeting was held in Los Angeles. I attended the meeting, and there I assumed the responsibility for doing a certain amount of organizing, primarily on the campuses, because I was at UCLA at the time, to inform people as to what was happening to George Jackson, John Clutchette, and Fleeta Drumgo.

Williams: This affected you a great deal because you participated very strongly in it. You became extremely close to one of the participants of the Soledad Brothers, namely, George Jackson. What was George Jackson really like?

Davis: I became very close to the members of George's family in the process of trying to organize around the Soledad Brothers defense committee, all of George's family—Jonathan, Mrs. Jackson, Mr. Jackson, and George and Jonathan's sisters, who were all extremely beautiful and extremely strong people. They were all involved in the political activity around the case. I did come to have a certain amount of contacts, primarily and directly, of course, with George. The only time I saw him was at a hearing I attended in Salinas, but it was almost impossible not to see the strength and the love that George Jackson had within himself, a love that expressed itself a million different ways, a love for his people, a love for oppressed people, a love for all the people with whom he had any contact. He used to call them all "the innocents," all the people who had not already actively aligned themselves with the forces of oppression.

Williams: I remember reading one of his letters, where he said that he had no self, he had no image, he had no ears, no eyes; he went on to talk about this, but some of those interesting letters were the ones that you and George changed. They were moving letters. You've undoubtedly had some kind of understanding as people who were struggling together. Were there some common strings there, in the struggle, that you felt very strongly about, you and George?

Davis: George was a revolutionary. George considered himself a communist revolutionary, and he felt that his revolutionary beliefs and the struggles that he had to wage were far more important than his own life. That's why he spent eleven years in prison for a crime that was so insignificant.

Williams: What was it, $70?

Davis: Seventy dollars. And if he had had at that time a good lawyer, and if racism had not been what it was, he never would have been in prison in the first place. And that's what was so ridiculous about it. I don't think that I would say that George was lacking in a personal image; that was one of the things that was so beautiful and so incredible about him, that he was able to perfectly merge his political life with his personal life. There was no conflict between the two, and the one was very much enhanced by the other. Within his political struggles, there was a very profound personal love and identity and solidarity with all his sisters and brothers, with all his comrades, and every personal relationship he had was determined by and infused with the struggle for liberation.

Williams: The interesting thing about it is the fact that George Jackson was killed August 21, 1971, and at that particular time we saw some new directions occur in the prison system: for instance, there was Attica, there was San Quentin. How did you perceive the penal institutions at this particular time in regards to what they call "rehabilitation" and other directions that they may be taking, now the death of George has occurred and Attica has broken loose and possibly the other prisons as well?

Davis: Things have been festering under the surface of a prison system for a long time. In fact, when I became involved with the Soledad Brothers defense committee in Los Angeles, we simply took it upon ourselves at first to defend George Jackson, John Clutchette, and Fleeta Drumgo. But we later realized that the question was much broader than that. It wasn't simply a matter of three individuals who were being subject to the repressive forces of the penal system. It was the system itself that had to be abolished so that we eventually broadened the field of our activities to include an assault on the prison system as a whole.

Williams: What you're strongly implying, I gather then, is that the character of justice is not really changing that much. Even though we've seen Bobby Seale, Ericka Huggins, Huey Newton just recently, who have been freed. Is the character of justice really changing that much?

Davis: What is justice; I mean, what does justice mean? Does justice simply mean that a person who has been charged with the crime is going to be acquitted? And that's what happened, of course, to Ericka and Bobby and Huey and the New York 21 and partially in the case of the L.A. Panthers who were just recently on trial. They were acquitted, or the charges dismissed against them, but that appears to me to be a purely formalistic view of what justice is—it's empty, it has no content. If you can show, or pick out someone, single a Black person, a Black revolutionary out, charge him with an unbailable offense, put him or her in jail for two years or two and a half years, as in the case of the New York 21, I think, and then afterwards get up with the case that you have that doesn't hold any water at all and have the jury acquit them, is that what justice is all about? The accused have lost years of their lives. See, what has happened in those cases is that the Black revolutionary leaders have been effectively silenced. They have been separated from their people, isolated from the community, for one year, two years, three years.

Williams: Do you see this as a contrived, calculated effort on the part of the ruling class to make sure that they're separated from their people?

Davis: There are a lot of ways in which repression can express itself. It does not necessarily mean being shot down; it does not even necessarily mean being sentenced to prison. It can mean being detained for so long that one cannot be effective in the community. It could mean being forced into exile as Eldridge Cleaver was forced into exile, and we see what has happened to Eldridge and what his exile has meant for this ability to be effective in the Black liberation struggle here. There are a myriad of ways in which you can repress a developing liberation movement.

Williams: I guess the thing that concerns me very much has to do with those unnamed Blacks, Chicanos, Asians, Indians, poor people, who go to the courts every day, who are sentenced and, in fact, we don't read about them, we don't know about them, they are imprisoned. Someone suggested some time ago that so many, so many people in prison did not really have the kind of adequate defense, legal defense, legal counsel, that they needed. Time after time, we have been told that people who were going before the courts have been told to plead guilty and they'd only get three months, and of course this meant an extensive amount of time in prison. But I've heard you talk about the nameless prisoners who have no recourse, because they did not have adequate representation.

Davis: One of the things that is so incredible—and I don't imagine that most people are aware of this fact, I myself wasn't aware of it until recently— is that of all the people who are arrested in this country and charged with crime, only 1 percent are ever tried by a jury! Which means that the vast majority of people in this country who are brought before a court end up pleading guilty on the advice of a public defender who doesn't have the time, who does not identify with his client, who has the interests of an over- crowded court system uppermost in his mind. The public defender counsels the accused to plead guilty, and, as you said, he tries to make a deal. And sometimes that doesn't work.

Williams: I wonder, do you really see this as a means of engaging in a contrived effort on the part of those who make the decisions to eliminate Black people? Is this a form of suppression also? To make sure, in other words, that Black people are railroaded into prisons, into jail?

Davis: In the whole history of the United States, the impact of racism has been to attempt to contain Black people, has been to attempt to stifle the desires towards liberation. One of the ways in which this is accomplished is by trying to convince people that they're completely powerless before this huge apparatus and that the police can just come into the community and pick someone out, kill them, as they have done on many, many occasions in the past, charge then with something they didn't do, railroad them to prison, send them to the gas chamber. This is just one of the many ways that the system suppresses Black people, and it's not a contrived effort in the sense that it's done consciously by a few men at the top; it's built into the system. It's built into the nature of society. And getting back to the question of what a revolutionary is, a Black revolutionary realizes that we cannot begin to combat racism and we cannot begin to effectively destroy racism until we've destroyed the whole system.

Williams: Now, I guess the amazing thing is that we noticed that in the state of California they have what is called the indeterminate sentencing of prisoners. The adult authority has the power to determine when a person is paroled, what time that person is paroled, if in fact that person is paroled. I know, I've talked to a number of prisoners who've said this is another means set up by a racist system to control the affairs and the destiny of Black people. Do you see this as a certain direction of providing controls on the lives of those prisoners who are in prison?

Davis: It's interesting that when the indeterminate sentence law was first enacted, it was presented as one of the most progressive reforms in the prison systems. That's one of the reasons, among many others, that California today is ironically considered to be the most progressive section of the American penal system. Originally, or at least it was stated that originally, the purpose of the indeterminate sentence law was to allow for the greatest flexibility in rehabilitation. That meant that if a prisoner was, say, charged or convicted of any offense that carried, say, a straight ten-year sentence, he would not get ten years, but he might get, say, two to fifteen because it's possible that in two years he might have rehabilitated himself. And it would have been overly inhuman to force him to spend eight more years in prison.

But how does this function in reality? In reality, the indeterminate sentence law had done precisely what you say it has done. It has provided an effective, a brutal, means of control over the lives of sisters and brothers who are in prison. What does this mean? It means that there's an eight-man board composed of—and I was just looking at this paper that was done on our prisons not too long ago, it gives a rundown on who's on the Adult Authority, and it says that there are six whites on the panel—and check this out, it includes a former assistant commander of the Los Angeles Police Department Detective Bureau, a former FBI agent in charge of the San Francisco Office, a former deputy United State attorney for the Southern

District of California, a former district attorney for Fresno, a former police chief of Richmond, California, and a former guard at Chino. And there's one Black man on the Adult Authority now. However, he was a former civil servant in the prison system. There's one Chicano; however, he was also in the prison system before he was appointed. Now, what does this mean? This means that they're ex-police, ex-agents, ex-prosecutors, all of whom have come from a background which is directly opposed to the prisoner, and of course they're going to take the side of the system, they're going to take the side that's directly opposed to the interests of the prisoners, and these people have the right to set a date, a parole date for prisoners.

And of course now with the increased surge of political activity and with the increasingly aggressive posture the prisoners are assuming in prison, the indeterminate sentence is used as a form of retaliation; it's used as a form of repression, because prisoners are either told or else they realize that if they continue to engage in any kind of political activity, they aren't going to get a date.

Williams: It had been suggested by the executive director of the Correctional Institutions of California that lobotomies, brain surgery, be used on those inmates who have violent tendencies. Also, we know that at two institutions like Atascadero and also Vacaville, certain drugs have been used on prisoners. This trend, we note, had taken place, and yet there was also a very strong suggestion by the executive director that lobotomies be engaged in.

Davis: Um hum. What does that sound like? I mean what does that remind you of? It evokes in my mind all of the horrors of Nazi Germany, all of the experiments that were done in the concentration camps. People who accuse us when we say that there are very definite fascist tendencies in America today ought to reconsider a moment. When the director of the Department of Corrections can get up and suggest that human beings have brain surgery to prevent them from feeling, to prevent them from reacting, because what does a lobotomy do?

Williams: Yes, I understand that it damages the front section of the brain.

Davis: It destroys it by means of attaching electrodes to the brain. It destroys very vital sections of the brain. Of course, I'm not a doctor, but from what I've learned, once you receive this lobotomy, you become practically a vegetable. Of course they maintain that it prevents the patient from being aggressive and violent, but what they're really talking about is stifling the political militancy that exists on the inside of the prisons.

Williams: Yes, I understand that lobotomies have been used, and this is, undoubtedly, well founded, to suppress pain.

Davis: You know, I really believe they would have actually initiated this policy of brain surgery had not there been the kind of reaction that there was. Probably. The way the news leaked out was an attempt to test what public reaction was going to be like, and had it not been what it was, more than likely a whole series of those kinds of experiments would have been initiated. But there's something that has not received very widespread publicity, and that is the use of these drugs in Vacaville and Atascadero that you were talking about before. Apparently the drug that is most widely used is called anectine. And it is used in what they call aversion treatment, I think.

Williams: Yes, that's right.

Davis: Isn't that the term they use?

Williams: Yes. Aversion treatment. Right.

Davis: To avert the prisoner from any kind of assertive activity. From what I've read, the experience of taking that drug is so frightening and so horrible. When they administer it, it causes, for a period of about sixty seconds, the sensation of dying; it completely relaxes, it completely arrests the breathing.

Williams: Sort of like suffocation?

Davis: You feel like you're suffocating, you feel like you're drowning, you feel like you're dying. Then, apparently, there's a psychiatrist who sits next to you and discusses what you've done. It's used as a disciplinary measure, so that the next time you get ready to strike out at a guard or do whatever you're charged with doing, you think about what it feels like, because you're going to be injected with some more of this anectine. That's what they really tell them, and I can imagine that once a person goes through that kind of experience of the actual sensation of dying, it's going to begin to affect the mind.

You see, I think that we have to look at what's going on in the prisons today in that respect as being a signal of what might possibly come in the society as a whole. I think that it is probably a truism by now that in any given society what goes on in the prisons reflects very important elements of the society as a whole and that you can learn something about the nature of the society by looking at what happens behind its walls, among its captives.

Williams: Yes, perhaps one of the critical questions for the use of anectine as well as lobotomies has to do with who gives the proper consent for a person; does the person himself, or herself, who is the prisoner or the inmate, give proper consent or volunteer for that?

Davis: Well, that's what they say. They say this drug is used on an entirely voluntary basis, but what does that mean to a woman or to a man who's in prison? They know, and the prison officials know, that if they refuse to submit to this kind of drug treatment, this is just going to be one more strike held against them and we can get back to the indeterminate sentence.

Williams: Yes.

Davis: Because many of them are on indeterminate sentences, and every time there's a mark against them on their record, this is given to the Adult Authority, and therefore their sentence is prolonged.

Williams: It seems to me there's another thing also, Angela, and it has to do with the selection of persons. If, in fact, it's done for psychiatric reasons, who selects the persons who have the destructive . . .

Davis: Well, you know what's happening, now. Governor Reagan, of course, just recently talked about abolishing San Quentin, right? What they're doing at this moment is that the so-called violent inmates—and almost inevitably when they talk about violent inmates, they're talking about political activists in prisons—are being transferred from San Quentin, from Soledad, from Folsom, which are the three major maximum security prisons in California, they're being transferred to Vacaville. And I don't think it's coincidental that . . .

Williams: They're going to Vacaville.

Davis: These kinds of things are happening in Vacaville. They're sending them down there now supposedly for psychiatric observation. They're going to be there for six months, then they send them back, and they send another group in.

Williams: Maybe this is the selective process they're talking about.

Davis: I don't think it's coincidental that these two things are happening. At the same time. And there are probably at lot of other things which are going on now too that we just don't know about, simply because it's so difficult for prisoners to get news out to the people.

Williams: Angela, there's something that's taking place in the prisons. There's an awareness that's taking place in the prisons. There's an awareness that's taking place, but we heard the term political prisoner emerge in the last few years very strongly. What is a political prisoner? Are there different levels of political prisoners?

Davis: Well, of course, throughout the history of the world, there've been political prisoners. We could even talk about Socrates, who was also a political prisoner. But getting into the contemporary situation, I think that many people have failed to see that the political prisoner is not only Bobby Seale, Ericka Huggins, Huey Newton, or the Soledad Brothers. There are scores of thousands of unnamed political prisoners who are now being held captive in this country. I would say that I can lay out perhaps about four different categories of political prisoners. The first one's, of course, the political prisoner, the sister or the brother who's imprisoned purely because of his or her ideas and political activities in the struggle for liberation, with the crime for which that person's charged being almost inevitably a pretext for assaulting that person for his political beliefs. That would be the first kind of political prisoner. Then, of course, there's the political prisoner who, in a sense, has done what he or she is charged with by the authorities, and I can think of examples throughout the history of this country. I should point out that although he or she had probably done the thing of which they are accused, it's not a crime in the sense that the system defines it as a crime.

Nat Turner, for instance, was such a political prisoner. He was charged and he was hanged for murder, but, of course, from our perspective as Black people, he was a valiant fighter for the liberation of slaves, and therefore when he fought back and when he led a slave uprising, we would not call that murder. It is murder only from the point of view of the system which is trying to continue to oppress and enslave the people who fight back. Of course, I could give you a number of examples of that type of political prisoner, but I'll go on to the next level. And for this we have to go inside the walls of the dungeons, and we see thousands and thousands of sisters and brothers who have actually been arrested and convicted of offenses which don't necessarily have political contours, but once they get into prison and once they become aware of all of the cants and passions of Left liberation and the struggle for freedom for all people, they become aware of what it is that led them to commit those offenses in the first place. They've therefore transformed themselves into political beings and become active behind the walls and are therefore subject to retaliation by the prison authorities. We could talk about Ruchell Magee, we could talk about George Jackson, Fleeta Drumgo, John Clutchette, and there's one brother whom we haven't heard that much about, and I think it's very important to talk about him at this point. His name is Robert Wesley Wells.

Williams: He's been in for quite some time.

Davis: He's sixty-two years old now. He's been in for over forty years. He was convicted of stealing a car, and he's been in for over forty years. Robert Wesley Wells was and continues to be the type of Black man who will not allow himself to be dehumanized, who will not kowtow to prison officials and who asserts his rights as a Black man. Apparently, the Attorney General of California wrote a letter to the Adult Authority saying that they did not want a sentence set, a determinate sentence set for Robert Wells, they wanted the Adult Authority to leave it open because they knew that at some point, Robert Wells was going to become involved with a guard and might possibly assault a guard.

Then they could use this other horrible law that they have on the books in the state of California which makes the death penalty mandatory for a prisoner who assaults a non-inmate. This letter is on file. I was informed of the existence of this letter by Wesley Wells's attorney. Sure enough, he was provoked into a confrontation with a guard, at that time, through a cuspidor which hit the wall and ricocheted and hit a guard's head and drew a little blood. However, the guard was back to work in about a week or so.

Robert Wesley Wells was then charged with 4500 and received the death penalty. Charles Garry was his attorney. Leo Branton, one of my attorneys now, was also working on the case. With the help of a mass movement on the outside during the forties, this was towards the end of the forties, the death sentence was commuted, but it was commuted to life without possibility of parole. And to this date, the only way that Wesley Wells can ever get out of jail, the only way that he's going to avoid dying behind the walls of San Quentin, of Soledad, of some other prison in this state, is if Ronald Reagan would grant him executive clemency. Of course, we know what Ronald Reagan's like, and we know that he's not about to make that kind of a gesture. Yet I think it's going to be extremely important for all of us to try to map a campaign and force Reagan to let Wesley Wells out of prison.

Williams: Ruchell Magee went through some trying times. He's been in now some sixteen or seventeen years, hasn't he? He, I think, has been in San Quentin now some eight years; he is a very brilliant man, I must say, in many regards. He's certainly spoken out. Ruchell Magee will be, I guess, one who will find himself in similar circumstances, who has found himself in similar circumstances.

Davis: Ruchell, I think, is a very beautiful man and is a kind of symbol of what the Black people have been forced to experience in America. He was charged with a case of rape, and we know about all of the . . .

Williams: That was in Louisiana, as I recall.

Davis: . . . brothers who have gone to their death and who have spent large portions of their life in prison because they happened to look in the direction of a white woman. Ruchell is another very shining example, like George, and like Wesley Wells, and like all our, I could go on to infinity, sisters and brothers in prison who achieve the most remarkable heights of consciousness and commit themselves to struggling for the liberation of their people and because they do this, they are the ones on whom the repressive might of the prison system comes down so strongly.

Williams: Angela, I asked you to bring some letters which you had received, I know you just received thousands, but I did ask you to bring several letters. Could you read several of those letters for me at this time? Some are just fascinating.

Davis: Maybe I should say, as a preface, that being in jail, and I've been in for about fifteen months now, the thousands and thousands of letters that come from people all over the world expressing their solidarity with me and all other political prisoners, has been a remarkable source of strength, not only for me, but also for the sisters with whom I come in contact, because I always let them know what's happening on the outside, how the struggle for our freedom is advancing. This letter, it's a really beautiful letter written by a very, very young child, apparently, and it says, very simply, "Dear Angela Davis: My name is Sarah. I wish that you were free. This is a picture of you when you will be freed. Love, Sarah." And on the other side, there's a picture that she's drawn.

Williams: Is this Sarah or of you, when you will be free?

Davis: Well, she says that it's a picture of me. You see the smile on my face. I think that's supposed to be symbolic of freedom. I get lots of letters from very young children. This is something which is so very beautiful. A lot of people somewhere have the feeling that the movement is collapsing, but I think that what's happening is that the ideas that a few people have been expressing for a long time are penetrating to the masses of people, and you have sisters and brothers who are, say, five, six years old, who know of what has to be done. There's another letter that I brought along from a ten-year-old Black brother, and it's a really moving letter. He says, "Dear Miss Davis: My mother gave me $5 for Christmas and told me to give it away to someone else that I felt needed it. I am sending it to you because I read about what happened to you. I do not think you are guilty and I hope that you can get out of prison. I'm only ten years old and I'm Black but from what I've heard and read I think some people are trying to ruin your life. All those accidents, like the killing of George Jackson, were on purpose. Try to hang on. We'll have our fingers crossed. Yours truly." And he gives his name. It's a really beautiful, moving letter. And that's only one out of many that I've received from children that age. It makes very concrete something that José Martí, the Apostle of the Cuban Revolution, said. He said, "Los niños son nas esperandos del mundo." Translation: "Children are the hope of the world." And I think this is true that we do have a revolution moving along, and it can be seen in our children and our youth.

Williams: This really has quite an impact with you, then, doesn't it? It really means a lot to you.

Davis: What it does is it completely eradicates this feeling of isolation and this feeling of separation that the prisons and the jails are designed to create. And that's why it's so necessary for people on the outside to find, to seek and find ways of expressing their solidarity with sisters and brothers in prison. If it's only a letter. I received thousands of letters from sisters and brothers in prison, and I've been trying to answer, if only with a few lines, all the letters that I get from this side of the walls. Of course, that's just a very small gesture.

People on the outside have far more flexibility than we on the inside and should begin to develop aggressive and creative means of showing their solidarity and support and concern for all of the sisters and brothers who are in here.

Williams: Um, hum. You've got another letter there. I see it on the desk, and I want to hear from that one also, because I think you told me it was from a brother who was in prison.

Davis: This is one of the many, many letters that I've received from sisters and brothers in prison. This is from the Ohio Penitentiary, Ohio State Reformatory. And it says a friendship letter, where the relationship is, you know, they have to fill out forms, the letters are generally censored. The letter says, "I don't know if you'll receive this letter or even if you'll be able to answer it. But my admiration for you compels me to write this letter. As you can see, I'm also in confinement for which I have been confined for the past twenty-one months." Then he goes on to say, "Sorry to say, my crime was selfish and stupid, unarmed robbery. Since being confined, I've been allowed to go on speaking engagements. During my speeches, I have endorsed your actions, but most of these places I've spoken were churches, and they all asked one main question, which is 'Why is Angela Davis Communist?' This is a very hard question to answer, mainly because I don't think I've been taught the true meaning of communism. This is one of my reasons for writing you at the time."

Williams: Hold it right there. Why is Angela Davis a communist?

Davis: Actually, I think I answered that before when we were talking about what a revolutionary is.

Williams: And many times the term communist, because I think it's been used by so many different aspects of our society to put down rather than to let people try to understand, everybody shuns away from it. It's like it's a disease or something. What I'm trying to get through is that that person here, in that letter, is raising a question, and therefore in his question it seems that he's trying to say that there are some people who are plagued by that and they let that get in the way. They don't want to know Angela Davis as a person. Or, even if they do, that prevents them from coming to know Angela Davis as a person.

Davis: Well, you see now, that might be true for, say, the vast majority of white people.

Williams: Yes.

Davis: But one of the things which really impressed me when I was on the streets and fighting for my job at UCLA was that whenever I spoke to Black people, whenever I spoke in the Black community, very few people had hangups about communism. I can remember many times walking down the street and having someone stop me and say, "Are you Angela Davis?" and I would say yes, and they would express their solidarity and say, a lot of sisters and brothers would say, "even though I don't really know what communism is all about," just as a brother, he has said, "we know that there must be something good about it, because otherwise the man wouldn't be coming down on you so hard."

Williams: Um hum.

Davis: So I think that the resistance to understanding what communism is all about doesn't exist nearly as much in the Black community as it does in the country as a whole. This letter here is an indication of that. What he's saying is that although he realizes that this country has kept away from him, and many of our sisters and brothers, the knowledge of what communism is, he wants to know about it, and I'm sure when he says that that's one of the main questions that's asked, I doubt whether there are huge contours of hostility in the Black community.

Williams: Yes.

Davis: It's just the desire, the curiosity to know.

Williams: I think that's true.

Davis: What I generally say, and I've answered the brother and tried to explain in a few words why I was a communist, and I said, essentially, the same thing that I said when I told you why I was a revolutionary. Because I have very strong love for oppressed people, for my people, I want to see all oppressed people throughout the world free. And I realize that the only way that we can do this is by moving towards a revolutionary society where the needs and the interests and the wishes of all people can be respected.

Williams: There are a number of women in prisons, aren't there?

Davis: About fourteen thousand, I think.

Williams: And a lot of people, certainly, would not even be aware of that.

Davis: Well, that's because, of course, of all the forces of male supremacy to which women have been subjected for so long in this society. So not much attention has been directed towards women in prisons; there are a lot of sisters who are innocent, who shouldn't be there. There are sisters who are in jail because of their political beliefs. In fact, in my experiences in New York, and in Marin County, and here—I go to exercises a couple of times a week at the Women's Prison in Santa Clara County, so I do have some contact with sisters here—and one of the things that the sisters told me when I got over there was that they really wanted to spend their time while they were in jail studying so that they could make significant contributions to the liberation struggle, except that there was no available material. So one of the things that I asked some of the people from the National United Committee to do was to make an appeal to people on the outside to donate books to the sisters in Milpitas.

Williams: Yes, I know you asked my church to make contributions, and certainly they have been sending books to the sisters at Milpitas.

Davis: Let me give you one, I think, very striking example of the lack of attention to women's prisons. We know about the Tombs, we know about Attica, we know about San Quentin, but how much do we know about the demonstrations and the strikes that took place in the Women's House of Detention? How much do we know about the revolt that occurred at Alderson Federal Penitentiary in Virginia? How much do owe know about that? How much do we know about all the unnamed sisters who are in prison today?

Williams: And it's been your contention all along that Angela Davis is not to be looked upon as a hero, but Angela Davis, along with the sisters and brothers in all prisons, must be seen in light of the struggle that's going on, as it relates to the liberation of all people.

Davis: Well, I don't see myself as any different, any more important, than all of my captive sisters and brothers, and, in fact, what I have attempted to do within all of these restrictions that surround me has been to draw people who have expressed support and concern for me into the struggle for all political prisoners. I've said on a number of occasions that one of the first experiences that I had in this jail here, after being transferred from Marin County, was very revealing of what the mass struggle can do for sisters and brothers in prison.

When they drove me down in the wee hours of the morning and brought me into the cell here, they took all of my clothes and made me take my underwear off, and I was sitting up in the cell, huddled in some blankets, freezing. Suddenly a mass of letters came flowing into the jail here, protesting the conditions, and I don't know whether it was coincidental or not, but suddenly other conditions did begin to relax.

One of the things that struck me then, and of course I'm constantly aware of this, is that because of the movement that has galvanized around me, there is a lot of public attention on me and on my case, and there's certain kinds of things that I can directly appeal to people, but what about all of the sisters and brothers that we've been talking about during this interview? What about all of the other thousands and thousands who are in America's prisons today?

People should begin to realize that they have a responsibility to see to it that America does not head in the direction of fascism, and it begins right at the level of the prisons; that's why the prison struggle is so important, because I see it as being a signal as to what the entire society will be about in the future, and that's why I think it's in the interest of all people, many of whom may not know anyone personally in prison, but most Black people, of course, have had some contact with the prisons, people should really begin to express themselves aggressively and boldly and demand that something be done about the prisons in their society today.

Interview with Angela Davis

Mike Hannigan and Tony Platt / 1975

From *Crime & Social Justice*, Spring–Summer 1975, pp. 30–35. Reprinted by permission of *Social Justice*.

Introduction

The following interview with Angela Y. Davis was undertaken because the National Alliance Against Racist and Political Repression, of which Ms. Davis is a cochairperson, is the only nationally coordinated program by Left organizations to oppose government repression. Given the fragmented, locally oriented, and short-range nature of most antirepression campaigns, we think it is important to support and critically assess any program which attempts to develop long-range strategies. We welcome articles which critically assess the practical experiences and program of the Alliance.

The National Alliance Against Racist and Political Repression was organized in May 1973, to develop a popular movement against increasing government repression. According to the Alliance's statement of purpose, the formation of the Alliance is "a rejection of the divisions that have often been used to keep people's movements weak and defenseless. It seeks to bring together people of all ethnic groups: Black, Chicano, Native American, Puerto Rican, Asian, white. It joins church activists and Communists, men and women, unionists and community organizers, students and prisoners, GIs and civilians. No group in the coalition surrenders its own identity and program, but are all committed to bringing to life the maxim that an injury to one is an injury to all.

Ten forms of repression are the targets of the National Alliance's fight back: (1) attempts to isolate, persecute, and prosecute political activists, (2) attempts to destroy movements for change in the prisons, (3) legislation aimed at repressing our basic rights or that seeks to outlaw organizations that work for social changes, (4) attempts to deny the labor movement the right to organize, the right to strike, and any other forms of repressing labor, (5) police murders and other crimes against the people—especially oppressed people of color; (6) failure to grant general amnesty to those who resisted the war in Indochina, (7) attempts to crush movements for democracy and against racism in the military, (8) governmental moves to restore capital punishment, (9) the growing trend of government agencies to use prisoners and other victims, especially the poor, for human experimentation and behavioral control, (10) increasing harassment and deportation of the foreign born, especially those who escaped countries dominated by US imperialism.

The objective of the Alliance is to focus coordinated public attention on repressive situations, get the facts to millions of people and mobilize them to move together in a way that makes the government back off. The Alliance makes use of the written word through regular newsletters and pamphlets, graphic communications through slide shows and films, and the spoken word through tours and conferences. It also moves people into action through mass demonstrations, petition campaigns, filling the courtrooms. Where appropriate, legal actions such as friend-of-the-court briefs and affirmative action suits are joined with mass action.

The Alliance has singled out for special focus in its campaign the state of North Carolina, where repression of Black and Native American activists has been most intense. (For a detailed analysis of the situation in North Carolina, see "North Carolina: Laboratory for Racism and Repression"— available through the Alliance's national office at the address given below.)

The Alliance has used these organizing techniques to build support for the Attica Brothers Wounded Knee defendants, Carlos Feliciano, George Merritt and Gail Madden of Plainfield, NJ, Martin Sostre framed in New York, Ruchell Magee and the San Quentin Six, Los Tres del Barrio, the Puerto Rican National Party Prisoners, the Wilmington 10, Charlotte 3, Ayden 11, and other victims!

On the National Alliance Against Racist and Political Repression

The idea for the Alliance was born immediately after I was acquitted. Everyone involved in the movement for my freedom understood that the "not guilty" verdict was the result of a tremendous mass movement that involved literally hundreds of thousands of people throughout the country as well as other parts of the world. All of us were acutely aware that the same kind of movement had not yet been used to bring people's aid and assistance to many other political prisoners still behind the walls. So we decided to attempt to build a unified front organization that would be able to struggle for freedom of political prisoners, fight around issues involving prisons, and attack the mounting wave of racist repression as well.

The structure of the Alliance is something that, in terms of long-range struggle, has not really succeeded in the past. We attempted in the first place to bring existing organizations together. We found that in my case the most effective means of organizing the various campaigns—the bail campaign, the fight to improve the prison conditions that I was living under, and eventually the struggle for my freedom—was to reach people through existing structures. That way we were able to reach literally hundreds of thousands of people.

We began with the notion that progressive organizations, though they might have ideological differences, could be brought together on the basis of an understanding that the struggle against repression is one which affects us all. Many diverse political, labor, religious, and civic organizations—including the American Indian Movement, the Republic of New Africa, the Communist Party, the Puerto Rican Socialist Party, the National Conference of Black Lawyers, and the Women's League for Peace and Freedom—are part of the Alliance. We've all decided that when it comes to freeing political prisoners, fighting against repression, and building a shield between the government and ourselves, we must all unite.

There was a considerable struggle around the name of the Alliance, and it ended up being quite unwieldy. We did that very specifically because we felt that it's not quite right to draw artificial distinctions between somebody who is arrested and subjected to repression because he or she is Black, Chicano, Asian, or Indian and those who are arrested because of their political activity. We decided that there would be a constant dialectic between what we call racist repression and repression directed against people because of their class and activism. So many of the cases that the Alliance is working on involve racist repression. Joanne Little in North Carolina, for example, is perhaps the most well-known case at the moment.

The Alliance is also struggling around cases which involve individuals who are leaders of social movements. In North Carolina, for example, there was a move on the part of the government to crush all the existing movements and antiwar, and they singled out for repression the leaders of the students, GI movements. It's clear that it is necessary to mount a really tremendous campaign around them, not only because they're individuals, but because the government attempts through them to destroy movements. By defending them we are also defending the right of people in North Carolina to organize.

The Alliance does not attempt to substitute for any existing movement. We see the struggle against repression as extremely important but only insofar as this struggle defends movements which fight for jobs, movements which fight for revolutionary change, and movements which in general fight against exploitation and racism. One of the main purposes of the Alliance is to provide these movements with a shield against the government so that there is more room and flexibility to go out and organize masses of people. Therefore, we would never say to any person that you should leave your political work and join the fight against repression, because the two are very closely linked. We have never said that the Alliance is the vanguard of a revolutionary movement. It is rather an attempt to put a shield between all people's movements and the government.

We see now, through the revelations about Watergate, the FBI and CIA, that there is an urgent need for a movement against repression. As the economic crisis deepens—unemployment is continuing to rise, and people are finding it more and more difficult to survive—it means that if activists are organizing there is going to be a higher level of resistance. People are going to have to get out in the streets and fight in a mass way, and workers are going to have to go out and strike. If we expect to get through this period without working people having to bear the entire burden of the crisis, there are going to have to be many more struggles. This means that the government is going to bring out of the closet the weapons that it has used in the past, as well as develop new methods to attempt to destroy these movements. There's no doubt that the level of repression is going to rise. For example, in Los Angeles all seven thousand members of the Police Department are being trained to put down "food riots." Also, the fact that the FBI has been training SWAT squads is an indication of the degree to which the government is preparing itself to deal with people's movements. And if we don't have an antirepression and antiracism movement that's strong enough to repel some of that, it's going to make it very difficult indeed for any movement to get off the ground.

Therefore, we see the need for every effort to unify and bring together people and groups that are essentially fighting for the same thing. This doesn't mean that we try to level political differences, because we understand that political differences are going to remain. For example, we have both the Republic of New Africa and the Communist Party in the Alliance. As a communist, I see the struggle of Black people as being an important part of the fight to overcome capitalism. The Republic of New Africa, on the other hand, says that in order to achieve the emancipation of Black people, there must be a separate nation. We can sit down and talk about why we think the other is incorrect and fight ideologically, but then we understand that when we go into Alliance meetings, we must leave those differences behind. The only way you can really build a revolutionary movement is by each organization trying to prove the correctness of tis policies through practice and not by imposing a single ideology on everybody.

One of the major specific concerns of the Alliance in the past year and a half has been the exposure of the state of North Carolina, and to building of movements against repression in the state. We've come to the conclusion that there's more repression concentrated in that state than anywhere else in the United States. There are a number of reasons why this state is the site of the most intensive repression. It has the highest proportion of unorganized workers. Next to Mississippi, I think, it has the lowest per capita income. Something like 35 percent to 40 percent of all Black families living in North Carolina don't even have inside plumbing. At the same time, there has consistently been a very strong resistance movement there. And recently when there was a tremendous Black movement emerging and developing, there was an attempt to completely crush it, and within months literally scores of charges were brought against Black people, Indians, and some white people also. North Carolina is also a very strategic state. Two of the largest military bases, Fort Bragg and Fort Lejeune, are located there and have been involved in training Chilean soldiers. Within the tobacco, textile, and furniture industries, there has been a consistent policy of powerful repression against workers. Next to Georgia, North Carolina has more prisoners per capita than any other state, and it leads the nation in the number of prisoners on Death Row. Also, the Federal Bureau of Corrections selected North Carolina to be the site of their behavior research center at Butner, because they felt that this is where their work would be most easily facilitated with the help of local universities.

We don't take the attitude that people, for example, in California should struggle around North Carolina just because our sisters and brothers there are really in bad shape. We see a direct relationship between a victory over repression in that state and diminishing ability of every other state to consolidate its repressive apparatus. It is with this in mind that the Alliance is organizing nationally around the Wilmington Ten, the Ayden 11, the Charlotte Three, the Joanne Little case, and other political prisoners in North Carolina. The effort to prevent the behavior modification center from being established at Butner and to make the death penalty unconstitutional in the case of Jesse Fowler definitely has national implications. So we see the struggles in other states as being related in a very concrete sense to the fight in North Carolina.

On the Prison Movement

The struggle behind the walls is extremely important and is mounting. The accumulated experiences of the past few years are beginning to take effect. If you look at the evolution of the cases of George Jackson, Ruchell Magee, the Sam Quentin Six, the Attica Brothers, the Leavenworth Brothers, Marie Hall, and many others who are either targets of repression or who became targets after they were incarcerated, we can understand the level of resistance that is taking place. The personal history of Marie Hill is interesting in this respect. She epitomizes the development that many prisoners have undergone in the last few years. She was picked up on the streets about six years ago when she was fifteen and charged with murdering a white man in a little town in North Carolina. Now, of course, all of her legal rights were violated. She wasn't told that she had a right to see her lawyer; a confession was literally beaten out of her. At her trial the confession was the only substantial evidence, and consequently she was convicted. Not only was she convicted, but she was sentenced to death. Some lawyers from the NAACP Legal Defense Fund and others got together and built a movement and managed to get the death sentence overturned. But she is now facing a life sentence. When she went to prison, she was just a young Black sister who had never been involved in politics. But when these things happened to her, when people began to organize around her, she began to study and think, and she began to grasp something of the nature of racism. She began to have discussions with her sisters in prison and eventually became one of the leaders inside the walls of the Women's Prison in North Carolina. As a result of that she has been the subject of harassment and intimidation. She also has some severe medical problems now as a result of their consistent refusal to attend to her health. When we study the lives and political careers of George Jackson, Ruchell Magee, the San Quentin Six, and others, we see essentially the same dynamic at work.

It is unfortunate that there has been a kind of lull in support movements on the outside for prisoners. The struggle inside is continuing, and it's probably more intense now than it was in 1970–1971, when the prison movement was at its height. The Attica situation is especially important, and the recent conviction of the two brothers John Hill and Charles Pernasilice was a real setback. I think that we are going to have to escalate our efforts to support them, because their conviction was in a sense a renunciation of our right to organize.

I think that it's also extremely important to raise, separately and in conjunction with issues involving repression, the various ways in which women as women are special targets of persecution through the prison system and the whole criminal justice system. Unfortunately, the prison movement has been almost exclusively directed towards male prisoners. You hear people talking about "brothers in prison" and forgetting about the fact that there are sisters in prisons all over the country. Many people have the incorrect notion of women's prisons as essentially nonrepressive and nonpunitive. That notion of course is based on the notion that when a woman commits a crime, she is not so much going against the laws of society as she is transgressing against her status as a woman. Therefore, prisons are designed to reindoctrinate women through the cottage system, a "domestic" atmosphere, and teaching prisoners how to sew and cook. Traditionally, this is the attitude towards women in prison that has prevailed ever since the first women's prison was built in this country.

You don't hear about the level of brutality that exists in every women's prison. The California Institute for Women may look like a college campus, or it may look beautiful, but when you find out what is going on inside the walls, it's a completely different story. I think that recently there has been a marked increase in the level of consciousness of women, and there have been struggles going on inside women's prisons from CIW to the Women's House of Detention in New York and the Women's Prison in Raleigh, North Carolina. These struggles have not been publicized at all, even during the high point of media coverage of prison activities. For example, when the Tombs rebellion took place in New York, there was a similar kind of revolt in the Women's House of Detention, yet nobody read about it. There should be special attention paid to women in prison. The special forms of repression suffered by women in prison have to be understood and combatted.

We are trying to build a subcommittee of the Alliance that deals specifically with the women in prisons. In organizing around such cases as Marie Hill, Joanne Little, Ann Shepard, Lolita LeBron, and others we are trying to reach out to women's organizations, to get women's organizations directly involved in the fight against repression. Women who truly believe in the fight for emancipation of women must see the relationship between their struggles and those women who are the most repressed.

On the Prospects for Organizing Within the University

I think that the prospects are now very good. There is a lot of talk now in the media about apathy that is supposed to prevail on the campuses. While the level of struggle in general is much lower than it was a few years ago, I think that students now have an even deeper understanding of what's happening to this country. One problem which characterized the student movement of the late sixties was the incorrect notion that students could in and of themselves, apart from relating to working and community people, build and lead a revolutionary movement. The most extreme example of this was the idea that students were going to be the vanguard of the revolution because workers were no longer revolutionary. I think that was wrong. But when student activists also began to understand the incorrectness of that notion, unfortunately many of them left the campuses in order to organize in communities and workplaces. And this left students without leadership.

I think it's important to understand that when we talk about undergraduates, there is a constant turnover, and they are only around the campus for three or four years. For example, there are few students now in 1975 who can remember what happened around the Cambodian protests, and they are unable to learn from the experiences and sense of struggles that emerged then. The basic problem on college campuses is the lack of structure and direction. It is not a lack of concern or militancy. And I can talk about this from my own personal experience, because I do a great deal of speaking on campuses. I have spoken at literally scores of campuses over the last two years, and I've discovered that students turn out in incredibly large numbers throughout the country. Young people always want to know what they can do to help the struggle, how they can contribute to the movement against racism and repression. When we explain the existing economic crisis and the reasons why the crisis is irreversible, when we discuss what's happening on the world scene, the increasing isolation of the US government, and the increasing resistance by peoples of color against imperialism, and when we talk about the fact that socialism is the only real answer to existing problems, we find that students are really impressed and receptive. I'm not saying that we're going to have a widespread revolutionary student movement tomorrow, but I think that what has happened over the last couple of years has paved the way for this kind of receptivity. If student leaders and organizations can link the struggles of students with the fight against racism, unemployment, and other manifestations of the present crisis, then there is a possibility for an even greater and more sustained student movement than we have seen in the past.

On Academic Repression

Using repression in its broadest sense, I think that the universities are a very important instrument of repression for maintaining the existing capitalist society. They're designed to develop individuals who will be committed to perpetuating monopoly capitalism. Also, universities have always served as a recruiting ground for the repressive agencies, such as the FBI and the CIA. It's also important to point out the ways in which the universities serve as instruments of racism. Shockley, for example, is allowed to flit around the country and talk about genetics even though he isn't a geneticist. Under the guise of academic freedom, he is encouraged to advocate racist and even fascist solutions. Nobody would be allowed to do that in a socialist country, because those countries understand the relationship between form and content. They understand that the democratic right to free speech does not include the right to deny others the right to exist.

One of the very important issues confronting the campuses today is the fact that many of the democratic gains and victories that were achieved by Black students during the 1960s and the early seventies are being constantly withdrawn. According to a recent report, there has been an approximate 11 percent decrease in the number of Black freshmen in 1973. And if you include all students of color and white students from working-class backgrounds, there has been something like a 16 percent decrease. The racism of the campuses reflects racism in the society and goes hand in hand with what's been happening at Boston.

Another real problem is that many of the student leaders who remain on the campuses were coopted by the administration. That is what happened at Lumumba-Zapata College (at the University of California in San Diego). The number of Black and Chicano students is steadily declining there, and it's losing all vestiges of its original character. If you don't understand the relationship between what's happening on and off the campus, it's much easier to be co-opted. So while I think it's important to fight against repression on the campus, I think it is equally important to organize and inspire students to relate their own interests to what is happening to working people in the society at large.

Students tend to unconsciously imbibe false ideas about their position in society. When you get down and really talk about who wields power in this country, it's not the students or their families, even though a lot of students come from middle-class backgrounds. Their families aren't the Hugheses and DuPonts and Rockefellers; students don't control the economic and political power in this country. And so it is important to educate students that they have a direct interest in linking up what's happening to workers. Now a college graduate has just as much or even more difficulty finding a job as a worker, and they're going to be thrown in the workforce just like any other worker. A lot of students are beginning to understand this, and I think we should concentrate our organizing on those campuses where students would be naturally most receptive. I am presently looking for a job in a community college, because students there are both students and workers and they're forced to relate what they learn in the classroom to what happens to them in the community. It's really important to break through the elitism on the campuses. This doesn't only affect white students. They try to do the same thing to Black students straight from the ghetto who don't have any material reasons to think that they're better than their brothers and sisters who are working on the assembly line. The universities cultivate elitism, and we have to organize students to recognize that this does not serve their true, long-range interests.

On Criminal Justice System Workers

Most people who take jobs in the criminal justice system do so for economic reasons. There are probably a few who have very strong authoritarian and sadistic tendencies, but the vast majority is [sic] people who need a job. The problem is that in order to fulfill their responsibilities as guards or police, the criminal justice system requires them in one way or another to be repressive and authoritarian. There are probably a few who retain some degree of humanity, but this ultimately comes from relationships outside their work. There are some exceptions, like Officers for Justice in San Francisco and the Afro-American Patrolmen's League in Chicago. These are both Black groups which organized as a result of the fact that they felt all kinds of racism directed against them within the police departments. This kind of organizing should be encouraged, and we should try to support their efforts.

If you're a prisoner, it makes a difference if you have to spend every single moment of the day fighting with racist, sadistic guards. If there is a relaxation of repression on that level, then it becomes a little easier to endure the incarceration and maybe you can become more productive. I say this from my own experience, because when I was in the Marin County jail, practically all the matrons there were constantly screaming—I even had to fight to get my food. When I was transferred to jail in Palo Alto, I began to realize how tense I had been in Marin. And it was only in Palo Alto, where the guards were a little less brutal, that I began to loosen and to start writing again. So I think it's important to try to reach the guards on that level so that the brothers and sisters inside can have a little more flexibility and room to develop themselves. But we should not labor under the illusion that the nature of the institution will be fundamentally changed. So we can't see that as the central issue in our organizing.

On Socialism and Capitalism

I think it is very important to give people in this country a sense of what it means to be part of a struggle for socialism on the basis of the concrete of institutions and traditions in this country. Certainly, to fight for socialism means that we join an international community of struggle which includes all socialist countries. Be we can't look to the Soviet Union or China or Cuba to tell us specifically and in detail what a socialist United States of America will be like. For one thing, none of the socialist countries, when their revolutions triumphed, were nearly as industrialized as the United States. But I'm not suggesting that we cannot learn from socialism in other countries. For example, I've found that students can relate to the fact that in socialist countries you don't have to worry about paying for tuition in universities. You don't have to pay for books or medical care. There's no inflation. These are the kind of basic things that people in this country have to learn about socialism. If you compare the present circumstances of capitalism and socialism, it is very clear that socialism is vibrant, developing, and continuing to grow, whereas the situation in capitalist countries is very bleak indeed.

Complexity, Activism, Optimism: An Interview with Angela Y. Davis

Kum-Kum Bhavnani / 1988

From *Feminist Review*, no. 31, Spring 1989, pp. 66–81. © 1989 by SAGE Publications, Ltd. Reprinted by permission of SAGE Publications, Ltd.

July 1988, Berkeley, California

Kum-Kum Bhavnani: Perhaps we could begin by you saying a little bit about your membership of the Communist Party in the United States.

Angela Davis: I've been in the Communist Party for exactly twenty years. As a matter of fact, exactly twenty years this month.

KB: What led you to join?

AD: Well, actually, my relationship to the Communist Party prior to my joining came from two very separate directions. First of all, my parents were very close friends with Black members of the Communist Party around the time I was born and during the period of my childhood. Although my mother did not join the Communist party, she did join the Southern Negro Youth Congress, in which the Communists played a central role, and was a national officer and leading activist in that organization. In that capacity she participated in the campaign to free the Scottsboro Nine. When I was still quite young, anticommunist repression brought on by the McCarthy era descended upon the country, and my mother's friends, who were the parents of my friends, were forced to go underground. As far back as I can remember, I've had some relationship to the Communist Party.

As a teenager in high school, I became very much interested in Marxism. I had the good fortune to attend a school in New York during the late fifties and early sixties that was quite progressive at that time. We studied the *Communist Manifesto*, for example, without being compelled to accept the usual anticommunist analysis of this work. When I was fifteen years old, I became very active in a youth organization associated with the Communist Party. During the late sixties, I worked with Black Communists in the Black Liberation Movement and eventually joined the Communist Party myself.

KB: And how do you think about that period now?

AD: It was an era of passionate and innovative political struggles. And because we were cultivating new ground, there were myriad problems. There was a tendency, for example, to perceive different mass movements as utterly separate, as bearing no relationship to others. The Black movement, by the time I had returned to this country after studying for several years in Europe, had acquired a very influential cultural nationalist component. This was the era following the height of the civil rights movement, approximately around the time of the assassination of Dr. Martin Luther King in 1968. For me, as for most other Black activists of that period and for Black people in general who were politically minded, it was very invigorating to experience the cultural emphasis on our African past. We began calling ourselves "Black" as opposed to Negro and began to acknowledge our African heritage. Many people took on African names and began to wear African garb, and entire organizations were devoted almost exclusively to the restoration of the African past. In the process there was a distinct opposition to white involvement in the movement for Black liberation. And while I personally felt greatly relieved to be able to divest myself of all the cumulative decades of internalized racism—it felt wonderful to be able to call myself a Black woman without feeling any negative connotations attached to the word "Black," and it felt wonderful to feel a kinship with Africa—but I realized at the same time that the cultural rebirth could not by itself achieve the political aims of Black Liberation.

KB: Why not?

AD: Because the cultural nationalist emphasis, in focusing exclusively on race, failed to grasp the connection between racism as it oppressed Black people and other people of color on the one hand, and the exploitation inflicted upon the working class as whole on the other. They generally argued that white people in general were the enemy, implying that a white worker was just as much our adversary as a white corporate executive. Being reluctant to accept the cultural nationalist analysis, I came to respect the role of Black communists in the movement.

KB: Such as?

AD: Such as the campaign against polite repression. Numbers of young Black people were shot without provocation by the police—and of course it is still happening today in this country as well as in Britain and in Canada—and we organized mass protest campaigns in response to their specific cases. I was impressed by the leadership that some young Black communists were able to provide for those mass movements. The most dramatic movements were a response to the repression of the Black Panther Party.

KB: When they were shot in their beds?

AD: Yes, that was in Chicago. In Los Angeles the police attacked the Black Panther Party offices with automatic weapons, dropping a bomb on the roof of the building. But, to continue the story behind my decision to join the Communist Party, there were also very strong sexist tendencies in the Black movement. In the Student Nonviolent Coordinating Committee (SNCC), for example, we women were running the office, but when the time came to publicly represent the organization at press conferences and rallies, the men would appear, taking credit for our work. We knew that something was wrong!

I joined the Communist Party, in fact, after the Los Angeles SNCC chapter dissolved. It dissolved as a result of internecine battles over women's role in the organization. What is interesting about this is that it was occurring during the time that the first women's circles were being formed by white women in connection with the emerging feminist movement. We were aware of this development, but we completely disassociated ourselves from this women's movement. Ironically, at the same time, we were conducting an important fight for women's equality within the context of the Black Liberation Movement. Reflecting on this experience later, I realized that Black women and women of color were making important contributions to the effort to elevate people's consciousness about the impact of sexism. While we didn't define ourselves as women's liberationists, we were in fact fighting for our right to make equal contributions to the fight against racism. Parenthetically, let me mention a historical parallel. Maria Stewart, a nineteenth-century Black woman, raised similar issues within the context of the Black challenge to slavery. She became the first woman born in this country to deliver public lectures. Only recently has her part in developing a woman's consciousness in the nineteenth century been recognized. In the aftermath of these conflicts over women's role in Los Angeles SNCC, I became a member of the Communist Party. I joined an all-Black collective of the Communist Party called the Che-Lumumba Club.

KB: But you joined the Communist Party after SNCC went down, rather than moving into the Women's Liberation Movement . . .

AD: Oh, there wasn't a place for me there.

KB: Why?

AD: I felt no connection with what the white women's liberationists were doing. And this was the case with the overwhelming majority of Black women. The feminist movement, even though it was sparked in part by contributions made by Black women, did not attract Black women. This was true for other women of color as well—Chicana women, Puerto Rican women, Asian women, Native American women—who, in some instances, created their own women's organizations. The Black Women's Alliance, later called the Third World Women's Alliance, made it absolutely clear that the target of their efforts was tripartite in nature: racism, sexism and imperialism. Whereas with many of the white women's circles, the focus was personal experience. Their structures were largely designed to allow white women to psychologically overcome the sense of inferiority which they had internalized as a result of the gender-role socialization they had experienced. What was very interesting at that particular juncture . . .

KB: The late sixties?

AD: We're talking about the late sixties. What's very interesting is that Black women were being attacked as being too aggressive and too assertive. In 1965 Daniel Moynihan authored a government report called "The Negro Family: The Case for National Action," in which he argued that Black oppression could be attributed to a tangle of pathology at the center of which is the matriarchal structure of the family and the community. It was simply an official government report, but its ideas were widely propagated by the media and were also integrated into the scholarly work of sociologists and other social scientists. Black women were represented as domineering vis-à-vis Black men. In reality Black women *had* experienced a different kind of gender-role socialization than white women. The socialization process within the Black family most often encouraged young girls to become independent. For example, my mother always urged me never to get married before I could support myself, whereas with middle-class white women it was "find a man who will support you." You see?

KB: So, the Moynihan Report, you're saying, twisted into blaming Black women for the ills of racism?

AD: Yes, exactly. I think that the Moynihan Report attempted to exploit and distort the male–female relationship with the Black community, which, while of course it was informed by sexism, at the same time had a much more egalitarian quality than in the white community. This was a historical consequence of slavery, when Black women essentially did the same work that Black men did—there was no gender-based division of labor during slavery. And in the aftermath of slavery, proportionately far more Black women worked for a living than white women, even if it was the case that they worked in white people's houses, cleaning their kitchen and taking care of their children. The economic subordination that most white women experienced was not as great a factor in the Black community. All of which is to say that we Black women activists—most of us at least—did not really have to learn how to be assertive. In fact, we were being accused of being *too* assertive and *too* aggressive! Therefore, we did not feel we needed to involve ourselves in the process by white which women were learning how to emerge from their socially imposed passivity, but I think there has been a great deal of progress since the late sixties and early seventies. Ever larger numbers of women of color are associating themselves with the feminist movement today. Initially the feminist movement was considered an all-white movement, which did not address issues which working-class women and women of color felt were critical issues. In the early seventies, when I was in jail, one of the organizers of the National United Committee to Free Angela Davis told me that they had approached a feminist organization—I do not remember which one—and the response was, "Well, Angela Davis is not associated with the women's movement, she's associated with the Black movement," as if one had to make a choice between the two, as if one was either a feminist or an antiracist. In all fairness, I should point out that white feminists were active around my case. Gloria Steinem, for example, was treasurer of my legal defense fund. There has been a great deal of dialogue about the influence of racism and class bias in the women's movement. In the latter 1980s, we are making sense of the confused and groping efforts of the era and are recognizing the connections between the various struggles in which we were involved. And of course now we understand very well that there is no absolute opposition between the women's movement, the Black movement, the labor movement. And even though there are enormous obstacles that remain within the women's movement preventing us from fully tapping our potential to create the foundation for a truly multiracial women's movement, nonetheless the issues are understood with a great deal more clarity today than were even ten years ago.

KB: Are you optimistic?

AD: I'm very optimistic. This is the era of coalitions. The Jackson campaign is the epitome of the kind of coalition work we are capable of doing. There is the challenge of coalition work we are capable of doing. Here is the challenge of coalition work; but there is also another challenge—to build and expand women's organizations that are truly integrated multiracial women's organizations. Multiracial coalitions are essential, as are coalitions involving working-class women, but if we wish to tap the full potential of the women's movement, we must have many more multiracial and working-class-based women's organizations. In my opinion women's organizations that are exclusively white will never be able to make profound contributions to the quest for women's equality.

KB: Because?

AD: Well, first of all, if we wish to shed the attitudinal forms of racism and class bias inevitable in any racist society, white middle-class women cannot continue simply to work among themselves. It will not happen as a result of white women attending workshops, learning how to unlearn racism. I'm not trying to completely dismiss those workshops, but white women must learn in activist contexts how to take leadership from women of color. And it may sound like a simple issue, but it isn't. Not at all. The need for white women to accept leadership from women of color flows from the objective relationship between the forms of oppression white women suffer—white middle-class women, white working-class women—and the forms of oppression suffered by women of color. If we actually look at the structure of sexism, it has a racist component which affects not only women of color but white women as well. Ku Klux Klan–instigated violence against Black people incites, for example, violence against women who attempt to use the services of abortion clinics. Low wages for women of color establishes a standard which leads to low wages for white women. So that white women are the victims of any upsurge in racism. But it has taken a long time to understand why white women should be active around issues affecting Black people not from a missionary vantage point, but rather because they are, in the process, defending their own interests.

Perhaps Jesse Jackson's campaign has clarified that connection somewhat. During the last election in 1984, when Jesse Jackson was a candidate, it was assumed that he was a Black candidate, speaking on behalf of Black people, right? And of course the foundation of his support was the Black community—there was nowhere near the kind of mass white support in 1984 that he received in 1988. The 1988 campaign demonstrated the extent to which Jesse Jackson, a Black person who emerged from the struggles of Black people in the country, was able to be an effective spokesperson for all oppressed people in this country, whether they be Black or Latino or Native American or white, whether they be gay or straight, whether they be workers or students. And it is not coincidental that the first candidate of a major political party truly able to address issues affecting all of us, was a Black person. I'm not saying that every Black person or every Black woman will necessarily exhibit that understanding, but I think that there is something in the nature of racism's role in this society that permits those who have come up through the ranks of struggles against racism to have a clearer comprehension of the totality of oppression in this society. White women must learn to acknowledge this. When white women are asked the questions "Why don't you have any women of color involved in your organization, why is your conference all white?" they should no longer offer excuses like "Well, we invited them, but they didn't come, they didn't seem interested."

KB: What don't you like about that?

AD: It indicates failure to reflect upon the extent to which the issues they generally raise have been articulated in accordance with the structure of white middle-class women's oppression.

Let's talk about the antirape movement. In the very beginning, going back go the late sixties or early seventies, when the antirape movement was one of the two major activist movements within the Women's Liberation Movement, there was a tendency to represent rape as inflicted by men upon women because they are men. And of course this period coincided with the infancy of the women's movement, and women's studies scholarship, so that no real theoretical clarity about sexual violence had been acquired. But Black women's historical experience taught us that the charge of rape has frequently been used as a tool of repression in the Black community. Lynchings of large numbers of Black men—and even Black women—were broadly justified by the accusation that Black men were rapists. This historical experience was not taken into consideration by those who initially organized the antirape movement. So many Black women took the position "Even though I may myself have suffered sexual abuse, and I may want to do something about it, I don't want to get involved in a movement that's going to bring down repression on the community." When white women raised the strategic demand for more police, longer prison sentences, the Black community would bear the brunt of this.

In 1975 there was the Joanne Little case—she was raped by a white jailer when she was herself incarcerated. As an act of self-defense, she killed her rapist. We mounted an effective mass and legal defense. When Joanne Little was acquitted, she issued a call to all the women who had been involved in her case to support a young man who was obviously framed up in Florida on charges of having raped a white woman. But virtually all of the white women's groups we approached at that time took the position that they didn't want to have anything to do with an accused rapist. (Later, I should point out, some groups changed their position). With that kind of disparity of perspectives, there was very little possibility for Black women and white women to come together during the early days of the feminist movement.

Another example is the abortion rights movement. Black women again had a much greater stake in decriminalization of abortions. Proportionately far fewer Black women, because of their impoverished economic positions, were able to take advantage of safe illegal abortion services. Therefore, Black women had to resort to the back-alley abortionists, and thus they were the ones who most frequently died as a result of botched abortions. It was clear that Black women stood to gain a great deal more from the decriminalization of abortion. But feminist activist circles frequently failed to take the special situation of women of color into account. As a matter of fact, during that period many abortion rights activists tended to say to Black women and Puerto Rican women and poor women in general, "Well, you really need to help us with this fight because you, more than any other group, are in need of the right to abortions; the more children you have, the greater your poverty." They were saying, basically, that Black women were responsible for their poverty because they gave birth to so many children, and that therefore *if* abortions were available, they could arrest this process. The categories may not have been available at the time for a clear analysis of this position, but Black women instinctively grasped that what the abortion activists were saying was, "You are duty bound to have abortions; and you don't have the right to have more than a certain number of children." This problem surfaced early on in the movement. Compounding this problem was the failure of the abortion rights movement to challenge sterilization abuse. This drove another wedge between white middle-class women and women of color.

Even though many of these problems still exist, at least now no white activists in the women's movement can pretend not to be aware of the need to integrate an analysis of racism in the overall analysis of sexism. In this sense I think that the work that we as Black women and progressive white women have done has reaped some very important fruits. The nature of feminist theory and feminist practice is beginning to reveal progressive changes. As I speak a great deal at women's conferences and to women's audiences on college campuses, I can see concrete manifestations of those changes.

KB: It's quite exciting . . . ?

AD: Yes, it is, and whereas previously white women used to be quite anxious and quite defensive, they expressed feelings of guilt when the issue of racism was raised, now they reflect more seriously on the problem. I recently spoke at a conference in Milwaukee organized by an organization called the National Association of Women's Centers. The member groups are community women's centers and campus women's centers. Their mission statement was very good. It pointed out the need to develop multiracial, multi-ethnic women's centers and to structure the services in such a way that they reflected the experiences and the needs of women of color. But then the problem was that while there were some women of color present at that conference, it was a majority-white conference. So I raised the issue there of what they were going to do in order to translate this understanding into strategy and tactics. It is exciting that we can now talk about strategic and tactical approaches.

KB: Angela, you've referred to when you were in jail, and I also know, and you probably know, the there's a quite well-known poster of you, with a quote from underneath the picture saying that the real criminals are not those who populate the prisons but those who own and control wealth. Do you want to say a little bit about why you were in jail, about the murder of George Jackson, and also how you feel that relates to issues about Black women—if you feel there is a connection.

AD: Yeah, there definitely is a connection. Let me see, where do I start?

KB: Well, there are also all the issues about your job at UCLA . . .

AD: Yes, it started there. Because of my membership in the Communist Party, I was fired by Ronald Reagan, who at the time was the governor of California, from my position in the Philosophy Department at the University of California, Los Angeles. While I was defending my right to teach, I became very involved in the organizing of a mass defense for the Soledad Brothers, three prisoners who had been falsely charged with killing a guard. They were George Jackson, Fleeta Drumgo, and John Clutchette. As a result I became acquainted with members of George's family, his brother Jonathan Jackson, his mother Georgia Jackson, and his sisters Penny and Frances Jackson, who attended the committee's meetings. Jonathan became involved in some of the other work we were doing. He began to do security for me. I should mention that during that period I had to have armed security everywhere I went.

KB: Why?

AD: Because I received daily threats on my life, sometimes as many as ten threats in one day. And while, on the campus, the campus police were supposed to be protecting me—off campus, there were friends, comrades, who did security for me. I had to have someone live with me as a bodyguard. And I purchased a few weapons that were kept in my house and used by the people who did security.

Well, in any event, Jonathan Jackson took the guns and went into a courtroom in Marin County in Northern California, near San Francisco, and, along with three prisoners in one courtroom, took hostages—the judge and members of the jury. However, once they took them into a van which was waiting in the parking lot, the San Quentin guards fired on the van, killing the judge, killing Jonathan Jackson and two of the prisoners, James McClain and William Christmas, and very seriously wounding the district attorney, some of the members of the jury, and Ruchell Magee, another prisoner, who was later my codefendant. For the sole reason that those guns were registered in my name, they charged me with murder, kidnapping, and conspiracy, even though I was nowhere in the vicinity of the site of that uprising. I was on the FBI's Ten Most Wanted list for two months; they finally captured me and charged me with three capital crimes—murder, kidnapping, and conspiracy.

During this time that I was active in the campaign around Soledad Brothers, before I was arrested, I had begun a correspondence with George Jackson, who was developing a very important theory concerning the relationship between prisons and society. George and I corresponded about those issues. What disturbed me about George's attitude was that he seemed to have internalized the notions of Black women as domineering matriarchs, as castrating females, notions associated with the Moynihan Report, which I discussed earlier. I could detect this in the comments he made in his letters, especially comments about his mother. So I began to challenge his perspective. I knew that there was something wrong with what he was saying. I knew that he was wrong, but I did not have the categories at hand to allow me to make a convincing opposing argument.

This is why I began to do research in jail on the role of Black women during slavery. The matriarchy thesis was actually based on E. Franklin Frazier's work during the 1930s, and on a number of theories which argued or attempted to prove that the Black family had been virtually destroyed during slavery, and that the woman remained the only real vestige of family life. This was why, according to these theories, Black women became domineering creatures who oppressed their men. When I was in jail, I tried to look at the role of Black women during slavery. At that time, very little had been written on Black women during slavery, and it was hard to get the books that were available. I couldn't just go out to the library and see what was there! I had to depend on people to bring books in to me. I was able to receive these books only because I was defending myself in court as a co-counsel in my case, and I informed the jail authorities that I had the right to whatever literature I needed for the preparation of my defense because in my trial I focused a great deal on the misogynist character of the prosecution's case. The theoretical work I did on Black women actually assisted me to develop a strategy for my own defense.

KB: So your article "The Role of the Black Woman in the Community of Slaves," it is a very significant article for you.

AD: Yes, it had a considerable personal significance for me.

KB: So, you have been involved, and you are still involved, in the Communist Party, and you are also involved in movements for women by women—*all* women. Some people argue that there's a contradiction or a tension between membership or sympathy and allegiance to Marxist politics, and sympathy and allegiance with women's politics. If someone said to you, "Oh, you can't be a proper feminist because you're a Marxist," or "You can't be a proper Marxist because you're a feminist," how would you deal with that kind of challenge?

AD: For a long time I was very reluctant to refer to myself as a feminist precisely because there appeared to be a this contradiction. But of course over the last twenty years there has been an effort to redefine feminism, or the various feminisms which have emerged. There are feminists who might embark upon a campaign to open the executive suites of the corporations to women, regardless of the fact that these corporations are exploiting people in South Africa. That is quite a different feminist from one that I espouse. It is our responsibility—those of us who are Marxists—to participate in that process of defining and redefining feminism.

Let me give you an example of the problems to be encountered within the context of feminism which defines itself very broadly as encouraging women's—any women's—victories over sexist-based discrimination. There is a woman now on the Supreme Court for the first time in history in this country, a Reagan appointee by the name of Sandra Day O'Connor. There are those who might argue that this is a women's victory, a feminist victory, but in actuality Sandra Day O'Connor's role on the Supreme Court has encouraged a distinctly backwards trend. She is opposed to abortion—really! The distinction of being the first woman on the Supreme Court has not advanced the condition of women in general. On the contrary, it has been retarded, I think. On the other hand, when women who are oppressed not only by virtue of their gender but by virtue of their class and their race win victories for themselves, then other women will inevitably reap the benefits of these victories. This is one example of the way in which it is possible to be a Marxist, emphasize the central role of the working class, but at the same time participate in the effort to win liberation for all women. Of course it's not that simple, and a lot more work needs to be done in the area of integrating within Marxist theory an understanding of women's oppression.

Of course the existing socialist countries are still involved in a real serious effort to throw off the cumulative effects of gender-based oppression. I was very excited in the seventies about the antisexist campaigns in Cuba. When I visited Cuba in 1969 for the first time, I became very excited about the general revolutionary process there, but it was clear that there were still very serious problems with respect to the inferior position women still held in that society. Together with the other women in the delegation, I raised this issue. We were very impressed by the openness there, which permitted criticism without the stigma of being considered antirevolutionary. The answer we received at that time was that the main emphasis in the campaign for women's equality was in the economic sphere. They were not dealing with attitudes, nor with institutionalized sexism in other realms. During that period I was visiting Cuba very regularly. I went in 1969, then I went in 1972 right after my trial was over, I went in 1973, I went in 1974, so I could see concrete changes occurring. I noticed during a later trip that they were talking about very serious problems such as absenteeism from the workplace among women, and women quitting jobs. This was an era of great economic difficulty for Cubans; there were very few consumer goods available, which meant that people were earning money they couldn't spend. In households where both husband and wife worked, because they were accumulating money for which there were no corresponding product on the market, the woman would frequently quit. And so they had to deal with the problem of the assumed economic superiority of the male. So in order to bring women into production, mass campaigns against sexism had to be conducted. At the same time they had to begin to address related areas of women's lives that are affected by their involvement in work outside the home, for example, childcare and housework. When women work outside the home, they work an eight-hour shift on the outside, only to come home and work in a second shift of eight hours or more. As a result of that very practical experience, the Cubans developed what they called at that time an attack on the second shift, which involved both institutional changes such as the expansion of childcare centers, as well as ideological campaigns. Since they were not economically in a position to institute socialized housework, the men had to be convinced to participate in household tasks in order for women to work. Among other things, they made use of film. There was this wonderful film called *Portrait of Teresa*, about a woman caught between her desire to work and a husband who refused to assist at home. There were billboards all over, skits or television encouraging men to participate in housework, in rearing the children, and so forth. Eventually they were able to pass a new Family Code, which wrote men's participation in housework and childrearing into law. To me, that was quite exciting, an example of how one can use the basis of socialism in order to advance the quest for women's equality. I have never been one to assume that the advent of socialism by itself will emancipate women or automatically free Black people from the constraints of racism. But socialism does provide a much more effective basis on which to develop campaigns that can eventually wipe out both the institutional and the attitudinal expressions of sexism.

KB: Angela, as well as your prisoners' rights work and your membership of the Communist Party, I am also aware that you are active on issues of health. Would you say a little bit about this?

AD: Sure. I'm a member of the board of directors of the National Black Women's Health Project, an organization founded by Byllye Avery in 1983. Our work focuses on physical, mental, and spiritual health needs of Black women. Until recently the emphasis has been on "self-help" as adapted from the larger feminist health movement but geared to the particular conditions of Black women. The most exciting aspect of this organization is its ability to unify Black women beyond the limitations of age, social class, occupation, and geographical origin. A typical gathering includes girls as young as thirteen and women as old as seventy-five, rural women on welfare and women who are lawyers or university professors, women from the most rural areas of the South and women from urban centers like New York. We are presently planning an international conference to be held in June 25–30, 1990, in Atlanta. We expect that the attendance will be at least five thousand women and men from all racial and ethnic backgrounds. The theme of this conference will be the politics of Black women's health, reflecting our desire to be able to bring about changes in the area of public policy. It goes without saying that your sisters in Britain are invited to participate in the celebration and strategy sessions.

KB: We'll look forward to it. Changing the focus slightly, you know there are a number of discussions which have occurred recently about the contribution of Jewish feminists within women's organizations. What do you think about these discussions?

AD: It is of course very important for Jewish feminists to attempt to integrate their particular historical and cultural heritage into theories and strategies for women in politics. In this country a strong connection with the early labor movement ought to be acknowledged, for Jewish women were in the forefront of working-class struggle during the early part of this century. In other words, there is a prominent progressive pattern in the historical experiences of Jewish women. The issue of Jewish feminists' relationship to Israel is of course a point of considerable controversy. Jewish women who are progressive feminists are not afraid to oppose the government of Israel for its sexist, racist, and imperialist policies, for its collaboration with apartheid in South Africa, as well as with other reactionary governments around the world . Progressive Jewish feminists must find ways to express solidarity with their Palestinian sisters, whose families have been cruelly divested of their land and their rights by the state of Israel, and, in turn, all of us who are active in the women's movement must look on anti-Semitism as a priority in our work. Black women in particular must reveal the strong ties between racism and anti-Semitism.

KB: Angela, there's something that struck me in Jesse Jackson's speech at the Democratic Convention last week—when he was talking about oppressed groups, he raised the issue of sexuality. It was interesting for me, that Jackson was prepared to take on what I think could be defined as an unpopular issue, at a time when there is much tightening, narrowing, and constraining of attitudes toward sexuality. What do you think about that?

AD: This is a very interesting era, an era, as I mentioned before, of coalition building. The coalition established by the Jackson campaign was to unify virtually all the progressive movements in this country today. This unity has compelled people to look at many issues in a qualitatively different way. Of course one of these issues is homophobia, which, by and large over the last period, has not been challenged through a *mass* effort—certainly in the gay and lesbian communities, perhaps by the women's movement—but it hasn't been taken on as a *mass* issue. The impressive march on October 11 of last year of approximately half a million people was an indication of the extent to which organized forces within the gay and lesbian communities have grown to encompass working-class people and racially oppressed people. Jesse Jackson was the only potential presidential candidate to speak during this, and his involvement directly reflected the grass-roots support of gay and lesbian groups for his campaign. Here in the San Francisco Bay Area, there was a very large gay and lesbian organization for Jackson. I think he has indeed learned that he must take his leadership from grass-roots movements, and that, in my mind is what is most impressive about Jesse Jackson. In 1984 at the very beginning of the campaign, if he had talked about gays and lesbians, he probably would have had little to say, but as a result of that interaction that has occurred over the last period, he felt comfortable enough to raise that issue at the Democratic Convention in front of millions and millions of people.

An article about the October 11 march on Washington by Paul Horowitz, in the journal *Outlook* (Spring 1988) pointed out that even though as many as six hundred thousand people participated, the tendency toward "ghettoization" of the gay and lesbian movements was evident for the overwhelming majority of people were themselves gay or lesbian. He speculated on what might have been possible if, say, every gay man and lesbian who attended the march had invited six of their straight friends or coworkers or colleagues to attend. This could have substantially transformed the nature of the struggle against homophobia. We have a long way to go in order to develop consciousness around the importance of representing homophobia as an adversary of progressive people in general, not just of gays and lesbians. But it is a victory that we have reached the point now where it is possible to begin that process. However, we have reached the point where it is possible to take on a question that ten years ago would have been an issue. It's always important to understand the process, to know how to define victories in such a way as to establish them as the foundation for moving forward, rather than simply expressing one's discontent—often very emotionally—at what we have not yet achieved.

Forty years ago it could not have been predicted that Jesse Jackson would accomplish what he did in this present election campaign. No one would have predicted that he could become a serious candidate, and that he would receive support not only from Black people and other racially oppressed people but from a broad section of the population; that during the primaries he could, for example, win the state of Nevada, which is overwhelmingly white, or Vermont or Alaska. No one would have dared to predict this. If one looks at the extent to which the women's movement has been accelerated as a result of increased working-class militancy, and other such interconnections, I would predict today that it won't be too long before there is a collective acknowledgment of the need to challenge homophobia.

KB: Say a bit more . . .

AD: Fundamentally, the roots of homophobia are very much connected to the roots of racism, which are connected to the roots of sexism, and to the roots of economic exploitation. It is not coincidental that the same forces that will picket an abortion clinic or inflict violence on abortion providers are the same ones who have tried to prevent integrated schools. These ultra-right forces—the most extreme being the Ku Klux Klan and the Nazis—are also the same forces responsible for violence against gays and lesbians, and for a fraudulent analysis holding homosexuals responsible for the so-called breakdown of the family. If one simply looks at the ties established among our enemies, there should be a greater awareness of the need to build a united movement. After all, we are challenging a common adversary. Unfortunately, I don't think we have enough time to talk about the connection between the repression of sexuality—the repression of heterosexuals' sexuality, and the repression of the sexuality of gays and lesbians. And racism has played a central role in creating this type of repressive sexual environment.

KB: OK, just to wind up. This issue of *Feminist Review* is about looking back over twenty years, but also looking forwards. What do you think think the future holds, what would you want to be fighting for, and, also, how does your academic and activist work fit in with each other?

AD: In a sense this is a more exciting era than twenty years ago, which is oftentimes romanticized and idealized—at least in this country—as a period when everyone was a radical or revolutionary! For those of us involved in the Black movement during the sixties, those were difficult times. One could easily lose one's life as a result of involvement in that struggle. It was a period during which we were constantly dodging bullets and wondering who was going to be killed next, wondering whose funeral we would be attending tomorrow. There was a great deal of confusion during that period as well. Today we have achieved a measure of lucidity, based on those historical experiences, based on an understanding of our errors as well as our achievements. Why I find this era exciting is not only related to the particular evolution of theory and practice in the United States, but also to the process by which international issues have become local issues. I think it was Jesse Jackson who said that we need to think globally and act locally. There's much more extensive consciousness of that dialectic between the concrete work that we do, the activist work, and the international context. People who are involved here in the anti-apartheid movement think about it in a qualitatively different way than those who were involved in the movement against the war in Vietnam. There is a great deal more respect for the people of South Africa and their struggles, and their ability to conduct those struggles and actually to give leadership to all of us, wherever we are. During the Vietnam war era, people tended to see the Vietnamese as anonymous, faceless, oppressed people. The structure of racism was built into the attitudes toward the people of Vietnam. I think that we've come a long way in this process of forging consciousness.

What lies ahead, I think, is the challenge of making the transition from consciousness to action, from theory to practice. In my opinion, while theoretical work, intellectual work, is extremely important, the work of the activist will determine whether or not we will move to a new stage. That's why I often say when I lecture across the country that everyone should learn how to become an activist on some level, in some way. Everyone who considers herself or himself a part of this overall progressive movement must establish some kind of organizational ties, and must definitely participate in one or more movements. This especially holds true for women, if we are to realize the enormous potential at this particular moment in the history of the women's movement. We have to get out there and do it for ourselves! Basically this is what I would say—and it's exactly eight o'clock!

KB: Thank you.

Note

Both Angela Y. Davis and Kum-Kum Bhavnani have edited this interview. Thanks to Stephanie Mack and Janet Hall for their help and comments.

Kum-Kum Bhavani is a member of the *Feminist Review* editorial collective.

Interview with Angela Davis

Terry Rockefeller and Louis Massiah / 1989

Conducted by Blackside, Inc. for *Eyes on the Prize II: America at the Racial Crossroads 1965–1985*. Henry Hampton Collection, Washington University Libraries. Reprinted by permission.

Editorial notes:

Interview, conducted by Blackside, Inc. on May 24, 1989, for Washington University Libraries, Film and Media Archive, Henry Hampton Collection. The transcripts contain material that did not appear in the final program. Only text appearing in bold italics was used in the final version of the interview.

Question 1

Interviewer: In 1967 what made you make the decision to come back home, and how would you characterize the mood of the Black Liberation Movement and how you began to get involved with it in those years?

Angela Davis: I decided to study in Europe in 1965, which was the year of the Watts uprisings, and the following year the Black Panther Party was founded. So I found myself in Europe at a time when the Black Liberation Movement was undergoing a very important transformation. I felt very drawn to that movement and felt very frustrated during the entire period I spent in Europe because I was forced to watch things from afar. In 1967 I decided to discontinue my academic work in Europe and return to this country specifically in order to become involved in the Black movement. I chose to go to San Diego because Herbert Marcuse, with whom I had studied at Brandeis, was teaching there. But I also knew that in California there was a great deal of organizing occurring in the community as a result of the emergence of the Black Panther Party and other organizations. So, as soon as I arrived in San Diego, I began to investigate what was happening in the community, what organizations existed. A number of organizations were active. The Black Congress, and there was an organization headed by Ron Karenga called "US Organization." Finally, however, I decided that the organization I wanted to join did not really exist. So I became active on the campus in founding the first Black Student Union there, which eventually developed into a movement demanding Black studies on the campus and an entire college devoted to the needs of Black students, as well as Latino students and white working-class students.

Question 2

Interviewer: Can you talk a little bit about the forces that came together behind the idea and the vision of that college?

Davis: Well, actually, we were quite unique during that period. That was an era during which Black people were seeking to identify with a lost heritage. And it, of course, it was extremely important that we understand what was necessary in order to feel comfortable calling ourselves Black, in order to talk about our African ancestry in a very positive way, so that many of us took on African names. My name during that time was Tamu. We wore African garb. And we were very much concerned about developing our Black identity. But at the same time I felt, perhaps because of my background, the way my parents reared me, that there had to be coalition work with other groups, that we could not so encapsulate ourselves that we were not aware of what was happening in the Chicano community, we were not aware of what was happening with white working-class people who were also oppressed. So, I convinced a couple of students to begin organizing the Black Student Union. When finally we had gotten enough Black students together, and I should say there were, there was only a handful on the campus at that time then we approached Chicano students who began to organize and created a Chicano student organization. We realized that we had to come together, because separately we were so few that we would accomplish absolutely nothing. We connected with a group of progressive white students on the campus and decided that we would demand that the next college to be established on the campus of the University of California, San Diego, be called Lamumba Zapata College and that its curriculum as well as its faculty reflect the specific needs of Black students, Chicano students and white working-class students. It was a very militant movement, I should say. We were forced to break in, at one point, to an academic senate meeting and of course ignore all of the decorum that is usually reserved for such meetings. And we simply demanded that the professors listen to us about the needs of those of us who had been marginalized so long within academia. The professors eventually listened. They were, of course, absolutely outraged that we would dare to disrupt their deliberations. But they listened. And some of them joined us. Eventually we decided to occupy the registrar's office. And Herbert Marcuse was the first person to walk through the door. We figured if the most revered professor on the campus participated in the occupation, that would legitimize our struggle. So that eventually we were able to muster support among the majority of the students on campus. We had a successful strike. And the third college, although it was never called Lamumba Zapata College, eventually came into being.

Question 3

Interviewer: I'd now like to have you talk about your decision to join the Communist Party and the vision for a movement that was inspiring you in that decision.

Davis: When I returned to this country from Europe I was very, very anxious to throw myself into organizing work in the Black community. I eventually became active in SNCC, Student Nonviolent Coordinating Committee in Los Angeles, even though I was commuting between San Diego and Los Angeles. And I was very excited about the work that we were able to do in the community. Within a very short period of time we had hundreds of active members of the organization. I was the head of the Liberation School, which I found extremely exciting, because I had always felt somewhat uncomfortable in the purely academic environment there. I was able to teach Marx to community people, to young people. Eventually we had some problems within the organization, Los Angeles SNCC; they had to do with the part played by women in the organization. It was a very difficult period. Eventually the organization became defunct. It was at that time that I decided to join the Communist Party. I joined the Communist Party because I had come into contact with a number of communists, Black communists in particular, in working with SNCC and doing community work in San Diego and Los Angeles. And I was always very impressed by their vision, which seemed to go much further than what was happening at the moment, which seemed to be much broader than specifically the issues confronting Black people at that particular moment in history. They had a long-range vision. They also had a sense of how to involve other progressive people, and I associated myself in general with their vision. For example, when we were in San Diego, there was the case of a young Black man by the name of Ed Lynn, at that particular time—his name, he eventually changed his name—who was charged with—I can't remember the exact charges—but he—

Interviewer: Let's just stop for a second. I'm not sure.

Davis: That you want to, OK, well.

Question 4

Interviewer: How would you characterize the growing opposition that the movement was confronting?

Davis: There was terrible repression during that period. I had never experienced anything like that in my life. And I realize, looking back, that we lived in a war zone. I could receive a telephone call from someone with whom I was active in SNCC, for example, and she or he might say, "My house is surrounded by the police. Call as many people as possible because we need support." That was quite usual. So that we expected every moment that we might be confronted with an armed attack. And I don't know if I can get that across, that feeling today, except by saying that it was as if were involved in battle. Now, many people during that era, precisely because of the organized police attack on the Black Liberation Movement and specifically on the Black Panther Party. We know that J. Edgar Hoover orchestrated a national assault on the Black Panther Party in particular and other organizations that were militant representatives of the Black community at that time. There were many people who, as a result of that repression call the period fascist. I was one of those who was opposed to arguing that we lived in an era of full-blown fascism.

Interviewer: I'm just going to run out of film on this.

Question 5

Interviewer: Again, how would you characterize the opposition you were facing, and what did that make you feel, and how would you deal with that fear?

Davis: Well, it was a very frightening phase of my own life, as I'm sure it was of all of those who participated during that particular moment of our movement. We were confronted with the possibility of being attacked by armed police at any given moment. I purchased a weapon. Most people had guns, and we bought guns, not because we were intending to use them in any offensive way, but because it, we needed them in order to protect ourselves, to defend ourselves. We learned how to use weapons because we had to guarantee that we would not be senselessly shot down by the police as were so many people during that period, the police or infiltrators. We knew that there was a nationally coordinated effort to wipe out the Black Panther Party and to wipe out the militant Black movement in general. And of course many people argued that because of the nature of this repression, we lived in a society which had embraced a full-blown fascism. I, personally, was not one who argued that that era was a fascist era. I felt that the repression was definitely fascistlike in character. But there were still things that we were able to do within the traditional channels of the society. There was still some democratic rights that we enjoyed, and we had to take advantage of those. Those who argued that we lived in a fascist country, if they followed the implications of that, would then say that our organizing had to be clandestine, that we must arm ourselves and we must engage in guerrilla activity. And of course there were those who felt that way at that time. But I felt that we could openly organize. The people with whom I worked were for organizing in an open manner in the community doing the kind of work we did with SNCC, for example, bringing people together around instances of police brutality, organizing the community to fight back whenever there was a police killing in the community or when a liquor store owner, for example, might kill a young Black man whom he thought was about to rob his store. So that was the kind of work that we were doing then despite the repression.

Question 6

Interviewer: I would like to now move on and have you relate what happened to you and your job at UCLA and how that, because of the notoriety it brought you, drew you into the prison movement. You made that wonderful link before about George Jackson contacting you, and the other Soledad Brothers contacting you.

Davis: Well, I was hired to teach in the Philosophy Department at UCLA in the fall of 1969. I had joined the Communist Party a year earlier. Before I had the opportunity to teach my first class, I was fired by the regents of the University of California, an ex-officio member of which was Ronald Reagan. As a result of the enormous amount of publicity that was focused on me by virtue of that firing, I received letters countless numbers of letters from prisoners all over the country. George Jackson wrote me. Ruchell Magee, who was my codefendant, wrote me, and later I began to recognize through the work that I did in the case of the Soledad Brothers that it was very important to bring into the movement of that period a consciousness of what was happening to people in prison. Previously we had worked primarily around political prisoners, or primarily around people who had been arrested because of their political beliefs and political activities: Huey Newton, Ericka Huggins, Bobby Seale, the New York 21, the L.A. 18, all of those cases. But we hadn't really taken a look at the function of the prison system in our society. As a result of working to free the Soledad Brothers, I became increasingly aware of the need to integrate an understanding of the social function of the prison system into the work that we were doing, calling for political equality the work that we were doing in the community against police crimes and police brutality, so that when I fought for my right to teach on the campus of UCLA, I always included in that analysis the fact that there were three young Black men who were victims of the very same repression which I was confronting, but they stood to lose their lives as a result of the political work they had done within the prison system. I stood to lose my job as a result of my political activities and my work.

Question 7

Interviewer: Tell me, can you describe how—you were talking before about how the definition of a political prisoner expanded. Can you relate that, that transformation that went on within the prisoner movement?

Davis: Well, initially, when we talked about political prisoners, we referred to those who had been sent to prison as a result of their work, their political work in the community. And of course we had scores of Black Panthers who were political prisoners. I was a political prisoner because I was arrested and charged with murder, kidnapping, and conspiracy—not because I had committed those crimes but because of my political work. We began to realize that the definition of political prisoner also needed to include those who did not necessarily go to prison because they had been politically involved but who became politicized within the prison system and therefore were subjected to long prison terms and other forms of repression as a result. George Jackson, for example, who was sent to prison as a result of being convicted of a $70 robbery. When I met George Jackson, when I became aware of his case and became active in the Soledad Brothers' case, he had been in prison for ten years, for $70. And it was clear that they had refused to release him on parole because he was trying to organize his colleagues in prison. He was doing the kind of work that was very threatening to the prison system because he was calling for unity. He was calling upon people to demand better prison conditions, better food, the right to read whatever they wanted to read. So, definitely George Jackson was a political prisoner even before he was charged with the killing of the Soledad guard. And then we came to realize that there was a whole category of prisoners who may not have been politically active in the community, may not have been politically active in prison but were in prison for political reasons. They were in prison because of the function of racism in the society. They were in prison because of the function of class exploitation. We took a look at the prison system and realized that if you were wealthy, you didn't go to prison. If you did at all, you went to what we used to call the country club prisons—you know, where you could play tennis and ride horses and that type of thing. So that expanded into a movement of support within the community, taking on the function of the prison system in general and calling for the abolition of the prison system as it exists as it existed then as it exists today.

Interviewer: Can you talk about—

Question 8

Interviewer: What was the prison movement in terms of, and how did you see the prison movement fitting into your overall notion of, the revolutionary movement or a full class liberation movement in this country—what was the part it had to play?

Davis: Well, though in the Black community at that time virtually everyone had some personal contact with the prison system, I know in my family I could count several cousins who had gone to prison. But it was one of those things that we never approached politically. We never integrated what was happening to thousands and thousands of Black people and other poor people into our analysis of the exploitative and oppressive character of this society. So, George Jackson, for example, was very enlightening in his ideas when he, you know, pointed to the—

Interviewer: I'm sorry.

Question 9

Interviewer: How did the prison movement fit into the larger vision of the Black liberation struggle?

Davis: Well, virtually every Black person had some personal relationship to the prison system. In my family I had several cousins who spent time in jails and prisons. And that was the case with virtually everyone. However, we had not analyzed the prison system with a view towards integrating it into our overall conception of the function of racism in the society, of the function of class exploitation. We had talked about police brutality, the Black Panther Party talked about the police as an occupying force in the community, but we had not really understood the extent to which the whole criminal justice system, the police, the courts, the prison system, is very much intertwined with the economic, economic oppression of Black people [1] Eyes on the Prize II: America at the Racial Crossroads 1965–1985; Episode. 206–30. There are no jobs for certain numbers of young people in our community. What happens to them? There's no recreation available. The schooling is not the kind of enlightening process that it should be. So what happens to these young people? They might go out and get involved in petty criminal activity as a result of the lack of these facilities in the community. And they end up, of course, spending, many of them, the rest of their lives in prison. George Jackson was charged with and convicted of a $70 robbery. He went to prison, incredibly, on a sentence which ranged from one year to life. He received an indeterminate sentence, and had George Jackson not been assassinated, I'm convinced he would have spent the rest of his life in prison. So what does that mean? How does the prison system function to reinforce the economic exploitation of our people? How does it function to prevent the kind of organizing challenging these injustices? These are questions that we had not really explored until, as a result of working around the case of the Soledad Brothers, we began to become acquainted with some of George Jackson's ideas on the relationship between prison and society, on the functions that the prison system has in relationship to the perpetuation of racism in a larger society.

Question 10

Interviewer: I'd like you to go back and talk about George Jackson, his initial sentence and then what he faced, without foreshadowing his death, because as we watch the film, the viewer will learn about his death. So, I don't want to introduce him as a person who is already dead. But if you could talk about the sentence he received and then how the sentence was extended.

Davis: We learned about the indeterminate sentence.

Interviewer: Can you start again?

Davis: We learned about the indeterminate sentence as a direct result of being acquainted with George Jackson's background. And it seems as if we should have been aware of this before, but many of us were absolutely shocked, seasoned activists as we were, to learn that George Jackson had been initially arrested in connection with a $70 robbery but had received a sentence ranging from one year to life. One year to life for a $70 robbery of which he says he was not even guilty.

Question 11

Interviewer: Can you speak some about the collection of letters, *Soledad Brother*, and the impact that had had on the prison movement inside the prisons and for those of you who were working for prisoners?

Davis: When *Soledad Brother* was published, the collection of George Jackson's letters, it was an extremely important moment for the prison movement, both inside and outside. For the first time, there was an attempt to develop an analysis of the relationship between what was going on in our communities, in the streets, in the factories, in the schools, on the campuses and what was happening inside the prison. Large numbers of prisoners, of course, could relate to what George Jackson said in his letters, the stories about the horrible repression that he suffered, the fact that he was never able to spend time with his younger brother Jonathan outside of the manacles and chains that he wore. So that there was a very important emotional effect of this book on people, both inside prison and, perhaps more importantly, outside, because those of us on the outside had generally not taken the time to try to understand what the experience was. We might have, at that time, been fighting for the freedom of political prisoners or challenging the prison system. But [what] George Jackson managed to do was to make that experience palpable, make it concrete so that it became something that people could relate to as human beings. There's always this tendency to push prisons to the fringes of our awareness, so that we don't have to deal with what happens inside of these horrifying institutions [2] Eyes on the Prize II: America at the Racial Crossroads 1965–1985: Episode 206–32. And there is the tendency also to look at prisoners as having deserved what they have met with there. So that the criminal is a figure in our society who has very little credibility. And what George Jackson demonstrated with his letters was that prisoners are human beings, prisoners are intelligent human beings, prisoners have families, they have feelings. And at the same time it seems he laid the basis for an important political analysis which was lacking. I was very moved when I first saw the published version of the letters. I was in jail myself by that time because I had worked on the manuscript and worked with those who were involved in publishing it. I received a copy of the book when I was in jail in New York in the Women's House of Detention. And at that particular time, the authorities banned that book from the jail population. They allowed me to read it in a library to which no other prisoners were allowed entrance at the time I was reading the book. Eventually we were able to get a clandestine copy, a copy which was brought in by one of the women officers who felt that we had the right, or the other women had the right, to read this. So the book circulated all over the corridor where I lived, all over the floor, all over the jail, as a matter of fact. And there were often long discussions about what George Jackson wrote about in that book.

Interviewer: Cut for a second.

Question 12

Interviewer: How did your own prison experience expand your notion of what the prison movement had to be?

Davis: When I went to jail in New York, it immediately occurred to me that there were whole areas that we had totally neglected within the prison movement having to do with women's imprisonment. While we had developed a solidarity movement designed to support prisoners, we had not taken on issues like the separation of mothers and their children, like the treatment of, the specific treatment of, women who were pregnant. As a matter of fact, women had been relatively invisible in the prison movement. It was as if there were no women who ever went into prison. And this, of course, reflected the lack of awareness within the movement and the nature of women's oppression. So that I began immediately to write to Ericka Huggins, who was in jail at the same time. We shared our experiences being women in prison. We could see very concretely the open role of racism. In New York over 90 percent of the women were either Black or Puerto Rican, so that racism became something that was very palpable and very visible and very hurtful, because we could see white women come in and go out immediately on their own recognizance, not that the white women were responsible for that, but the judges who would not give Black women O.R., or the right to leave on their own recognizance. I learned what many of the people whom I had been working around must have to go through every day for weeks and months and years. I was in solitary confinement for approximately one year, and as hard as that was for me to endure, I realized that there were many others who did not have the opportunity to make their cases heard as I did. At least I was aware of the fact that there were hundreds, thousands of people out organizing for me, all over the world. So.

Interviewer: Stop. What I'd like to do is pick up with—

Question 13

Interviewer: What were the particular reactions of some of your fellow inmates to some of the contents of George Jackson's book?

Davis: Well, the women in the New York Women's House of Detention who had the opportunity to read George's book felt extremely enlightened by his ideas. But they were also disturbed by his negative attitudes toward women, and in particular his mother, but specifically his attitudes toward Black women. And, of course, that was a direct reflection of the ideological climate. The period following 1965 saw concerted, systematic propagandistic and ideological attacks on Black women. We were called emasculating females. We were being held responsible for collaborating in the oppression that hurt Black men. And George Jackson unfortunately accepted some of these ideas in an uncritical fashion, which come through in *Soledad Brother*.

Question 14

Interviewer: What was the response that you heard, and what was the discussion around those issues?

Davis: Well—

Interviewer: Let's just wait for this to pass.

Interviewer: What was the response to those?

Davis: Well, they couldn't understand what George Jackson had against his mother, for example. And, you know, why is it that Black women are being held responsible for a system of oppression that emanates from people who are wealthy from, you know, white men, the ruling class? And of course this was very intentional. I think that George later realized as a result of a correspondence that I carried on with him, and as a result of discussion with other people that he had unwittingly accepted ideas that were designed to create that kind of division within the community. And that, as a matter of fact, Black women were playing extremely important roles. The civil rights movement would not have been what it was without the roles of Fannie Lou Hamer and Daisy Bates and Ella Baker and Ruby Doris Robinson. And Jo Ann Robinson, and we can go on and on and on. So that the women in the jail in New York had the same reaction that I did, which confirmed my own criticism of George's notions of Black women. And I should say that George changed. He began to critically examine his acceptance of ideas that emanated with the government. The Moynihan Report, for example, which was published in 1965. And eventually he did agree that he had been influenced in a very negative way by these ideas and that women should play equal roles in the community, and Black mothers should not be held responsible. Black mothers who care for their sons and their daughters should not be held responsible for preventing, or should not be accused of preventing, their sons from being warriors in the struggle for Black liberation. Because Black women have won a lot of those battles themselves.

Question 15

Interviewer: What allowed your legal victory in your case, and what did it forecast?

Davis: Well, it was very important to be able to win victories during that period. It was a very difficult juncture of our history. It was—

Question 16

Interviewer: Can you start by defining that period? I mean, saying the period when I was in prison or the period of the late sixties, early seventies.

Davis: OK, the period, the period of the late sixties and the early seventies was a very painful period. The repression was so total that no one could escape being hurt in some way or another by the death of someone, an activist who was killed in the communities. I, when I look back on that period, I see myself attending funerals, and it was important at that time that we recognized that we could be victorious, that we were not simply the targets of repression but that we were active, historical agents who could set an agenda, fight for that agenda, and win. And that is why I think my particular case, my legal case and the organizing that went on around it, was so important, because it did demonstrate that with organizing, with coalition organizing, it was possible to defeat the agenda of the president of the United States, because Richard Nixon was very much involved in creating the impression that I was a terrorist. It was possible to defeat the agenda of Ronald Reagan, who was the governor of the state of California at that time. People responded at first spontaneously to my case. And I think that a lot of it had to do with the fact that I was out there as an activist, that I was attempting to organize people to defend the rights of political prisoners, to free Huey Newton, Ericka Huggins, Bobby Seale, George Jackson, John Clutchette, Fleeta Drumgo, and that, as a matter of fact, I had often said that we all need to be involved in this movement because we don't know who will be the next to go. And if we don't build the basis for a strong movement, and if one of us happens to be hit by the repression, we won't be able to count on the support that we will personally need. And of course at that time I had no idea that I would be one of the next who would be imprisoned in that way. I think that the spontaneous response was important. But alone it would not have guaranteed the victory. Because the response initially would have petered out. It would have withered away. My case spanned a period of almost two years. And certainly organization was needed in order to build the kind of movement that would endure throughout that period from the fight for bail, for example, to the actual legal acquittal. I think that we were successful because those who were organizing around my case.

Interviewer: We're at the very end of the roll.

Question 17

Interviewer: What was the importance of the coalition that made your ultimate legal victory possible? What was the importance historically to this period? What was that coalition?

Davis: Well, there was a spontaneous response; the spontaneous response was not sufficient to serve as the basis for a movement that had to endure two years of support activities. So that what was key to achieving my acquittal was the organizing, very serious organizing work that took place on a community basis, in factories, in churches, in schools, in every existing institution in our country. Some 250 committees were organized from one end of the country to the other, and those committees were always multiracial. The committee was a multiracial community. It was a committee which brought together workers and students, a committee that brought together religious activists and people who might be involved in the women's movement, the peace movement. It was an important lesson, because the lesson learned was that we could indeed be successful if we could bring together all of the progressive forces in this society. And of course I shouldn't be saying "we," because I sat in jail during the time all of this work was going on. I did have a part in developing the strategy, both the legal strategy and the political strategy. And I was not always correct in the suggestions that I made. I can remember that I was opposed to organizing around bail movement. Because at that particular time, I was charged with three capital crimes, and at that time of course if you were charged with a capital crime, you were not eligible for bail. But there were those in the committee who argued that a bail movement should be established. There might be people, for example, who would be willing to stand up for my right to bail but who might not yet be willing to call for my freedom outright. And I felt at that particular time that was not a realistic goal, because the legal possibilities of achieving bail did not exist. As it turned out, I was wrong. Because the California Supreme Court overturned capital punishment, which made me then eligible for bail. In the meantime people all over the country and all over the world had gathered thousands and thousands of signatures, so that as soon as the California Supreme Court overturned capital punishment, there were letters and telegrams and telephone calls flowing into the judge, who then did establish bail. But he set bail at $100,000, which was absolutely exorbitant during that period. We didn't have $100,000. And a white farmer from a rural area of California came forth and said he would put up his farm as bail.

Question 18

Interviewer: What was the lesson of that coalition for this period in the history, in your thinking? What, where, what did that signify in terms of what was possible in this very dark period?

Davis: At a time when there was not a great deal of unity embracing people from various racial and ethnic backgrounds, embracing, you know, workers and students, there tended to be unfortunately a kind of competition among those of us who considered ourselves as the oppressed. One group would argue that they were oppressed. The other group would say, "No, you know, women are more oppressed than Black people." And unfortunately that's the kind of climate that prevailed during that era, to a certain extent. In any event, there was not a great deal of multiracial organizing going on. There was not a great deal of efforts designed to allow people to cross bridges from various political points and various personal experiences. And those who organized the campaign for my freedom reached out to everyone and were able to figure out a strategy which allowed everyone to feel connected with my case. The women's movement and of course the Black movement, the working-class movement. I was a union member as a faculty member at UCLA. I belonged to the union, the church movement. And I think it was a real lesson on how to achieve the maximum possible political force. And a lesson in pointing out that even though there may be differences separating various groups of people in our society, how there are also things that we have in common. And if we are in some way the target of an oppressive socioeconomic system, we should be able to figure out how to stand together. And by bringing literally tens of thousands, hundreds of thousands, millions of people together, it was possible to build a movement which did seep into the courtroom and did influence people, not in terms of the jury deciding, well, there is this movement that is going to get me if I do not vote for the acquittal of Angela Davis, but rather because the jurors themselves recognized that it was not a question of simply being accountable to me as one individual, that they would have to be accountable to enormous numbers of people. They would have to be accountable to their own church members. They would have to be accountable to their own union members. They would have to be accountable to their, to the students who attended college with their sons and daughters. It was by building that kind of movement that it was possible to achieve victory.

Question 19

Interviewer: How did the victory feel? How did that moment feel?

Davis: Well, it was the happiest day of my life. When I was arrested, I didn't know whether I would ever again see what it was like to live on the other side of the walls. I knew the repression of that era was a very destructive repression and that many people had fallen. And I did not know whether I would survive.

So that on that day when I was pronounced officially not guilty, I celebrated. But at the same time it occurred to me immediately that we needed to keep that movement together, so that all of the sisters and brothers whom I had left behind could benefit from this organized might of the people of this country.

Interviewer: Cut. That's great.

Question 20

Interviewer: When did you hear Malcolm speak? What was that occasion?

Davis: I heard Malcolm X speak when I was a student at Brandeis University, and it was one of the most enlightening moments of my life. I was attending a university which was predominately white. As a matter of fact, I had spent two years in a high school that was predominantly white. And I had come to feel very alienated in a way that I could not even articulate myself, because we had not yet developed the language that allowed us to talk about the way racism functions in those kinds of unspoken situations. So that I had been attending this university, doing well and feeling OK. But, at the same time, feeling very alienated, feeling OK in my academic life but feeling very alienated. Because I didn't see myself anywhere. I didn't see myself in the courses that I taught. I didn't see myself in the faculty members. I didn't see myself in the students. And so when Malcolm came and spoke and affirmed what it was to be Black and talked about the quest for Black equality in a very passionate and militant way, it made me feel good. It made me feel OK. It made me feel that as a human being I was as important as were all of the white people sitting around me. As a matter of fact, at that particular time, Malcolm spoke to the white audience, and in a very—I would say—negative kind of way. He spoke, he astonished the largely white audience, because he called them all kinds of names and ran down the list of their, his historical crimes. And you know, while I wonder what good evoking guilt really does in terms of creating the right kind of basis for, of a movement, I can say, at that time, it made me feel good, because he said a lot of the things that I probably would have wanted to say if only if I had been in possession of the language that would have allowed me to say them at that time.

Question 21

Interviewer: What was the response of the white—

Interviewer: What was the response of the predominantly white audience to Malcolm's speech?

Davis: Well, they were very shocked that—

Interviewer: Can you say "the predominantly white audience" just so that—

Davis: OK the response of the predominantly white audience, at that address given by Malcolm X was utter shock, as a matter of fact. They applauded very amply after he spoke, but I think that they simply could not deal with the fact that here was a Black man that had the courage to stand up and not, you know, only criticize the system of racism but talked about white people and the historical crimes for which they are responsible in a way they had never heard before. I don't think they took him as serious as he should have been taken. Because at that particular time he was not seen as the spokesperson for a movement that would be able to make good on the words that were coming across during that speech. But I think that later on they probably recognized, as I did, that what Malcolm was doing was representing patterns of political thought that would later become accepted by large numbers of people in this country and would mark the beginning of an entirely new approach to the movement for Black liberation in this country.

Interviewer: Ok, great.

Question 22

Interviewer: What was your family's response and the community that you come from, grown [*sic*] up in, response to the turn that you took to the left?

Davis: My mother was active in Left causes as a young person. She was active in the NAACP, which eventually became an illegal organization in the state of Alabama. She was active in an organization called the Southern Negro Youth Congress, which had been initiated by Black communists. And as a matter of fact, my mother had many friends who were members of the Communist Parties. I didn't not initially join the Communist Party when I first became a political person, because I had a tendency to see communists as being my parents' age. And no, I didn't see it as an option for myself as a young person. In a few years, of course, I changed my mind. But my mother had been active in Left causes for many years. And she had always, when I was growing up, told me that I should dare to be different, and she reminds, she reminded me of that over and over again, that I should not be afraid to stand up for what I believed. So that, even though there were difficulties, my mother immediately supported me. My father immediately supported me. There were members of our community in Birmingham, Alabama, who, particularly during the time I was in jail, played very important roles in the movement. My mother traveled all over the country speaking on my behalf. My father spoke. My brother spoke. As a matter of fact, my brother, who was a professional football player at the time, had very serious problems with his own career because he had decided to take a stand on my behalf. So, if there is one thing I had during that period, that was family support, and it was community support. Many people, of course, did not understand what it meant to be a communist. I encountered many Black people who said that they really were not aware of what it meant to be a communist, but they did know that every time anyone attempted to do something for the Black community, that person was called a communist. So they knew there must be something positive about it. So there was support. Despite the real vicious anticommunism that combined with the racism and, as I always point out, also the sexism, to make me a target from three different directions, there was always a very strong support.

Question 23

Interviewer: Last question. I'm wondering if you can give us a concise statement of how it was that the prison movement expanded the notion of what a political prisoner was. How it went from someone explicitly in prison for political activity to understanding that that was a lens through which to understand the whole society.

Davis: Well, initially as we began to organize on behalf of political prisoners like Huey Newton and Ericka Huggins and Bobby Seale and the Los Angeles 18 and the New York 21 and the Soledad Brothers, we were not aware of the extent to which many, many more people who happened to be in prison were victims of a political system. We expanded the definition of political prisoners to include also those who had been in prison on nonpolitical charges or whose imprisonment resulted from no political activity on their part but who became politicized while they were in prison and were subjected to long prison terms and other forms of repression as a result. We also recognized that we needed to understand the function of racism. And class exploitation within the prison system, because of the fact that a grossly disproportionate number of the prisoners at that time were Black, Puerto Rican, Chicano, Asian, Native American, and virtually none were wealthy, so that you could almost be sure that every single prisoner came from a working-class or poor background. So that we had to talk about the political function of the prisons as well as political prisoners. And we began to see all of those who were in prison or the majority of those who were in prison as being affected in some way by the particular political institutions which determine the nature of the prison, such as racism classism, et cetera.

Interviewer: OK.

Nappy Happy

Ice Cube / 1992

From *Transition* 58, 1992, pp. 174–92. © 1992. Reprinted by permission, Indiana University Press.

A Conversation with Ice Cube and Angela Davis

You may love him or loathe him, but you have to take him seriously. O'Shea Jackson—better known by his *nom de microphone*, Ice Cube—may be the most successful "hardcore" rap artist in the recording industry. And his influence as a trendsetter in Black youth culture is unrivaled. According to some academic analysts, Ice Cube qualifies as an "organic intellectual" and (in Antonio Gramsci's famous phrase) someone organically connected to the community he would uplift.

He is, at the same time, an American success story. It was as a member of the Compton-based rap group NWA that he first came to prominence in 1988 at the age of eighteen. Less than two years later, he left the group over a dispute about money and went solo. *Amerikkka's Most Wanted*, his gritty debut album, went platinum—and the rest is recording history.

Ice Cube is also a multimedia phenomenon. Artless, powerful performances in films by John Singleton and Walter Hill have established him as a continuing screen presence. That, combined with his streetwise credibility, has been a boon for St. Ides malt liquor, which has paid generously for his ongoing "celebrity endorsement." Naturally, it's a relationship that has aroused some skepticism. Public Enemy's Chuck D, for example, has inveighed against an industry that exacts a tragic toll in America's inner cities, even suing a malt liquor company that used one of his cuts to promote its product. Ice Cube defends his role in touting booze in the 'hood—even though, having joined the Nation of Islam, he says he's now a teetotaler. "I do what I want to do," he says of his malt liquor ads.

Some of his other celebrity endorsements have raised eyebrows as well. For example, at the end of a press conference last year, Ice Cube held up a copy of a book entitled *The Secret Relationship between Blacks and Jews*, which purports to reveal the "massive" and "inordinate" role of the Jews in the genocidal campaign against Blacks. "Try to find this book," he exhorted, "*everybody.*"

But then, Ice Cube is no stranger to controversy, and his second album, *Death Certificate*, has certainly not been without its critics. The album, which has sold over a million copies, delivers a strong message of uplift and affirmation . . . unless you happen to be female, Asian, Jewish, gay, white, Black, whatever.

So, for instance, in the song "No Vaseline," Ice Cube calls for the death of Jerry Heller, his former manager, and imagines torching NWA rapper Eazy-E for having "let a Jew break up your crew." In "Horny Lil' Devil," Cube speaks of castrating white men who go out with Black women. ("True Niggers ain't gay," he advises in the course of this cut). In "Black Korea," he warns Korean grocers to "pay respect to the black fist, or we'll burn your store down to a crisp." You get the picture. Not exactly "It's a Small World After All."

Still, Ice Cube's champions—and stalwart defenders—are legion. "I have seen the future of American culture, and he's wearing a Raiders hat," proclaimed the music critic James Bernard. "Cube's album isn't about racial hatred," opined Dane L. Webb, then–executive editor of Larry Flynt's *Rappages*. "It's about have-nots pointing fingers at those who have. And the reality for most Black people is that the few that *have* in *our* communities are mostly Asian or Jewish. And when a Black man tells the truth about their oppressive brand of democracy in our community, they 'Shut 'Em Down.'" "When Ice Cube says that NWA is controlled by a Jew," Chuck D protested, "how is that anti-Semitism, when Heller is a Jew?" The journalist Scott Poulson-Bryant pointedly observed that most of Cube's critics are unconcerned when he advocates hatred and violence toward other Blacks. "All the cries of Ice Cube's racism, then, seem dreadfully racist themselves," he argued. "Dismissing the context of *Death Certificate*'s name-calling and venom, critics assume a police-like stance and fire away from behind the smoke screen."

Not all Black intellectuals have been as charitable. Thus, Manning Marable, the radical scholar and commentator, questions the rap artist's "political maturity and insight" and insists that "people of color must transcend the terrible tendency to blame each other, to emphasize their differences, to trash one another. . . . A truly multicultural democracy which empowers people of color will never be won if we tolerate bigotry with [*sic*] our own ranks, and turn our energies to undermine each other."

And what of the legendary Angela Y. Davis? In some ways, hers too was an American success story, but with a twist. Raised in Birmingham, Alabama, Davis went on to graduate magna cum laude from Brandeis University and work on her doctorate under Herbert Marcuse at the University of California, San Diego and teach philosophy at the University of California, Los Angeles. In a few short years, however, her political commitments made her a casualty of the government's war against Black radicalism: the philosopher was turned into a fugitive from justice. In 1970, by the age of twenty-six, she had made the FBI's Ten Most Wanted list (which described her as "armed and dangerous") and appeared on the cover of *Newsweek*—in chains.

Now a professor in the History of Consciousness program at the University of California, Santa Cruz, Davis has made her mark as a social theorist, elaborating her views on the need for a transracial politics of alliance and transformation in two widely cited collections of essays, *Women, Race & Class* and *Women, Culture, & Politics*. Cautioning against the narrow-gauged Black nationalism of the street, Davis is wont to decry anti-Semitism and homophobia in the same breath as racism. "We do not draw the color line," she writes in her latest book. "The only line we draw is one based on our political principles."

So the encounter between them—a two-hour conversation held at Street Knowledge, Cube's company offices—was an encounter between two different perspectives, two different activist traditions, and, of course, two different generations. While Davis's background has disposed her to seek common ground with others, these differences may have been both constraining and productive. Davis notes with misgivings that *Death Certificate* was not released until after the conversation was recorded, so that she did not have the opportunity to listen to more than a few songs. She writes, "Considering the extremely problematic content of "Black Korea," I regret that I was then unaware of its inclusion on the album. My current political work involves the negotiation of cross-cultural alliances—especially among people of color—in developing opposition to hate violence. Had I been aware of this song, it would have certainly provided a thematic focus for a number of questions that unfortunately remain unexplored in this conversation."

Angela Y. Davis: I want to begin by acknowledging our very different positions. We represent different generations and genders: you are a young man, and I am a mature woman. But I also want to acknowledge our affinities. We are both African Americans, who share a cultural tradition as well as a passionate concern for our people. So, in exploring our differences in the course of this conversation, I hope we will discover common ground. Now, I am of the same generation as your mother. Hip-hop culture is a product of the younger generation of sisters and brothers in our community. I am curious about your attitude toward the older generation. How do you and your peers see us?

Ice Cube: When I look at older people, I don't think that they feel they can learn from the younger generation. I try and tell my mother things that she just doesn't want to hear sometimes. She is so used to being a certain way: she's from the South and grew up at a time when the South was a very dangerous place. I was born in Los Angeles in 1969. When I started school, it was totally different from when she went to school. What she learned was totally different from what I learned.

AYD: I find that many of the friends I have in my own age group are not very receptive to the culture of the younger generation. Some of them who have looked at my CDs have been surprised to see my collection of rap music. Invariably they ask, "Do you really listen to *that*?" I remind them that our mothers and fathers probably felt the same way about the music we listened to when we were younger. If we are not willing to attempt to learn about youth culture, communication between generations will be difficult as it has always been. We need to listen to what you are saying—as hard as it may be to hear it. And, believe me, sometimes what I hear in your music thoroughly assaults my ears. It makes me feel as if much of the work we have done over the last decades to change our self-representations as African Americans means little or nothing to so many people in your generation. At the same time, it is exhilarating to hear your appeal to young people to stand up and to be proud of who they are, who we are. But where do you think we are right now, in the 1990s? Do you think that each generation starts where the preceding one left off?

IC: Of course. We're at a point when we can hear people like the L.A. police chief on TV saying we've got to have a war on gangs. I see a lot of Black parents clapping and saying: Oh yes, we have to have a war on gangs. But when young men with baseball caps and T-shirts are considered gangs, what these parents are doing is clapping for a war against children. When people talk about a war on gangs, they ain't going to north of Pico or Beverly Hills. They are going to come to South Central L.A. They are going to go to Watts, to Long Beach, to Compton. They are going to East Oakland, to Brooklyn.

That war against gangs is a war against our kids. So the media, the news, have more influence on our parents than we in the community. The parents might stay in the house all day. They go back and forth to work. They barely know anybody. The gang members know everybody up and down the street.

AYD: During the late sixties, when I lived in Los Angeles, my parents were utterly opposed to my decision to become active in the Black Panther Party and in SNCC [Student Nonviolent Coordinating Committee]. They were angry at me for associating myself with what was called "Black militancy" even though they situated themselves in a progressive tradition. In the thirties my mother was active in the campaign on behalf of the Scottsboro Nine—you know about the nine brothers who were falsely charged with raping three [*sic*] white women in Scottsboro, Alabama. They spent almost all of their lives in prison. My mother was involved in that campaign, confronting racism in a way that makes me feel scared today. But when she saw me doing something similar to what she had done in her youth, she became frightened. Now she understands that what I did was important. But at the time she couldn't see it. I wish that when I was in my twenties, I had taken the initiative to try to communicate with my mother, so that I could have discovered that bridging the great divide between us was a similar passion toward political activism. I wish I had tried to understand that she had shaped my own desire to actively intervene in the politics of racism. It took me many years to realize that in many ways I was just following in her footsteps. Which brings me to some observations about Black youth today and the respect that is conveyed to the popular musical culture for this who came before—for Malcolm, for example. What about the parents of the young people who listen to your music? How do you relate to them?

IC: Well, the parents have to have open minds. The parents have to build a bond, a relationship with their kids, so Ice Cube doesn't have control of their kid. They do. Ice Cube is not raising their kid. They are.

AYD: But you *are* trying to educate them.

IC: Of course. Because the school system won't do it. Rap music is our network. It's the only way we can talk to each other, almost uncensored.

AYD: So what are you talking to each other about?

IC: Everybody has a different way. My first approach was holding up the mirror. Once you hold up a mirror, you see yourself for who you are, and you see the things going on in the Black community. Hopefully, it scares them so much that they are going to want to make a change, or it's going to provoke some thought in that direction.

AYD: Am I correct in thinking that when you tell them, through your music, what is happening in the community, you play various roles, you become different characters? The reason I ask this question is because many people assume that when you are rapping, your words reflect your own beliefs and values. For example, when you talk about "bitches" and "hoes," the assumption is that you believe women are bitches and hoes. Are you saying that this is the accepted language in some circles in the community? That this is the vocabulary that young people use, and you want them to observe themselves in such a way that may also use them to think about changing their attitudes?

IC: Of course. People who say Ice Cube thinks all women are bitches and hoes are not listening to the lyrics. They ain't listening to the situations. They really are not. I don't think they really get past the profanity. Parents say, "Uh-oh, I can't hear this," but we learned it from our parents, from the TV. This isn't something new that just popped up.

AYD: What do you think about all the effort over the years to transform the language we use to refer to ourselves as Black people and specifically as Black women? I remember when we began to eliminate the word "Negro" from our vocabulary. It felt like a personal victory for me when that word became obsolete. As a child I used to cringe every time someone referred to me as a "Negro," whether it was a white person or another "Negro." I didn't know then why it make me feel so uncomfortable, but later I realized that "Negro" was virtually synonymous with the word "slave." I had been reacting to the fact that everywhere I turned I was being called a slave. White people called me a slave, Black people called me a slave, and I called myself a slave. Although the word "negro" is Spanish for the color black, its usage in English has always implied racial inferiority.

When we began to rehabilitate the word "black" during the mid-sixties, coining the slogan "Black is beautiful," calling ourselves Black in a positive and self-affirming way, we began to criticize the way we had grown accustomed to using the word "nigger," "Negro" was just a proper way of saying "nigger." An important moment in the popular culture of the seventies was when Richard Pryor announced that he was eliminating "nigger" from his vocabulary.

How do you think progressive African Americans of my generation feel when we hear all over again—especially in hip-hop culture—"nigger, nigger, nigger"? How do you think Black feminists like myself and younger women as well respond to the word "bitch"?

IC: The language of the streets is the only language I can use to communicate with the streets. You have to build people up. You have to get under them and then lift. You know all of this pulling from on top ain't working. So we have to take the language of the streets, tell the kids about the situation, tell them what's really going on. Because some kids are blind to what they are doing, to their own actions. Take a football player—a quarterback. He's on the field, right in the action. But he still can't see what's going on. He's got to call up to somebody that has a larger perspective. It's the same thing I'm doing. It's all an evolution process. It's all going to take time. Nothing's going to be done overnight. But once we start waking them up, opening their eyes, then we can start putting something in there. If you start putting something in there while their eyes are closed, that ain't doing no good.

AYD: Your first solo album, *Amerikkka's Most Wanted*, went gold in ten days without any assistance from the radio and the normal network, and went platinum in three months. Why do you think young sisters and brothers are so drawn to your voice, your rap, your message?

IC: The truth. We got a lot of brothers who talk to a lot of people. But they ain't saying nothing. Here's a brother who's saying something—who won't sell himself out. Knowing that he won't sell himself out, you know he won't sell you out. We have a brother who ain't looking to get paid. I'm looking to earn, but I'm not looking to get paid. We've got a lot of people in the position of doing music, and all they want to talk about is "baby, don't go, I love you," "please come back to me," and "don't worry, be happy."

AYD: What's the difference between what you tried to do in *Amerikkka's Most Wanted* and on *Death Certificate*?

IC: Well, in *Amerikkka's Most Wanted*, I was still blind to the facts. I knew a few things, but I didn't know what I know now. I've grown as a person. When I grow as a person, I grow as an artist. I think that this new album, *Death Certificate*, is just a step forward.

AYD: Perhaps you can say how this album is evidence of your own growth and development in comparison to *Amerikkka's Most Wanted*.

IC: I think I have more knowledge of self. I am a little wiser than I was. In *Amerikkka's Most Wanted*, even though it was a good album—it was one of the best albums of the year—I was going through a lot of pressure personally. With this new album, *Death Certificate*, I can look at everything, without any personal problems getting in the way. It's all about the music.

AYD: I am interested in what you've said about the differences between side A and side B.

IC: *Death Certificate* is side A. Most people liken it to "gangster rap." "Reality rap" is what it is. Side A starts off with a funeral, because Black people are mentally dead. It's all about getting that across in the music. A lot of people like the first side. It's got all that you would expect. At the end of the first side, the death side. I explain that people like the first side because we're mentally dead. That's what we want to hear now. We don't love ourselves, so that's the type of music we want to hear. The B side—which is the life side—starts off with a birth and is about a consciousness of where we need to be, how we need to be, how we need to look at other people, how we need to look at ourselves and reevaluate ourselves.

AYD: Let's talk about "party politics." When kids are partying to your music, they are also being influenced by it, even though they may not be consciously focusing on what they need to change in their lives.

IC: I wouldn't say my music is party music. Some of the music is "danceable." But a lot of it is something that you put on in your Walkman and listen to.

AYD: But what kind of mood does it put you in? Isn't it the rhythm, the beat that captures you, that makes you feel good?

IC: You should feel good when you learn it.

AYD: I have talked to many of my young friends who listen to you and say, "This brother can rap!" They are really impressed by your music, but they sometimes feel embarrassed that they unthinkingly follow the lyrics and sometimes find themselves saying things that challenge their political sensibilities. Like using the word "bitch," for example. Which means that it is the music that is foregrounded, and the lyrics become secondary. This makes me wonder whether the message you are conveying sometimes escapes the people that you are trying to reach.

IC: Well, of course it's not going to reach everybody in the same way. Maybe the people that are getting it can tell the brother or the sister that ain't getting it.

I think what my man's trying to say here is called *breakdown*. You know what I'm saying? Once you have knowledge, it is just in your nature to give it up.

AYD: I took your video—"Dead Homies"—to the San Francisco County Jail and screened it for the sisters there who recently had been involved in a series of fights among themselves in the dorm. They had been fighting over who gets to use the telephone, the microwave, and things like that. The guards had constantly intervened—they come in at the slightest pretext, even when somebody raises their voice. Your video, your song about young people killing each other, provided a basis for a wonderful, enlightening conversation among the women in the jail. They began to look at themselves and the antagonisms among them in a way that provoked them to think about changing their attitudes.

IC: Let me tell you something. What we have is kids looking at television, hearing the so-called leaders in this capitalist system saying: It's not all right to be poor—if you're poor you're nothing—get more. And they say to the women. You got to have your hair this way, your eyes got to be this way. You got to have this kind of purse or that kind of shoes. There are the brothers who want the women. And the women have the attitude of "that's what we want." I call it the "white hype." What you have is Black people wanting to be like white people, not realizing that white people want to be like Black people. So the best thing to do is to eliminate that type of thinking. You need Black men who are not looking up to the white man, who are not trying to be like the white man.

AYD: What about the women? You keep talking about Black men. I'd like to hear you say Black men and Black women.

IC: Black people.

AYD: I think that you often exclude your sisters from your thought process. We're never going to get anywhere if we're not together.

IC: Of course. But the Black man is down.

AYD: The Black woman's down too.

IC: But the Black woman can't look up to the Black man until we get up.

AYD: Well, why should the Black woman look up to the Black man? Why can't we look at each other as equals?

IC: If we look at each other on an equal level, what you're going to have is a divide.

AYD: As I told you, I teach at the San Francisco County Jail. Many of the women there have been arrested in connection with drugs. But they are invisible to most people. People talk about the drug problem without mentioning the fact that the majority of crack users in our community are women. So when we talk about progress in the community, we have to talk about the sisters as well as the brothers.

IC: The sisters have held up the community.

AYD: When you refer to "the black man," I would like to hear something explicit about Black women. That will convince me that you are thinking about your sisters as well as your brothers.

IC: I think about everybody.

AYD: We should be able to speak for each other. The young sister has to be capable of talking about what's happening to Black men—the fact that they are dying, they're in prison; they are as endangered as the young female half of our community. As a woman I feel a deep responsibility to stand with my brothers and to do whatever I can to halt that vicious cycle. But I also want the brothers to become conscious of what's happening to the sisters and to stand with them and to speak out for them.

IC: We can't speak up for the sisters until we can speak up for ourselves.

AYD: Suppose I say you can't speak up for yourselves until you can also speak up for the sisters. As a Black woman I don't think I can speak up for myself as a woman unless I can speak up for my brother as well. If we are talking about an entire community rising out of poverty and racism, men will have to learn how to challenge sexism and to fight on behalf of women.

IC: Of course.

AYD: In this context, let's go back to your first album. I know that most women—particularly those who identify with feminism or with women's movements—ask you about "You Can't Faze Me." Having been involved myself with the struggle for women's reproductive rights, my first response to this song was one of deep hurt. It trivializes something that is extremely serious. It grabs people in a really deep place. How many Black women died on the desks of back-alley abortionists when abortion was illegal before 1973? Isn't it true that the same ultraright forces who attack the rights of people of color today are also calling for the criminalization of abortion? Women should have the right to exercise some control over what happens to our bodies.

■ ■ ■

AYD: What do you think about the "don't do drugs" message you hear over and over again in rap music? Do you think that it's having any effect on our community?

IC: Maybe, but it's message without action.

AYD: Message without action?

IC: We've got to start policing and patrolling our own neighborhoods. There's got to be a day when we go into the drug house and kick down the door. Snatch the drug dealer, take his drugs. Destroy his drugs. Take the money and put it into the movement. That's what we gotta do. We can't dial 911, call Sheriff Bill or Deputy Tom who don't care about the community or the drugs.

AYD: But where are the drugs coming from?

IC: Oh, it's coming from them.

AYD: So don't you think that Bill will always be able to find someone who will be able to do their dirty work?

IC: Yes, but there's got to be a time when we say: You can do your dirty work, but you're not going to do it here. You are not going to occupy our court.

AYD: Let's get back to your music. Would you say you're trying to raise people's consciousness?

IC: We get the minds open so we can start feeding into them, break down. The mind revolution has to go on before anything happens.

AYD: So how does the song "Us" help us to achieve this mind revolution?

IC: It makes us look at ourselves again.

AYD: Talk about that.

IC: "Us" is a record saying: "Look at who were are. Let's look at ourselves." Because every time you look at the other man, you've got to look at yourself, too. See how we reflect him. They fight each other; that's why we fight each other. He's still in our mind. No matter how much we deny it, he's still in our mind. As long as we accept this mentality, we're going to do exactly what the slave did when the master said, "I'm sick, "and the slave said, "We're sick." The house is burning, and he tries to throw water on the house faster than the slave master does. They put us in this trap. Now we're living just like they're living.

AYD: What is the role your music plays in assisting young people to develop an awareness of the self-hatred that they have grown up with? Whether you like it or not, you're out there as a teacher.

IC: My job is to teach what I know and then point to *my* teacher.

AYD: And then there will be the sister or brother who listens to you and who will use your message as the basis for teaching somebody else.

IC: Of course. And then they will point that someone else to their teacher, and then I'll point them to my teacher.

AYD: So what you're talking about is education?

IC: Of course, the revolution.

AYD: So education is the mind revolution.

IC: That's right, education is the mind revolution.

AYD: There's a long tradition of music as education and of situation education at the center of our social struggles. Frederick Douglass, for example, talked about how important it was for enslaved Black people to educate themselves. Because once they began to educate themselves, they would no longer be slaves.

IC: But we wouldn't educate ourselves; we wanted the slave master to educate us.

AYD: But we created our own schools. Immediately after the abolition of slavery, we began to create our own schools.

IC: But you're still being taught by the slave master. Because whoever's the teacher had to be affected by slavery in one way or another. Reverend Pigfeet ain't giving us what we need to know. He's not telling us what we need to know about who we are. He telling us about the life after this one. Why can't we have heaven right here? Why can't we have heaven here and heaven in the life after?

AYD: What do you think about African American history, and the contemporary lessons we can learn from our history? I raise the question because we often fail to grasp the complexity of our own culture. The comment you just made about the role religion has played in our history has often been the basis for an unfounded criticism of the spirituals that were created and sung by slaves. When, for example, slaves sang, "Swing low, sweet chariot, coming for to carry me home," they may have appeared to be evoking freedom in the afterlife, but wasn't it true that they were also singing about Harriet Tubman—the chariot, Harriet, who rescued so many women and men, helping them to discover freedom in this life? How do we remember what came before us? How do we maintain a historical memory that helps us to build on the accomplishments and insights that came before us, even if we adopt a critical attitude toward those accomplishments? How do we avoid reinventing the wheel over and over again? As a rap artist, what do you think about the images and icons representing historical personalities that abound in hop-hop culture? Take Malcolm, for example.

IC: Malcolm's a student. You don't know about Malcolm until you go to Malcolm's teacher.

AYD: I know that as a result of rap music, young people, especially young African Americans, became interested enough in Malcolm to read his autobiography. This is important, because there is a generation between my generation and yours who didn't know who Malcolm X was—had never heard of him. Now the younger generation at least knows his name, has read the autobiography, and perhaps knows a little of the surrounding history. The question I want to ask you is whether you think it is necessary to probe more deeply into our history, to go beyond the music, as many young people have been stimulated by the music to read Malcolm's autobiography? And especially to look at the women who have still not become a part of our collective historical memory. To look, for example, at Ida B. Wells, the Black woman who was the single most important figure in the development of the campaign against lynching. To encourage, for example, an awareness of this woman who traveled all over the country, sometimes nursing her baby on stage, organizing throughout the Black community, in villages and towns. Ida Wells was responsible for Black people realizing that we can stand up and say that we were not going to allow the Ku Klux Klan to deliver tens of thousands of brothers and sisters into the hands of lynch mobs . . .

IC: Like I said, you've got to go to the teacher. Malcolm was a student. You've got to teach all the kids that they can become Malcolm, but you've got to go to the teacher. Malcolm can teach you what he knows, but he should point you in the direction for the teacher. Same thing with me and my process. I'm just now starting to look at the Nation of Islam. That's how I've learned all that I know, indirectly. So in "Watch Out" at the end of my record, I point to my teacher.

AYD: Continuing the discussion of your latest album, what is "Lord Have Mercy" about?

IC: "Lord Have Mercy" is like a prayer, but it's a rap song. This song evaluates the situation and asks the Lord to help us in our struggle. It's saying, when he sends down the ladder, don't forget us.

AYD: Where do the ideas expressed in this song come from?

IC: They come from my belief in God. Today they say you've got to go to a church. I think I've been to a church six times in my life. A church should not be like—shhhh quiet, you're in a church—you know what I mean?

AYD: But there are some churches that don't require you to be quiet. In the African tradition, a church is a place where you dance, you move, you sing, where you celebrate in a collective spirit.

IC: Yes.

AYD: Also, in our history, the church is the site where we organized and planned our rebellions.

IC: But we could have done that anywhere.

AYD: What do you mean we could have done it anywhere?

IC: I mean, we could have done it anywhere—in the house . . .

AYD: I'm talking about slavery. The religious gathering was the only place we had that was collective and not subject to surveillance. The church had to become a lot of things. That's why ministers became social, political leaders. I know there are a lot of your "Reverend Pigfeet" around. But there is also another tradition . . .

IC: But now, in the 1990s, are they real leaders?

AYD: What do you think about Reverend Jesse Jackson?

IC: I should say this to him in person, though I don't know when I'm going to see him.

But I call him "Messy Jesse." I don't believe Jesse Jackson is a leader. I don't look at him as a leader. I look at him as a follower, but he's following the wrong leader. I'm a follower, but I believe I'm following the right leader.

AYD: Well, what do you think about running for political office in more general terms? Jesse Jackson's claim to leadership is based on the fact that he ran twice for president on the Democratic ticket.

IC: That's cool, as long as you don't become a puppet. As long as you don't become a token. I look at him, the relationship between him and Minister Louis Farrakhan. The FOI [Fruit of Islam] security was protecting Jesse with their lives, and Jesse publicly denounced Farrakhan, at the same time that he was meeting with Farrakhan behind closed doors in the alley, in the back ways of South Side Chicago. Around the same time, he shook hands with George Wallace. How can you not talk publicly to a man who protected your life but shake hands on TV with a man who murdered your people?

AYD: Are there any Black politicians you respect—who you feel are doing a good job? Take Ron Dellums, for example. During the late sixties, he was elected to the Oakland City Council and then to Congress based on the work he did in defense of the Black Panther Party.

IC: I really don't follow politicians. I really can't talk to a politician who would hold up the flag.

AYD: What about the ones who don't?

IC: Who don't hold up the flag? Are they down for the movement? Down to get our people tight? Or are they using them as a stepping-stone for themselves?

AYD: I would say that there are a few—like Dellums and Maxine Waters—who are not out for themselves, but for the people. But people shouldn't expect them to accomplish anything progressive without the community demanding it. The election of Maxine Waters to Congress was an important moment in our history. A progressive Black woman, solidly backed by her community, whose record as an elected official in California is strong as it can get. People in South Central Los Angeles can vouch for that. We also need organizers.

IC: Of course, our leaders are organizers.

AYD: Often the leader or the spokesperson can't do everything, and we don't often give credit to those who do the backstage work of organizing. It's unglamorous work; it is not work that people read about. And who usually does that work? Who usually does that housework of the movement?

IC: The people do that work. They need a sense of direction. That's all we need to give our kids, is a sense of direction, a goal that you want them to meet, that you demand them to meet. So then the housework gets done.

AYD: But that work requires you sometimes learn the skills necessary to do it. You have to learn how to do it.

IC: You have to be taught, you need guidance, direction.

AYD: Take Rosa Parks, for example. People usually think of her only as the woman who refused to sit in the back of the bus in 1955. According to the myth—memorialized in the Neville Brothers song "Sister Rosa"—she was tired. But she had been tired for a long time and was therefore not only motivated by her feelings. She made a conscious political decision, as an organizer. Rosa Parks is a woman who helped pull the community together, who therefore did the work of the backstage organizer. We need to learn how to respect those who do the behind-the-scenes work in the same way that we respect the orators, the theorists, the public representatives of the movement. Often, the people who do the organizing, the people who don't get credit for their work, are women. Everybody knows Dr. Martin Luther King as the public representative of the civil rights movement, but not very many people know that it was a group of women who organized the boycott in Montgomery. If it hadn't been for them, nobody would have known who Dr. King was. Shouldn't we pay tribute to those women, whose names are known by only a few of us, and realize that we need organizers in the tradition of the Montgomery women today as well?

IC: You have people who fight for integration, but I'd say we need to fight for equal rights. In the schools, they want equal books, they don't want torn books. That was more important than fighting to sit at the same counter and eat. I think it's healthier if we sit over there, just as long as we have good food.

AYD: Suppose we say we want to sit in the same place or wherever we want to sit, but we also want to eat food of our own choosing. You understand what I'm saying. We want to be respected as equals, but also for our differences. I don't want to be invisible as a Black woman, I don't want anyone to tell me I have to eat like white people eat, or have the same thoughts, or do my academic work only in the tradition of Western European philosophy. Which doesn't mean that I am not interested in Western philosophers, but I am also interested in African philosophical traditions and Asian and Native American philosophies . . .

IC: It's all about teaching our kids about the nature of the slave master. Teaching them about his nature, and how he is always going to beat you no matter how many books you push in front of him, no matter how many leaders you sent to talk to him, no matter how much you try and educate him. He's always going to be the same way. We've got to understand that everything has natural enemies. There's the chicken and the chicken hawk.

The ant and the anteater. They are enemies by nature. That's what we got to instill in our kids.

AYD: Would you say that there are creatures who are "friends by nature." As human beings, how do we recognize our friends? Shouldn't we be friends with Native Americans?

IC: Oh yes. But that isn't who I'm talking about. You have people trying to love their enemy. That's where the problem is: trying to get them to accept us, trying to get them to "get together" with us. It has never been the intention of the government of the United States to integrate white and Black people.

AYD: It may be the government's intention today to integrate a certain kind of Black person into the power structure—the Colin Powells and the Clarence Thomases . . .

IC: What everybody thought would work is not working. What you have is people who go to school and go to college, and they are running from their people when their people need them the most.

AYD: Speaking of shock, what do you think about the fact that in some schools, rap music is being academically studied? My niece Eisa is a student at Harvard. She wrote her junior thesis on rap music. So what do you have to say about the way hip-hop culture is now being examined and analyzed in the context of university studies?

IC: Rap music is a school system itself, and one of the best school systems that we have. It's entertainment, but it's also a school system. Right now we are more unified on the surface than we have been. I'm not just saying that we know the same thing, but the brothers that got the bald head in Mississippi the same brothers who got the bald head in Los Angeles. All over, we're starting to know the same thing, we're starting to say: Hey, we're trying not to identify with the slave master. Putting the contacts in, the Jheri curls in, trying to be like somebody you shouldn't ever want to be like, ain't cool. Cut 'em off. Take 'em out.

AYD: Is that why you cut off your Jheri curl?

IC: Yes, that's why I cut off my Jheri curl. I was trying to identify with the slave master. I like it now. I'm nappy happy. You know what I'm saying? I'm nappy and happy.

AYD: So am I.

IC: You know, that's the thing that we got to break down. We've got to break that down, and start teaching about ourselves, and stop teaching us about who they are. They learned civilization from us. Once you instill that in Black kids and let them know who they are and who we are, all the problems will start to improve.

AYD: So what responsibilities do we have to Africa? South Africa, for example?

IC: We can't help South Africa. That's just like the blind leading the blind. We can't help them because we can't even help ourselves.

AYD: If you were to talk to Nelson Mandela, he would say that the solidarity of African Americans has been extremely important. The work of anti-apartheid activists here was certainly not the primary factor that led to Mandela's release, because Black people inside South Africa had been fighting for his freedom for twenty-five years. But Mandela himself has said that if it hadn't been for the fact that we have organized a powerful anti-apartheid movement here in the United States, it would have taken them much longer to get where they are now. If we don't do what we can—and I would say that African Americans have a special responsibility here—to continue to encourage a political consciousness in favor of an end to the white regime and for a free and democratic South Africa, it will probably take them a lot longer to achieve these goals. My position is that we need to stand up and say no.

IC: It's true, we do need to stand up and say no.

AYD: You were saying that nothing has been offered to us on a silver platter—we have always had to fight for what we have achieved.

IC: It's all about taking. They ain't never going to give us nothing. Nothing but heartaches and the blues. That's the only thing they are ever going to give us.

AYD: We have already taken quite a bit. But it seems that the more we take, the more we lack.

IC: We've taken a whole lot, but more is ours. More is ours. We deserve more. We ain't taken enough.

AYD: So how do you think we can convince our young people to realize that instead of directing so much of their rage and violence against each other . . .

IC: They have to learn how to love themselves. They don't love themselves. If they don't love themselves, how are they going to love me and you? We need an organization that teaches them to love themselves.

AYD: How do we build this organization? Although I personally doubt that history can be repeated, there are people who say that we need another Black Panther Party. They point out that during the late sixties, there was an abundance of gang violence between some of the same gangs that are around today in South Central Los Angeles—the Bloods, the Crips, etc.—and the Black Panther Party eliminated gang antagonisms. The more widespread the influence of the Black Panthers became, the more the gang structure began to collapse. I can say from personal experience that it was empowering to witness young Black people give up gang violence and begin to respect each other, regardless of their neighborhood allegiances.

IC: Did anybody in the Black Panther organization smoke?

AYD: I'm sure they did.

IC: Did anybody drink?

AYD: I'm sure they did.

IC: That ain't loving yourself.

AYD: Well, people didn't know that then.

IC: But now we do.

AYD: I'm not arguing that we need another Black Panther Party, because I think that would be a simplistic solution. History is far more complex. Each generation has to find its own way. You are standing on our shoulders, and it is up to you to reach much higher.

IC: And somebody is going to end up standing on ours and build something better than what we had. It's all about having a Black Panther Party, just making a more advanced Black Panther Party. Do you know what I mean? A more organized Black Panther Party. That's the key. More people in the party.

AYD: Would you say that your music calls upon young people to move from a state of knowing, a position of being educated, to a state of doing and a position of political activism, a position of transforming this society?

IC: Yes, of course. To me, the best organization around for Black people is the Nation of Islam. It is the best organization: brothers don't drink, don't smoke, ain't chasing women. They have one job. They fear one person, though I wouldn't say it's a person—they fear Allah, that's it.

AYD: What about the women in the Nation?

IC: They fear Allah. Don't drink, don't smoke. Know who they are. Love themselves. Respect themselves. Love each other, respect each other. You know what I mean? That's what we need. But we don't need no Rodney Kings. I mean we won't have that incident. You pull your piece and try to take my brother's life, you going to have to take all of our lives. That's how it got to go.

AYD: What is the difference, as you see it, between your role as an artist and your role as a political teacher—as a purveyor of political consciousness? You create and perform your music, and at the same time you have a political agenda. How do you negotiate between the two positions?

IC: It is very delicate. I can't preach, so to speak, because I don't want to turn people off. I have to walk a thin line. I have to sneak the message in there until they open up. When they open up is when I get to shove. You know how you open babies' mouths? Until they open up, you can just get a taste on their lips, but when they do open up, you just put it in there. It makes them feel good inside.

AYD: So what can be expected from you as an artist, as a musician?

IC: It's going to be raw. I'm starting to get the baby's mouth open. Now it's all about me learning and studying, so I can know the right thing to put in it—and so I can know more as a person. I have to learn more as a person before I can pass it on to the kids who are buying my music.

An Interview with Angela Davis

Nina Siegal / 1998

From *Ms.* Magazine. September/October 1998. Reprinted by permission of *Ms.* magazine, @1998.

In 1970 radical scholar Angela Davis was accused of murder, kidnapping, and conspiracy in connection with her involvement in a campaign to release three Black men from Soledad prison. A jury found insufficient evidence for conviction, but Davis spent almost two years behind bars awaiting trial, from 1970 to 1972. She never forgot the women she left behind in those jails or the plight of women in prison in general, and since her incarceration, she has become one of the nation's leading experts on female incarceration and also one of the world's most outspoken prison abolitionists. Now a professor at the University of California, Santa Cruz, in September, Davis will cohost Critical Resistance: Beyond the Prison Industrial Complex, a conference at UC Berkeley that will bring together activists, scholars, policy makers, and cultural workers to encourage progressive organizations and individuals—especially feminists—to help halt the exponential expansion of the prison system. In this interview with writer Nina Siegal, Davis shares her perspective on women in prison.

Nina Siegal: How do you account for the fact that most women in prison are women of color and poor women?

Angela Davis: The popular notion of crime has been constructed in such a way that crime is equated with very specific behaviors generally for which people of color and poor people generally are under constant surveillance. According to many studies, most people have committed some kind of "criminal" activity during their lifetimes. But it is largely people in poor communities who are targeted by criminal justice systems and held legally responsible for these acts.

NS: According to statistics, about 80 percent of women in prison are mothers. What kinds of long-term effects do you predict their incarceration will have?

AD: For many women, being sent to prison in the US leads to a permanent loss of parental rights. This is not the case in Cuba, whose prison system is constantly criticized in the US media. Last summer I conducted a series of interviews in Cuba with women in three women's prisons and discovered that one of the most dramatic differences was the consistent attention in Cuba to mothers and their children. Imprisonment never leads to the loss of parental rights, except in cases of severe abuse. Infants remain with their imprisoned mothers, and prison authorities are responsible for facilitating regular visits—including overnight visits inside and outside the prison—between mothers and their children. When one compares this to the fact that in some penal institutions in the US, women are separated from their children by Plexiglas during visits and thus are not even allowed to touch them, we see the extent to which the US government engages in gross abuses of human rights.

NS: What are the main concerns of abolitionists?

AD: The main critique of the prison system by abolitionists is that it attempts to address problems that cannot be solved through incarceration. Abolitionists thus propose a range of alternatives. One of the most obvious alternatives would be the decriminalization of drug use, which would vastly reduce the prison population—especially for women, who, even more than men, tend to be imprisoned for drug-related charges. I certainly agree with the suggestion made by the former surgeon general Joycelyn Elders that a public dialogue on the decriminalization of drugs is absolutely necessary. As it stands today, people are punished because they have done harm to themselves. The "crime problem" can only be addressed ultimately by the eradication of poverty, by the eradication of the circumstances that lead people to commit the kinds of crimes for which most are sent to prison.

NS: Why is it important for us to talk about women in prison?

AD: In many important respects, women in prison are the most vulnerable people in our country. The assault on the rights of women prisoners points to the systematic assault on democratic possibility in this country. To stand up for the rights of women in prison is to challenge racism and poverty and resist becoming an incarcerated society. To stand up for the rights of women in prison is to defend the possibility of a democratic future in this country.

Globalism and the Prison Industrial Complex: An Interview with Angela Davis

Avery F. Gordon / 1998/1999

This is published courtesy of the Institute of Race Relations, London, which first published the interview in *Race & Class*, vol. 40, nos. 2–3, 1998/1999.

Angela Y. Davis is professor of History of Consciousness at the University of California, Santa Cruz. A prolific speaker and internationally renowned activist, Davis is the author of several books, including *Women, Race & Class* (Vintage, 1983), and *Blues Legacies and Black Feminism* (Pantheon, 1988). For almost thirty years, Angela Davis has been working to radically change the US penal system. During the last ten years, her teaching, writing, speaking, and organizing efforts have been intensively focused on exposing the prison industrial complex and on working for its abolition. Most recently these efforts culminated in a large national conference and strategy session, Critical Resistance: Beyond the Prison Industrial Complex, held on September 24–27, 1998, at the University of California, Berkeley; *Dispossession and Punishment: Essays on the Prison Industrial Complex and the New Abolitionism*, a forthcoming book, presents Davis's recent research and writing on prisons, some of which is excerpted here. In July, Avery Gordon, author of *Ghostly Matters: Haunting and the Sociological Imagination* (University of Minnesota Press, 1997) and other works, spoke with Angela Davis about the prison industrial complex and its threats.

Avery F. Gordon teaches in the Department of Sociology, University of California, Santa Cruz.

Avery Gordon: I'd like to begin by asking you to describe what is meant by the "prison industrial complex."

Angela Davis: Almost two million people are currently locked up in the immense network of US prisons and jails. More than 70 percent of the imprisoned population are people of color. Approximately five million people—including those on probation and parole—are directly under the surveillance of the criminal justice system. Three decades ago, the imprisoned population was approximately one-eighth its current size. While women still constitute a relatively small percentage of people behind bars, today the number of incarcerated women in the state of California, where we live, alone is almost twice the entire state and federal women's population of 1970. In fact, the fastest-growing group of prisoners are Black women. According to Elliott Currie, "the prison has become a looming presence in our society to an extent unparalleled in our history—or that of any other industrial democracy. Short of major wars, mass incarceration has been the most thoroughly implemented government social program of our time."[1]

Penal infrastructures must be created to accommodate this rapidly swelling population of caged people. Goods and people must be provided to keep imprisoned populations alive. Sometimes these populations must be kept busy, and at other times—particularly in repressive super-maximum prisons and in Immigration and Naturalization Service (INS) detention centers—they must be deprived of virtually all meaningful activity. Vast numbers of handcuffed and shackled people are moved across state borders as they are transferred from one state or federal prison to another. All this work, which used to be the primary province of government, is now also performed by private corporations, whose links to government in the field of what is euphemistically called "corrections" reveal dangerous resonances with the military industrial complex. The dividends that accrue from investment in the punishment industry, like those that accrue from investment in weapons production, only amount to social destruction. Taking into account the structural similarities and profitability of business–government linkages in the realm of military production and public punishment, the expanding penal system can now be characterized as a "prison industrial complex."

Gordon: That the prison industrial complex produces "social destruction" is an important point, since it challenges the ubiquitous rhetoric of prisons as a necessary solution to what's now—after the US defeat of the "communist threat"—taken to be the major social problem facing the United States, and that is crime.

Davis: Imprisonment has become the response of first resort to far too many of the social problems that burden people ensconced in poverty. These problems are often veiled by being conveniently grouped together under the category "crime" and by the automatic attribution of criminal behavior to people of color, especially Black and Latino/a men and women. Homelessness, unemployment, drug addiction, and illiteracy are only a few of the problems that disappear from public view when the human beings contending with them are relegated to cages. Prisons thus perform a feat of magic. Or rather the people who continually vote in new prison bonds or tacitly assent to a proliferating network of prisons and jails, have been tricked into believing in the magic of imprisonment. But, as you've suggested elsewhere, prisons do not disappear problems, they disappear human beings, and the practice of disappearing vast numbers of people from poor, immigrant, and racially marginalized communities literally has become big business.

As prisons take up more and more space on the social landscape, other government programs that have previously sought to respond to social needs are being squeezed out of existence. In fact, the dismantling of the welfare state and the growth of the prison industrial complex have taken place simultaneously and are intimately related to one another. In the process of implementing the prisonization of the US social landscape, private capital has become enmeshed in the punishment industry in a variety of ways, and precisely because of their profit potential, prisons are becoming increasingly central to the US economy. If the notion of punishment as a source of potentially stupendous profits is disturbing by itself, then the strategic dependence on racist structures and ideologies to render mass punishment palatable and profitable is even more disturbing.

This political economy of prisons relies on racialized assumptions of criminality—such as images of Black welfare mothers reproducing criminal children—and on well-documented racist practices in arrest, conviction, and sentencing patterns to deliver up bodies destined for profitable punishment. Colored bodies are the main raw material in this vast experiment to disappear the major social problems of our time. Once the aura of magic is stripped away from the imprisonment solution, however, what is revealed is racism, class bias, and the parasitic seduction of capitalist profit within a system that materially and morally impoverishes its inhabitants, while it devours the social wealth needed to address the very problems that have led to spiraling numbers of prisoners.

Gordon: You're suggesting, then, that the prison industrial complex accomplishes two interrelated vanishing acts. It disappears ever larger numbers of poor colored people, especially women and youth, into the shadow society of the prison, where they are expected to live behind, as you put it, "layer upon layer of razor wire," in a literal state of social dispossession.[2] It also hides from public view the racialized capitalism that underwrites and drives the development of the prison industrial complex.

Davis: Yes. Let me try to connect these two dimensions. Because of the tendency to view it as an abstract site into which all manner of undesirables are deposited, the prison is a perfect site for the simultaneous production and concealment of racism. The abstract character of the public perception of prisons militates against an engagement with the real issues afflicting the communities from which prisoners are drawn in such disproportionate numbers. This is the ideological work that prison performs; it relieves us of the responsibility of seriously engaging with the problems of late capitalism, of transnational capitalism. The naturalization of Black and brown people as criminals also erects ideological barriers to an understanding of the connections between late twentieth-century structural racism and the globalization of capital.

Gordon: Would you elaborate on that connection?

Davis: The vast expansion of the power of capitalist corporations over the lives of people of color and poor people in general has been accompanied by a waning anticapitalist consciousness. As capital moves with ease across national borders, legitimized by recent trade and invest agreements such as NAFTA, GATT, and MAI, corporations close shop in the United States and transfer manufacturing operations to nations providing cheap labor pools. In fleeing organized labor in the US to avoid paying higher wages and benefits, they leave entire communities in shambles, consigning huge numbers of people to joblessness, leaving them prey to the drug trade, destroying the economic base of these communities and thus affecting the education system, social welfare—and turning the people who live in those communities into perfect candidates for prison. At the same time, they create an economic demand for prisons, which stimulates the economy, providing jobs in the correctional industry for people who often come from the very populations that are criminalized by this process. It is a horrifying and self-reproducing cycle.

Gordon: This is a disturbing twist on the notion of dependency and an example of what Helen Quan, in the context of studying neo-imperialism in Brazil, has called "savage developmentalism."

Davis: It is more than a twist. Prisons themselves are becoming a source of cheap labor that attracts corporate capitalism in a way that parallels the attraction unorganized labor in Third World countries exerts. Let me read you a statement by Michael Lamar Powell, a prisoner in Capshaw, Alabama:

I cannot go on strike, nor can I unionize. I am not covered by workers' compensation of the Fair Labor Standards Act. I agree to work late-night and weekend shifts. I do just what I am told, no matter what it is. I am hired and fired at will, and I am not even paid minimum wage: I earn one dollar a month. I cannot even voice grievances or complaints, except at the risk of incurring arbitrary discipline of some covert retaliation.

You need not worry about NAFTA or your jobs going to Mexico and other Third World countries. I will have at least 5 percent of our jobs by the end of this decade.

I am called prison labor. I am The New American Worker.[3]

The "new American worker" will be drawn from the ranks of a racialized population whose historical superexploitation, from the era of slavery to the present, had been legitimized by racism. At the same time, the expansion of convict labor is accompanied in some states by the old paraphernalia of ankle chains that symbolically links convict labor with slave labor. Several states have reinstated the chain gang. Moreover, as Michael Powell so incisively reveals, there is a new dimension to the racism inherent in this process, which structurally links the superexploitation of prison labor to the globalization of capital.

In fact, many corporations that provide us with products we consume on a daily basis have learned that prison labor power can be as profitable as the Third World labor power exploited by US-based global corporations that have relegated formerly unionized labor forces to joblessness and prison. Some of the clients of companies that use prison labor are IBM, Motorola, Compaq, Texas Instruments, Honeywell, Microsoft, and Boeing. But it is not only the high-tech industries that reap the profits of prison labor. Nordstrom department stores sell jeans that are marketed as "Prison Blues," and T-shirts and jackets made in Oregon prisons. Maryland prisoners inspect glass bottles and jars used by Revlon and Pierre Cardin, and graduation caps and gowns made by South Carolina prisoners are purchased by schools throughout the world. In our own state, the California State University system is required to purchase a variety of furniture and equipment produced by prison labor under the auspices of the Prison Industrial Authority. Work now being performed on prison grounds includes computerized telephone messaging, dental apparatus assembly, computer data entry, plastic parts fabrication, electronic component manufacturing, security glass manufacturing, swine production, oak furniture manufacturing, and the production of stainless steel tanks and equipment.

Although prison labor is hugely profitable for the companies that use it, the penal system as a whole does not produce wealth. It devours the social wealth that could be used to subsidize housing for the homeless, to meliorate public education for poor and racially marginalized communities, to open free drug rehabilitation programs for people who wish to kick their habits, to create a national health care system, to expand programs to combat HIV and to eradicate domestic abuse, and, in the process, to create well-paying jobs for the unemployed. This amounts to a massive redistribution of social wealth and resources. For example, government contracts to build prisons have played a major role in bolstering the construction industry, and prison design has become a major business "opportunity" for architects. Technology developed for military use is marked by companies like Westinghouse for use in law enforcement and punishment. Moreover, corporations that appear to be far removed from the business of punishment are intimately involved in the expansion of the prison industrial complex. For example, prison construction bonds are one of the many sources of profitable investment for leading financiers such as Merrill Lynch.

Gordon: So, the rise of private prison companies is only the most visible component of the increasing corporatization of punishment?

Davis: Prison privatization is the most obvious instance of capital's current movement toward the prison industry. In March of 1997, the Corrections Corporation of America (CCA), the largest US private prison company, claimed 54,944 beds in sixty-eight facilities under contract or development in the US, Puerto Rico, the United Kingdom, and Australia. In response to the global pattern of subjecting more women to public punishment—although "private domestic" violence continues[4]—CCA recently opened a women's prison outside Melbourne.

Wackenhut Corrections Corporation (WCC), the second-largest US company, claimed contracts and awards to manage forty-six facilities in North America, the United Kingdom, and Australia. It claims a total of 30,424 beds as well as contracts for prisoner health services, transportation, and security. If these companies divulged statistics by race indicating who has slept in those beds, they would probably reveal an inordinate number of Black and Latino people in the US, Black and Asian people in the United Kingdom, and Aboriginal peoples in Australia.

Currently, the stocks of both CCA and WCC are doing extremely well. By the end of last year, CCA's revenues had increased by 58 percent—from $293 million in 1996 to $462 million in 1997. Its net profit grew from $30.9 million to $53.9 million. WCC, which is 54 percent owned by the

Wackenhut Corporation (which itself had revenues of over one billion dollars in 1997), increased its revenues from $138 million in 1996 to $210 million in 1997, amounting to a net profit increase from $8.3 million to $11 million. It hardly needs to be pointed out that such vast profits rely on the employment of nonunion labor to operate prisons.

Gordon: I'd like to go back to a statement you made earlier that Black people and people of color in general are the main human material with which the expansion of the prison industrial complex is being accomplished. In several articles and in your forthcoming book, you've been excavating the racialized and gendered history of punishment and penalty in the US, and you've identified at least four systems of incarceration that link "confinement, punishment, and race": the reservation system, slavery, the mission system, and the internment camps of the Second World War.[5] You've focused especially on the history of slavery and on people of African descent.[6] What are some of the main features of this history that you see as particularly important for understanding the prison crisis today?

Davis: Within the US—and increasingly in postcolonial Europe—the disproportionate presence of people of color among incarcerated populations has acquired a self-evident character.[7] But, this commonplace is a result of a long history of exploitation and state repression. Historically, people of African descent consigned to slavery in the US were certainly not treated as rights-bearing individuals and therefore were not considered worthy of the moral reeducation that was the announced philosophical goal of the penitentiary. Indeed, the slave system had its own forms of punishment, which remained primarily corporeal and of the sort that predated the emergence of incarceration as punishment.

Within the institution of slavery, itself a form of incarceration, racialized forms of punishment developed alongside the emergence of the prison system within, and as a negative affirmation of, the "free world," from which slavery was twice removed. Even if the forms of punishment inherent in and associated with slavery had been entirely revoked with the abolition of slavery, the persistent second-class citizenship status to which former slaves were relegated would have had an implicit impact on punishment practices. However, an explicit linkage between slavery and punishment was written into the US Constitution precisely at the moment of the abolition of slavery. In fact, there was no reference to imprisonment in the Constitution until the passage of the Thirteenth Amendment declared chattel slavery unconstitutional. The Thirteenth Amendment read: "Neither slavery nor involuntary servitude, except as punishment for crime whereof the party shall have been duly convicted, shall exist within the United States, or any place subject to their jurisdiction." The abolition of slavery thus corresponded to the authorization of slavery as punishment. In actual practice both emancipation and the authorization of penal servitude combined to create an immense Black presence within southern prisons and to transform the character of punishment into a means of managing former slaves.

In constructing prisoners as human beings who deserved subjection to slavery, the Constitution allowed for a further, more elusive linkage of prison and slavery, namely, the criminalization of former slaves. This criminalization process became evident in the rapid transformation of prison populations in the southern states, where a majority of Black Americans resided. Prior to Emancipation, prisoners were primarily white, but as Milfred Fierce pointed out, during the post–Civil War period, the percentage of Black convicts in relation to white was often higher than 90 percent.

The swift racial transformation of imprisoned southern populations was largely due to the passage of the Black Codes, which criminalized such behavior as vagrancy, breach of contracts, absence from work, and insulting gestures or acts. Theft and escape, for example, long considered effective forms of resistance to slavery, became defined as crimes. What during slavery had been the particular repressive power of the master became the far more devastating universal power of the state, as Black people were divested of their status as slaves in order to be accorded a new status as criminals. The criminal justice system, then, played a significant role in constructing the new social status of former slaves as human beings whose citizenship status was acknowledged precisely in order to be denied.

Southern prison populations not only became predominantly Black in the aftermath of slavery, penitentiaries were either replaced by convict leasing, or they were restricted to white convicts. This racialization of punishment practices determined that Black people were to be socially defined in large part by re-created conditions of slavery. In fact, as historian David Oshinsky has documented, convict leasing in institutions like Mississippi's Parchman Farm created conditions "worse than slavery."[8]

During the last three decades of the nineteenth century, southern criminal justice systems were profoundly transformed by their role as a totalitarian means of controlling Black labor in the post-emancipation era. Because so many of the particular crimes with which Black people were charged served more as pretexts than as causal factors for arrest, these punishment strategies were explicitly directed at Black communities and eventually informed the history of imprisonment outside the South as well.

Gordon: And today?

Davis: Today, the emergent prison industrial complex recalls the early efforts to create a profitable punishment based on the new supply of "free" Black male laborers in the aftermath of the Civil War. As Steven Donziger has argued, "the criminal justice system need[s] sufficient quantities of raw materials to guarantee long-term growth. . . . In the criminal justice field, *the raw material is prisoners*. . . . For the supply of prisoners to grow, criminal justice policies must ensure a sufficient number of incarcerated Americans regardless of whether crime is rising or the incarceration is necessary."[9] Just as newly freed Black men, along with a significant number of Black women, constituted a virtually endless supply of raw material for the embryonic southern punishment industry (as well as providing much-needed labor for the economies of the southern states as they attempted to recover from the devastating impact of the Civil War), so, in the contemporary era, do unemployed Black men, along with increasing numbers of women, constitute an unending supply of raw material for the present-day prison industrial complex.

By 1997 African Americans were the majority of state and federal prisoners. As the rate of increase in the incarceration of Black prisoners continues to rise, the racial composition of the incarcerated population is approaching the proportion of Black prisoners to white during the era of the southern convict lease and county chain gang systems. Whether this human raw material is used for purposes of labor or as the forced consumers of commodities provided by a rising number of corporations directly implicated in the prison industrial complex, it is clear that Black bodies are considered dispensable within the "free world" and that they are a major source of profit in the prison world. This relationship recapitulates in complicated new ways the era of convict leasing.

The privatization characteristic of convict leasing also has its contemporary parallels, as companies like CCA and Wackenhut literally run prisons for profit. Private prisons have multiplied at four times the rate of expansions of public prisons. It is now estimated that there will be three times as many private facilities by the turn of the century and that their revenues will be more than one billion dollars. In arrangements reminiscent of the convict lease system, federal, state, and county governments pay private companies a fee for each inmate, which means that private companies have a stake in retaining prisoners as long as possible, and in keeping their facilities filled.

Gordon: African American men, in particular, are also vastly overrepresented in state and federal super-maximum security prisons, of which there are an increasing number. You see these supermax prisons as exemplary of the increased repression characteristic of US society in general and also as part of the longer history you've been describing.

Davis: The danger of supermax prisons resides not only in the systematically brutal treatment of the prisoners confined there but also in the way they establish standards for the treatment of all prisoners. They solidify the move away from rehabilitative strategies, and they do so largely on the backs of Black men. Moreover, as prisons become more repressive and as this repression becomes more remote from, and by default accepted within, the "free world," they promote retrograde tendencies in educational institutions that serve the populations most likely to move from schools into prisons. These educational institutions begin to resemble prisons more than schools and are fast becoming prep schools for prison, molding Black children into raw material for punishment and coerced labor.

The extent to which Black men today function as the main human raw material for the prison industrial complex only highlights the many ways in which the prison system in the US in general resembles and recapitulates some of the most abhorrent characteristics of the slavery and convict lease system of the late nineteenth century. In fact, the rampant exploitation of prison labor in an increasingly privatized context is a modern-day form of convict leasing. And while Black men are not the only population vulnerable to this exploitation, the overwhelming numbers of Black men imprisoned in the US make them by far the most threatened members of our society when it comes to the new form of enslavement being implemented through the prison system.

That we can so easily draw these connections between latter twentieth-century imprisonment practices in the US and various systems and practices that were in place a century ago is, in large part, a result of the racism that consistently has been interwoven into the history of the prison system in this country. The ultimate manifestation of this phenomenon can be found in the supermax prison, whose main function is to subdue and control "problematic" imprisoned populations—again, comprised largely of Black men—who, having been locked away in the most remote and invisible of spaces, are basically no longer thought of as human. The absolute authority that is exercised over these disappeared populations by supermax administrators and staff—and the lack of accountability on the part of private corporations that are in the prison business and/or benefit from prison labor—is reminiscent of the impunity with which slave owners, overseers and, later, patrons of the convict lease system routinely disregarded the humanity connected with the Black bodies they systematically abused.

In this sense the supermax draws upon, even as it also serves to feed, the perpetuation of racism at every level of our society. This is true, in fact, of the entire prison system. The continued practice of throwing away entire populations depends upon those populations being constructed and perceived—fixed, really—within the popular imagination as public enemies. It is precisely this relationship between racism and imprisonment that necessitates coalitional work between antiracist activists and prison activists. On the eve of the twenty-first century, these two movements are inseparable.

Gordon: Let's move, then, by concluding, to discuss resistance to the prison industrial complex and the call for a new abolitionism. Would you begin by addressing the particular challenge that the geographical isolation of prison and the social invisibility of prisoners issues?

Davis: How many of us have stood outside a prison, let alone been inside one? This is a question that quickly separates people of color, and particularly Black people, from whites, and the poor from the affluent. Most people in the US do not have direct knowledge of the penal system, although the prison has inhabited the personal and political histories of Black and poor people continually. Most people have not pondered the razor wire, not imagined concretely what, or who, exists behind it. Instead, public perceptions about prison and prisoners are shaped by media (mis)representations, including the grossly sensationalized genre of Hollywood prison films. On a recent visit to Cuba, during which I interviewed three dozen women in prison there, I was only half surprised to learn that many of the women's preconceived notions about what prisons would be like were based on portrayals they had seen in Hollywood films.

In the US the growth of the punishment industry occurs against the backdrop of a ubiquitous reluctance on the part of most people on the outside to engage in critical discussions about jails and prison beyond the oversimplified and fatally inaccurate equation of prison expansion with the elimination of crime. Media and law enforcement agencies collude to create an increasingly crime-saturated atmosphere in which those who are least likely to be victims of crime are the very individuals most vocally supportive of harsher sentencing practices and prison expansion as a means of curtailing crime. In the public imagination, as fantastical notions of "the criminal" translate into fears of a Black male stranger who lurks in dark corners waiting to beat, rob, rape, or murder an unsuspecting victim, the resulting "lock-'em-up-and-throw-away-the-key" attitude (exemplified at the legislative level by three- and, in some states, two-strike laws) renders more and more invisible those who are imprisoned. The continued demonization of welfare mothers, particularly Black single mothers, and the dismantling of programs that assist poor women and their children, is carving out new gendered paths toward imprisonment.

Challenging the invisibility of incarcerated populations, and especially the hypervisibility [sic] of women prisoners who are twice-marginalized—invisible in the "free world" by virtue of their incarceration and largely overlooked even by prison activists by virtue of their gender—is central to resisting the social dispossession wrought by the prison industrial complex. It is also necessary to expose that magic trick I mentioned earlier.

The great majority of people have been tricked into believing in the efficacy of imprisonment, even though the historical record clearly demonstrates that prisons do not work. They have never really worked and they never will. The economic and social factors that lead certain individuals to commit offenses that are likely to land them in prison (as well as the criminalization process itself, which dictates what segments of the population become the objects of the widespread fear of crime) go unaffected by the number of prisons that are built in the US each year. Systemic social problems such as poverty, homelessness, illiteracy and child abuse—each of which renders its victims more likely to become entangled in the penal system—require aggressive and innovative solutions that bear no relationship whatsoever to incarceration. Yet these simple and rather obvious realities are obscure to most people for whom penal institutions are remote. For this reason, it is vital that those of us who are active around prison issues promote as much firsthand exchange as possible between the members of the "free world" and members of the imprisoned world. It is difficult to step inside a jail or prison, to talk with the people whose lives are confined to these facilities, without being deeply moved. In fact, I'm always struck by the profound contrast between the self-possession of so many prisoners and the social dispossession to which they are subjected, individually and collectively, as wards of the penal system. In the news and especially during elections, we constantly hear descriptions of prisoners as "animals" and prisons as "zoos," but to really hear the stories of incarcerated women and men is to recognize that little more than the luck of the draw—or, rather, of one's socioeconomic birthright—separates "us" from "them."

Today, the deepening influence of racism is largely responsible for the failure of a popular critical discourse to contest the ideological trickery that posits imprisonment as a stop-gap measure at a time when the focus of state policy is rapidly shifting from social welfare to social control. The emergence of a US prison industrial complex within a generalized context of cascading conservatism marks a new historical moment, whose dangers are unprecedented. At the same time, we need not succumb to the sense of powerlessness that ideological evocations of crime waves and the creation of new prisons tend to encourage. Considering the impressive number of grassroots projects that continue to resist the expansion of the punishment industry, it ought to be possible to bring these efforts together to create radical and internationally visible movements that can legitimize anticapitalist critiques of the prison industrial complex.

Gordon: Is the aim of this critique ultimately the abolition of the prison system as we know it?

Davis: Yes. Raising the possibility of abolishing jails and prisons as the institutionalized and normalized means of addressing social problems in an era of migrating corporations, unemployment and homelessness, and collapsing public services, from health care to education, can help to interrupt the current law-and-order discourse that has such a grip on the collective imagination, facilitated as it is by deep and hidden influences of racism. This late twentieth-century abolitionism, with its nineteenth-century resonances, may also lead to a historical recontextualization of the practice of imprisonment. With the passage of the Thirteenth Amendment, slavery was abolished for all except convicts—and, in a sense, the exclusion from citizenship accomplished by the slave system has persisted within the US prison system. Only three states allow prisoners to vote, and approximately four million people are denied the right to vote because of their present or past incarceration. A radical strategy to abolish jails and prisons as the normal way of dealing with the social problems of late capitalism is not a strategy for abstract abolition. It is designed to force a rethinking of the increasingly repressive role of the state during this era of late capitalism and to carve out a space for resistance.

Notes

1. Elliot Currie, *Crime and Punishment in America* (New York: Henry Holt, 1988), 21.

2. See Angela Davis, "A World unto Itself: Multiple Invisibilities of Imprisonment," in Michael Jacobson-Hardy, *Behind the Razor Wire: Portrait of an American Prison System* (New York: New York University Press, forthcoming).

3. "Modern Slavery American Style," unpublished essay (1995).

4. See Angela Davis, "Public Imprisonment and Private Violence: Reflections on the Hidden Punishment of Women," *New England Journal on Criminal and Civil Confinement* (Summer 1998).

5. See Angela Davis, "Racialized Punishment and Prison Abolition," in *Blackwell Companion to African-American Philosophy*, ed. Tommy Lott (London: Basil Blackwell, forthcoming).

6. See Angela Davis, "From the Prison of Slavery to the Slavery of Prison: Frederick Douglass and the Convict Lease System," in *Frederick Douglass: A Critical Reader*, ed. Bill Lawson and Frank Kirkland, (London: Basil Blackwell, forthcoming 1998); Angela Davis, "Race, Gender and Prison History: From the Convict Lease System to the Supermax Prison," in *Confronting Prison Masculinities: The Gendered Politics of Punishment*, ed. Terry Krupers, Willie London and Don Sabo (Philadelphia: Temple University Press, forthcoming).

7. See Kum-Kum Bhavnani and Angela Davis, "Fighting for Her Future: Reflections on Human Rights and Women's Prisons in the Netherlands," *Social Identities* 3, no. 1 (1997). On racism and the prison industrial complex in the US, see Angela Davis, "Masked Racism: Reflections on the Prison Industrial Complex," *ColorLines Magazine* (Fall 1998); and Angela Davis, "Race and Criminalization: Black Americans and the Punishment Industry," in *The House That Race Built: Black Americans, US Terrain*, ed. Wahneema Lubiano (New York: Pantheon, 1997).

8. David Oshinsky, *"Worse than Slavery": Parchman Farm and the Ordeal of Jim Crow Justice* (New York: Free Press, 1996).

9. Steven Donziger, ed., *The Real War on Crime: The Report of the National Criminal Justice Commission* (New York: HarperPerennial, 1996), 87.

Conversations: Prison as a Border: A Conversation on Gender, Globalization, and Punishment

Angela Davis and Gina Dent / 2000

From *Signs: Journal of Women in Culture and Society*, vol. 26, no. 41. Reprinted by permission of University of Chicago Press.

The following conversation on prisons between Angela Davis and Gina Dent took place in Oakland, California, on November 4, 2000.

Angela Davis (AYD): As I reflect on the history of our collaborative work around prisons, I remember your arrival in California two years ago amid the excitement preceding the inaugural Critical Resistance conference. The conference organizing committee was quite impressed by the way you immediately began to calmly work out some of the overwhelming problems that arose at the last minute, and also by your vision of what this gathering would potentially accomplish.

Gina Dent (GD): I remember that there was a good deal of discussion and trepidation among participants of the large committee. Before I arrived it was about whether or not we would be able to attract enough people to the conference. Later it was about whether or not a group of volunteers would be able to productively host and accommodate the enormous number of respondents. I remember saying then that I was certain that the people who came would be taken up, as I was, by the spirit and vision of the event, which foregrounded the questions of gender and globalization as starting points, rather than last instances, for a racial critique of the punishment industry. It seems to me that one of the real strengths of Critical Resistance remains this vision as it is reflected even in its structure as a loose network and a campaign, rather than a member organization, joining people whose work touches on prison issues but is not primarily defined by them (e.g., in education, health care, media, education, and the environment) with current and former prisoners, activists, and cultural workers to fight together against the prison industrial complex. As Critical Resistance is based on the idea of spending information about the socially destructive business of imprisonment—the links between the corporate economy and the punishment industry under globalization—it invites committed individuals and organizations to affiliate in a variety of ways, including by taking on the work and the name of Critical Resistance. Of course, this is also connected to the articulation and development of abolitionism as the vision, rather than just a goal, of the work—a programmatic program that also seeks to analyze its own limits in a racial critique of the punishment industry in these days of reform. I think it was this vision—connected to the nineteenth-century work of antislavery abolitionism—that also helped to change our working process when the seven of us met in Irvine as a research group.[1]

AYD: Yes, we are drawing on important legacies. In recently rereading Rosa Luxemburg's (1999) study on the relationship between capital accumulation and imperialism, I was struck by the way her work resonates powerfully with our contemporary critiques of globalization. It reminded me of the rich history of theoretical and activism opposition to imperialism—especially in the Marxist tradition—and how the forgetting of history can be so disempowering. Racial working-class formations—parties and unions, for example—do have a history of acknowledging the tendency of capital to disregard national borders and thus to internationalize their resistance. It is against this backdrop that we have been reconceptualizing the relationship between the prison industrial complex and globalization—from a discussion of how the prison is affected by the globalization of the economy (where the prison fits into globalization) to using the prison as a contingent historical institution that not only prefigures globalization but allows us to think today about the intersections of punishment, gender, and race, within and beyond the borders of the United States.

GD: Certainly, we return again and again to the impact of the prison as the paradigmatic institution of democracy—encapsulating democracy as a reform, with its attendant and necessary contradictions. Thinking about Gustave de Beaumont and Alexis de Tocqueville's 1831 research trip to the United States to study the new American penitentiary, we are reminded of the important context that produced the volume *Democracy in America* [(1835) 1990].[2] Of course, this is why we have had something specific to say about a concept and practice of decolonization that does not challenge the contemporary use of the prison around the world. We continue to find that the prison is itself a border. This analysis has come from prisoners, who name the distinction between the "free world" and the space behind the walls of the prison. This is an important interpretation that undoes the illusions of the powerful nation-states on one hand and the seeming disorganization and chaos of capital's travels on the other. There is a very specific political economy of the prison that brings the intersections of gender and race, colonialism and capitalism, into view.

AYD: Our own visits to prisons in Europe, South America, Australia, and the United States have allowed us to begin to think about the appeal of the prison across time and space as the most influential paradigm for punishment over the past two centuries. We need to draw on the history of the prison as a colonial institution profoundly linked to that earlier era of imperialism in understanding the ease with which new models of imprisonment developed in the United States—such as the supermax (super-maximum security facility)—travel around the world today. Don't you remember how stunned we were when we learned a company headquarters in Nashville, Tennessee (the Corrections Corporation of America), owns and operates the largest women's prison in Australia?

GD: And that white Australians, proud of a convict heritage, did not automatically link this history to the troubling contemporary circumstances for prisoners today—the overwhelming percentage of whom are Koori women (that is, aboriginal—approximately 2 percent of the total population but 30 percent of the prison population).

AYD: If I were to try to summarize my impressions of prison visits all over the world, and most of them have been to women's prisons, including three jails which I visited involuntarily, I would have to say that they are uncannily similar. I have always felt as if I am in the same place. No matter how far I have traveled across time and space—from 1970 to 2000, and from the Women's House of Detention in New York (where I was myself incarcerated) to the women's prison in Brasilia, Brazil—no matter how far, there is a strange sameness about prisons in general, and especially about women's prisons. This sameness of women's prisons needs to be measured against how important it has been for feminisms to divest themselves of the notion that there is some universal quality we can call *woman*. This makes me think about your work on the challenge for us to rethink the boundaries between social science and the humanities. As a means of thinking specifically about women in prison.

GD: Yes, I think our collaborative work also contests the hegemony of social science in producing knowledge about the prison—not only in the most obvious places but also in activism and popular culture. The assumptions that exist in these supposedly separate spheres have been remarkably consistent and mutually constitutive. Knowledge is never secured for use on only one side of the divide between science and the real of social life. I am always struck by the extent to which scholars, activists, and legal practitioners draw their assumptions not only from personal experience but from the experiences of popular culture as a source of understandings that are used like one's own life (assuming already that these understandings are not just drawn from other scholarship). Here these understandings are insufficient, we often assume they can't be addressed with the facts. But what process generates these facts? So we are forced to think seriously about the status of traditional social scientific paradigms (and their permeation in all kinds of arenas) as the more reliable, legitimate evidence. For example, in what sense could we produce knowledge about women in prison? How would this violate what we know about the shrouded conditions of imprisonment (where only the state permits access) and the missionary zeal that can be the most obvious sign of the desire to know about prison and prisoners? To what uses can we put knowledge produced under these conditions? This is not merely a question about how we have to rethink an abolitionist politics that starts from the position of those women on the underside of capital but does not put them in another cage.

AYD: Any conventional social scientific study of women prisoners introduces you to the typical women prisoner—generally characterized as a "mother," with a relatively low level of education, who is also a drug addict. We know that when we go into a women's prison in a European country, we discover—as in the case with men—a disproportionately large number of women who are immigrants, noncitizens, African, Asian, and Latin American. But, as you point out, this is not enough. We also have to consider the role that criminology and penology have played in giving us this striking similarity, not only in the populations but in the methods of control, architectural models, and custodial practices that devolve from the psychology of the criminal generalized around the world. In other words, the institution of the prison and its discursive deployment produce the kind of prisoners that in turn justify the expansion of prisons. As a matter of fact, the term *prison industry* can refer precisely to the production of prisoners even as the industry produces profits from increasing numbers of corporations and, by siphoning social wealth away from such institutions as schools and hospitals, child care, and housing, plays a pivotal role in producing the conditions of poverty that create a perceived need for more prisons.

GD: This is key to stating simply why more and more people are in agreement that the prison industrial complex underwrites the social problems that it purports to solve.

And we have to consider scholars' role in this and also find the means to make use of the written history of the prison to understand race, gender, and globalization anew.

AYD: Well, we could start with thinking about the strange but predictable way feminism has been embraced by custodial hierarchies. The demand for more women guards and high-level officers has been complemented by the demand to treat women prisoners the same as men prisoners. This has occurred as departments of corrections discover that through "diversity management"—incorporating men of color and women of all racial backgrounds—their prisons run all the more efficiently. Thus, putatively feminist positions have bolstered the trend toward more repressive imprisonment practices for women, and specifically the move from cottage/campus architectural model to the concrete fortresses being constructed today. An interesting example of this feminism that demands formal equality of men and women prisoners is some wardens' insistence that women prisoners have the right to be considered every bit as dangerous as men. Tekla Miller, the former warden at Huron Valley Women's Prison in Michigan, complained that the arsenal at the women's prison was inferior to those at men's institutions. She also successfully lobbied for the right to shoot women escapees.

GD: And we know these new recipes for equality—part of the legacy of the conjunction of capitalism and democracy—travel as a preeminent American export. It seems that we're back to the point that prisons have become not only terrain for our activism but also a challenge to our work as feminist intellectuals trying to think about the limits of feminisms and the terrain of new struggles. We can discuss, for example, the distinctions between an equality of sameness and an equality of difference, but what about an embodied theory that also contains agency? I'm thinking of two paradoxes that continue to haunt us. First of these is the incommensurability of women and the prison and the consequent symbolic use of women as the prison's excess. Amnesty International's campaign image of the woman giving birth in chains is only one example. What if we set that picture up against a second example? In California we know that one emerging "protection" for women is that no sexual relations between prisoners and guards will be considered consensual. The history of the resistance to women's subordination in prison also constrains us—inasmuch as they assume that these women are not agents. We know one means of rethinking this through feminism. Your references to the prison writing of Barbara Saunders, who compared life in prison to a violent domestic relationship—you can never be sure what will happen next and what it will require emotionally (cited in Chevigny 1999, vii)—are helpful here. If the expression of agency against domestic violence is leaving the relationship, we know that women in prison present a further challenge to us. Of course, this at the heart of why Critical Resistance took up the idea of "Go to Prison Week" to celebrate the thirty-fifth anniversary of the Civil Rights Act. Visiting prisons—not so much to gain information, as researchers or tourists, but to work with women prisoners—helps to create a firmer basis for future work. This also suggests that we need to be able to talk about how some men are then also in such a domestic violence relationship. Who these men are—in terms of class, race, and location—matters then in a different way.

AYD: Well, we know that the gendering of men's prisons equates violence with masculinity and that not only is violence expected but the violence of the institution produces the relations between prisoners and guards among prisoners themselves. As we saw in our visit to Calipatria State Prison in California, prisons—and this is the case in other states as well—a system of racial classification and separation prohibits Black prisoners from being housed with white or Chicano ("northern Hispanic" in the official vocabulary) but permits them to be housed with Mexican ("southern Hispanic") prisoners. This strict segregation inevitably produces violent clashes along racial lines. The historical gendering of racial contact in women's prisons intersects with policies governing sexual contact. Estelle Freedman (1981) points out that historical policies of racial segregation at Bedford Hills Prison for women in New York (which, of course, still operates and holds such political prisoners as Kathy Boudin) involved rules against racial integration of the prison population to prevent interracial lesbian relations. While sex contained by race was tolerated, sex across race was treated as a major threat.

GD: Yes, and this is why it is important to think of the prison: not only because of the very genuine concerns for those this are incarcerated but also because of its place in revealing the organization of the structures that we hold to be democratic and their connections to gender and globalization. We have also spoken in the past, for example, and in the context of US history, of miscegenation as a threat that is legitimated not only through a racially prescribed heteronormativity but also through the assumption that the site of reproduction—the "mixed" child—is the site of fear. Prisons teach us that this analysis is insufficient. Perhaps the more reverberating site of fear is that of the reproduction of a social world that would read along and against the boundaries of nation-states, races, genders, and sexualities—the solidarity that is produced and most surveilled in the prison. Isn't that precisely the site of the critical resistance of which we speak?

University of California, Santa Cruz (Davis)
University of California, Santa Cruz (Dent)

References

Beaumont de la Bonniere, Gustave, and Alexis de Tocqueville. (1833) 1964. *On the Penitentiary System in the United States and Its Application in France.* Carbondale: Southern Illinois University Press.

Chevigny, Bell Gale. 1999. "Introduction." *In Doing Time: Twenty-Five Years of Prison Writing*, ed. Bell Gale Chevigny. New York: Arcade.

Drescher, Seymour. 1968. *Tocqueville and Beaumont on Social Reform*: Harper & Row.

Freedman, Estelle. 1981. *Their Sisters' Keepers: Women's Prison Reform in America, 1830–1930*. Ann Arbor: University of Michigan Press.

Luxemburg, Rosa. 1999. *Rosa Luxemburg: Writings and Reflections*. Edited by Paul Le Blanc. Amherst, NY: Humanity Books.

Tocqueville, Alexis de. (1835) 1990. *Democracy in America*. New York: Vintage.

Notes

1. The other members of the research group from the University of California Humanities Research Institute are Ruth Wilson Gilmore (Berkeley), David Goldberg (Irvine), Avery Gordon (Santa Barbara), Sandra Baringer (Riverside), and Nancy Scheper-Hughes (Berkeley).

2. Works by de Beaumont and de Tocqueville (1833) 1964 and Drescher 1968 include work preceding the publication of de Tocqueville (1835) 1990.

Angela Davis

David Barsamian / 2001

From *The Progressive*, February 2001. Reprinted by permission of David Barsamian/alternative radio.org.

If you are of a certain age, the name Angela Davis is etched in memory. Close your eyes, and you can see her signature Afro and clenched fist raised high. But the Angela Davis of yore and the educator, scholar, and activist of today are quite different. Unlike some of her peers from the sixties who traffic in nostalgia, Davis has kept up with the times. Her pathbreaking work on the prison industrial complex has helped push this issue to center stage.

Davis was born and raised in Birmingham, Alabama. "Even though Birmingham was entirely segregated, I learned not to assume that that was the way things were supposed to be," she recalled. "I can remember my parents saying, 'This may be the situation now, but it will not be this way forever.' From a very early age, I managed not to feel imprisoned."

She graduated magna cum laude from Brandeis University in 1965 and pursued graduate studies at the Goethe Institute in Frankfurt and the University of California at San Diego, where she received her master's in 1968. A year later, she was fired from her teaching position as an assistant professor at UCLA by Gov. Ronald Reagan for her political activities in the Communist Party and the Black Panther Party. After a 1970 shootout in a courthouse in Marin County, California, Davis, who was not even in the area at the time, made the FBI's "Ten Most Wanted" list. After going on the lam, she was apprehended and jailed on charges of conspiracy, kidnapping, and murder. The trial, which was an international cause célèbre, resulted in her acquittal in 1972.

A tenured professor at the University of California Santa Cruz, she's the author of *Women, Race, and Class* (Random House, 1981) and *Women, Culture, and Politics* (Random House, 1989). Her latest book is *Blues Legacies and Black Feminism* (Pantheon, 1998). She is just finishing up a collection of essays on the prison industrial complex called *Dispossessions and Punishment.*

It's one thing to read Davis's work and quite another to hear her speak. Her voice is a musical instrument. I know of few speakers who use pauses and silences so effectively. She measures her words like a composer crafting a melody. She fills halls all over the world and is in such demand as a speaker, she should could probably lecture every night of the year. Still, she has a shyness and humility about her. She doesn't flaunt her celebrity or talk down to her audiences. She is like the classic Thelonious Monk tune "Straight, No Chaser."

I talked with her in early November.

Q: I think it's fair to say that you have almost iconic status, linked as you are to a legendary era when it seemed revolutionary change was possible. What's it like being Angela Davis?

Angela Davis: I don't think about that very much. I do recognize that people associate me with another time. It seems to me that when people approach me and say, for example, "I'm from the sixties," they tend to use me as a way to think about their own youth. That's OK, but it's not really about me, and it can be somewhat straining. I have tried over the years to grow and develop. I am not the same person I was in the early 1970s, when many people became familiar with my name. The impetus for radical social movements has always come from young people. I don't want to represent myself, as some people of my generation do, as the veteran with all of the answers.

Q: You ran for vice president twice on the Communist Party ticket in the 1980s. Did I hear you right recently when you said you're now a Green Party member?

Davis: I'm registered as a Green Party member. I've never been registered as a member of one of the major parties. I've been registered as a Communist, and I am now a registered member of the Green Party, and I do believe that independent politics basically are absolutely necessary. Independent politics provide us with the only vote for accomplishing anything significant within the electoral arena.

Q: W. E. B. Du Bois in his classic work *The Souls of Black Folk* wrote, "The problem of the twentieth century is the problem of the color line." Where is that color line today?

Davis: The color line about which Du Bois spoke is not nearly as clear as it was at the time. Racialization processes are now far more complicated. Class is an important category to consider as it intersects with race and gender. The prominence of Black middle classes today combined with the putative eradication of racism within the legal sphere means that we have to think in a much more complicated way about the structures of racism and how they continue to inform US society. We need to develop an analysis that incorporates gender and class and sexuality, as well.

Q: A lot of academics write about the criminal justice system, but you actually spent time in jail, sixteen months, most of it in solitary confinement. How has this affected your work?

Davis: Certainly the fact that I was once incarcerated has inspired me to do activist as well as scholarly work around prison issues. But no matter what particular work progressive people are doing today, it is incumbent upon them to discover some way to relate their scholarship, their activism, to the campaign against the prison industrial complex. This is not however, to underestimate the importance of involving people who have direct experience of the prison system. As a matter of fact, when one looks at the campaign against the death penalty, it certainly can be argued that Mumia Abu-Jamal is one of the most eloquent and most powerful opponents of it. When we organized three years ago the conference Critical Resistance: Beyond the Prison Industrial Complex, we attempted to involve former prisoners and people who were at that time in prison.

My approach to the study of prisons and also to prison activism is informed by prison abolitionism. In other words, I, along with many other people, believe that we should seek ways of minimizing the use of imprisonment. Therefore, when I talk about a prison that seems to be more attentive to the humanity of those it imprisons, it is against the backdrop of an abolitionist strategy.

Q: The current prison population is eight times what it was in 1970. More than two million people are behind bars—70 percent people of color, 50 percent African Americans, 17 percent Latinos. And Native Americans have the highest per capita rate of incarceration.

Davis: The role of race in creating the raw material for the prison industry is undeniable. While you've mentioned the statistics that relate to US prisons, one can also point to prisons in Europe or Australia. It's generally the case that you find a disproportionate number of people of color or immigrants. I recently visited a prison in Stockholm and discovered that large numbers of people there are refugees from Turkey and Yugoslavia, as well as people from Africa and Latin America. In the Netherlands you see a vast number of people of African descent, from the Caribbean, and from Indonesia, the former colony of the Netherlands. In Australia, while aboriginal

people constitute 1 to 2 percent of the population, in the prisons they constitute 20 to 30 percent. So the racialization of prison populations is not
simply a characteristic of the US system.

Unfortunately, in this era of globalization, the US prison model is being
exported around the world. When I visited Australia a year and a half ago, I
found that the largest women's prison there, which is outside of Melbourne, is
owned and operated by Corrections Corporation of America, which is head-
quartered in Nashville, Tennessee. It is not only the tendency to incarcerate
even greater numbers of people that one can see in European countries and
Australia, but also the super-maximum prisons have been exported. There are
super-maximum prisons in the Netherlands, South Africa, and even Sweden.
The security housing unit, which is a particularly repressive formation origi-
nating in the US, has invaded their prisons, as well. We're talking about countries such as the Netherlands, which for a very long time attempted to use
strategies of decarceration. Now, under the impact of the drug war and the
peculiarly North American ways of addressing the drug issue, one sees ever
larger numbers of people going to prison, and therefore the historical strategy
of decarceration has been basically dismissed.

Q: You've also looked at the prisons in Cuba. What's it like there?

Davis: In Cuba, at least in the women's prisons I visited, the women—
unlike women in the US or in other countries—did not feel disconnected
from the larger society. The effort to pay close attention to the UN standard
minimum rules for the treatment of prisoners was very obvious. Perhaps
the most impressive aspect of the system itself was the fact that prisoners
were allowed to continue to work in their fields if their offense was not related to their particular profession. I talked to a woman who was a veterinarian, for example, and she continued to be a veterinarian in the prison. I
talked to a woman who was a doctor, and she continued to be a physician in
the particular prison where she was incarcerated. That in itself was interesting because it inverts the hierarchies of prisoners and guards.

As the doctor she was in charge of civilian nurses, for example, and was
treated not as a prisoner, not as an inferior person, but rather as a doctor.
Furthermore, people who work—and virtually everyone works who is in
prison—receive the same wages and salaries as they would receive if they
were working in the same job on the outside. It was a striking difference
with respect to the US, where prisoners can receive as little as ten cents an
hour. It seems to me that the trade union movement in this country could
learn a great deal by looking at the integration of Cuban prisoners into
unions and not separating them as inferior workers.

Q: When you use the term "prison abolition," how do people react?

Davis: Many more people are willing to think seriously about the importance of decreasing the role of punishment in society. The vast expansion of the prison system, which happened largely without any major protest, has reached critical proportions. But, at the same time, over the last five years, the interventions of activists have been important in encouraging people to think differently about the prison system, particularly the use of the term "prison industrial complex" as an example of a new vocabulary that allows people to think critically rather than to respond based on their own emotional reactions.

Q: Would you favor incremental strategies of prison reform?

Davis: Reform is a difficult question. Certainly it is important to think about the kinds of reform that will, in fact, assist the people who are so unfortunate as to live behind prison walls. But at the same time, if one looks at the history, it is clear that reforms have played pivotal roles in actually bolstering the prison system.

Michel Foucault in his work *Discipline and Punish* points out that from the very origin of the prison, reform played that central role. As a matter of fact, imprisonment as punishment was a reform designed to replace capital punishment and corporal punishment. During the 1970s the very dramatic prison movement that emerged around the rebellion in Attica and the many other uprisings in prisons throughout the country gave rise to what many of us felt was significant reform, such as the abolition of the indeterminate prison sentence. However, we need to consider the fact that prison sentences have become far longer and that developments such as truth in sentencing and three strikes have relied precisely on this reform in sentencing practices. All of which is to say we need to be very cautious about supporting those reforms that have the potential of creating a more powerful prison system. I would suggest that we measure the reforms we propose against the potential for rendering the prison system less powerful.

Let me give you another example of the potential dangers of certain kinds of reforms. At the moment, there is very impressive movement against the death penalty. Many people now say it should be abolished pending the possibility of guaranteeing that there's not a single innocent person on death row. With the DNA technology, innocence is something that is demonstrated scientifically. I find that extremely problematic, because precisely in proving innocence through DNA, there's also the concomitant demonstration of guilt, so that what appears to be a progressive movement may well, in fact, make it even more difficult to abolish the death penalty as a form of punishment.

One other problem in the death penalty movement as it stands today is that there is a tendency to argue that life imprisonment should be offered as an alternative to capital punishment. The danger of seeing life imprisonment as the alternative is precisely that life imprisonment will be legitimized not only for people who would otherwise have been sentenced to death but for a whole class of people far beyond those who might have been subject to capital punishment.

Q: According to a report by Human Rights Watch and the Sentencing Project, 2 percent of all Americans have lost the right to vote because of felony convictions.

Davis: It's important to point out that we're talking about not only currently incarcerated prisoners who have lost the right to vote. In many states former felons are divested of their political rights, as well. In the state of Alabama, one-third of all Black men, according to that report by Human Rights Watch and the Sentencing Project, have permanently lost the right to vote and will be unable to exercise it unless they receive a pardon by the governor.

Q: A lot of your work has focused on women prisoners.

Davis: A number of activists and scholars, myself included, suggest that we think about other ways of punishing women in conjunction with the state apparatus of punishment. And we see that historically women have been punished in mental institutions, within the patriarchal structure of the family, or within intimate relations. There is a connection between violence against women in the domestic sphere and the punishment of women by the state. The recent reports by human rights organizations such as Human Rights Watch and a report by the United Nations Special Rapporteur on Violence Against Women have demonstrated that sexual violence is quite pervasive in US prisons. Some women prisoners point out that being imprisoned is structurally similar to being in a violent relationship. I make this point because the current movement against violence against women, which has become highly professionalized over the recent period, could benefit from an effort to engage with the politics of imprisonment. And, at the same time, the movement against the prison industrial complex needs to integrate an analysis of gender.

Q: In October there was a state hearing in Chowchilla, home of California's two largest women's prisons. One person testified that the health care there was "something the Three Stooges would do on *Saturday Night Live*. Breast lumps and vaginal tumors are left untreated for months. Treatable illnesses become terminal." What about the issue of health care and women in prison?

Davis: The issue of health care reveals how systematically US prisons violate the human rights of women. The prison in Chowchilla is the largest women's prison in the world, and numerous health violations have been revealed there by organizations such as the San Francisco group Legal Services for Prisoners with Children. I know of one particular case of a woman at the prison across the street, the Central California Women's Facility, who was diagnosed with a brain tumor shortly after she was incarcerated last February. But because there was no neurosurgeon on staff of the local hospital, the Madera Community Hospital, she has to be taken to a hospital in another city, Fresno. However, on the two occasions when she was transferred to that hospital, the prison failed to transfer the chart, and therefore her appointments were canceled, and she was returned to the prison undiagnosed. After many months of delayed treatment, the tumor had grown so large and had become entangled with her brain stem that they were not able to remove it. This is a horror story, just one of many.

Q: You've taught in the University of California system for years. Starting in the mid-1990s, California began spending more money on prisons than on its university system. What kind of impact has that had?

Davis: There is a vastly deteriorated educational system. The impact of Proposition 2019 has meant that affirmative action can no longer be used in admission processes in the state of California. On the other hand, affirmative action, it appears, is quite alive in the recruitment of prison personnel. As a matter of fact, people of color increasingly play major roles in the California correctional system. Certainly there is an invisible affirmative action program at work with respect to the population of the prisons. As the Justice Policy Institute reported a couple of years ago, a Black man in the state of California is five times more likely to be found in a prison cell than in one of the state colleges or universities.

Q: What's your sense of student activism today as you travel around the country?

Davis: I'm extremely impressed by the student activists. I don't envy them. The difficulties are far greater than they were during the sixties. The stakes are far greater today. The issues are far more complex. But I think that the younger generation will be able to go much further.

Q: I've seen the impact that you have, particularly on young women of color, at your public appearances. At the end of the speech, there's a rush to talk to you, to touch you and even embrace you.

Davis: That often happens, that's true. I try to trouble their attitude toward celebrity, and, at the same time, I try to encourage them to find their own way. I try not to provide answers and solutions but to raise questions and to encourage people to think differently about their own lives.

David Barsamian is the director of Alternative Radio in Boulder, Colorado. He interviewed Haunani-Kay Trask in the December 2000 issue.

Politics and Prisons: An Interview with Angela Davis

Angela Y. Davis and Eduardo Mendieta / 2003

From *Radical Philosophy Review*, vol. 6, no. 2, 2003, pp. 163–78. DOI: 10.5840/radphilrev 20036212. Permission to republish this article was granted on behalf of Radical Philosophy Review by the Philosophy Documentation Center.

Eduardo Mendieta: Angela Davis, you are probably one of the top five most important Black women in American History, and your books are continuously considered to be notable books of the year by the *New York Times*. Thirty years ago your autobiography was published by Random House, in 1974. Since then it has become a classic of African American letters. It is a book that has become central to the tradition of Black women writers and the tradition of Black political thought that in many ways harkens back to the tradition of Black slave narratives. How do you see this work now, with thirty years' hindsight?

Angela Davis: Well, first of all, thanks for reminding me that this is the thirtieth anniversary of the publication of my autobiography. At the time I wrote my autobiography, I did not imagine myself within any of those traditions, of course. As a matter of fact, I was initially reluctant to write an autobiography. I was too young. I was also aware of the fact that the celebrity, or whatever you want to call it, that I had achieved had very little to do with me as an individual. It was based in the first place on the mobilization of the state and its effort to capture me, the fact that I was on the FBI Ten Most Wanted list, of course. But also, and perhaps most importantly, I know that my situation was very much created by a massive global movement that successfully achieved my freedom. So the question was how to write an autobiography that would be attentive to the collective community of struggle. I decided then that I wanted to write not the conventional autobiography in which the hero furnishes lessons to the audience, to the readers. I decided that I wanted to do a political autobiography that would explore the way in which I had been shaped by movements and campaigners in communities of struggle.

EM: Since then this book also has become integral to the tradition of American letters. In what way do you think that the Black political biography plays a role within this tradition of American letters?

AD: Well, of course the canon of American letters has been contested previously; and if one considers the example of the autobiography of Malcolm X, which has found its ways in the canon, one can talk about the extent to which this has made a difference. But on the other hand, I wonder whether the canon itself has been transformed. It seems to me that these kinds of struggles to contest bodies of literature are similar to the struggles for social change and social transformation. What we manage to do each time we win a victory is not so much to alter the frameworks, but rather to create new terrains for struggle. And so I would argue that it is a good thing that this has happened, but certainly, as someone like Toni Morrison may point out, it has not altered the canon in a significant way.

EM: Since we are talking about canons, I actually came relatively late to your work, but once I read it, it seemed to me that it fit within another tradition, another canon, and it is the philosophical canon. If we think of the work of Boethius, of Jean-Paul Sartre, Martin Luther King, Dietrich Bonhoeffer, Antonio Gramsci, Primo Levi . . . there are philosophical figures who have reflected out of their prison experiences. Yet it is curious that philosophical reflection on imprisonment has been quite sparse. How do you see your work contributing to this, or do you see it as belonging to this tradition at all, this philosophical tradition of prison writing?

AD: Well, oftentimes prison writing is described as that which is produced in prison or by prisoners, and certainly Gramsci's prison notebooks provide the most interesting example. I don't know whether it's accidental that the conditions in prison, that the prison itself, the institution, has not been theorized by those who engaged in intellectual production while they were in prison. There are of course some exceptions. George Jackson is an exception. I don't know whether it would have been possible to think critically about the prison while I was a prisoner. So I suppose I follow in the tradition of some of the thinkers you mention. I did publish while I was in jail. I wrote an article called "Reflections on the Black Woman's Role in the Community of Slaves." I did another piece, a paper I wrote for the conference for the Society for the Study of Dialectical Materialism, associated with the American Philosophical Association, and it was called "Women and Capitalism: Dialectics of Oppression and Liberation." It was recently published in *The Angela Y. Davis Reader*. I did that and I also wrote an extended study of fascism, which was never published.

EM: We would love to see this.

AD: I think I have it somewhere with my papers at home. But it was only after I was released and after I felt I had sufficient distance, critical distance, that I felt it was possible to think critically about the institution of the prison, drawing of course very much on the work of the prison intellectual George Jackson.

EM: You were trained as a philosopher, yet you teach in a program called the History of Consciousness at the University of California, Santa Cruz. Do you think that philosophy can play any role at all in political culture in the United States? And, has philosophy influenced your work on aesthetics, jazz, and in particular the way in which you analyze the situation of Black women?

AD: Absolutely, absolutely, and I think that the influence of philosophy is a question of formulating, asking the kinds of questions that would otherwise be foreclosed. I suppose I can say that I learned a great deal from Herbert Marcuse about the relation between philosophy and ideology critique, political critique. His work, for example, *Counterrevolution and Revolt*, engages directly with the material conditions of the period, the late 1960s. But, at the same time, the framework is philosophical. The kinds of questions that are posed are those questions that otherwise would not be capable of formulation, and I think that is what I try to do. Because really it's not so much about the answers you discover, it's about the reach of the questions.

EM: You already mentioned Herbert Marcuse, who was your teacher and mentor, and there are beautiful pages in your autobiography about your relationship with him, but Herbert Marcuse was part of a school, the Frankfurt School. You spent some years in Frankfurt in the late 1960s. You studied with Theodor Adorno, with Jürgen Habermas, with Max Horkheimer. Do you see yourself as a critical theorist in the Frankfurt School sense?

AD: Well, I think I've certainly been inspired by critical theory, which precisely centralizes the role of philosophical reflection. But, of course, critical theory argues that philosophy cannot indeed accomplish that about which it alone is able to raise the questions. So that the mode of philosophical inquiry, when it is linked to other disciplines, other approaches, of course with Adorno and Marcuse it was literature, it was sociology, it was music, it was all these. They are, I think, the first . . . they constituted the first serious effort to build interdisciplinary inquiry and interdisciplinary theory.

EM: You were twice a Communist vice-presidential candidate in the United States, although you left the party in the 1990s. After the fall of the Berlin wall, after the demise of the Soviet Union, what role can communism play today? Is there a role for communism today, at all?

AD: Well, in a sense I would say there has to be a role for an alternative to capitalism; whether it's communism in the sense in which it was constructed by the socialist community of nations that no longer exists is another question. The importance of unhooking capitalism and democracy is right now essential. So I very much see myself as continuing in that tradition. Yes, there is, there ought to be a role.

EM: Do you think that the so-called antiglobalization movement, the anti-WTO movement, can take up the role that Karl Marx assigned to the proletariat? In other words, can we say, "Anti-globalists of the world, unite"?

AD: Well, I don't know whether the transition is so easy. But I do think that the importance of global solidarities cannot be contested. And there is a link, it seems to me, between the internalization of the era of Karl Marx and the new globalisms we are seeking to build today. Of course, the global economy is far more complicated than Marx may have ever attempted to imagine. But at the same time his analyses, it seems to me, are equally resonant today. *Capital* begins with a look at commodity. The capitalist commodity has penetrated people's lives in ways that are unprecedented. The commodity has entered . . . capitalism in general has entered structures of feeling, the intimate spaces of people's lives. I think actually of a song performed by Sweet Honey and [*sic*] the Rock. I cannot remember the name, but it's about the global assembly line, and it's about the fact that we are indeed connected, by virtue of the fact that we wear clothes that are produced in Africa, in Asia, in Latin America . . .

EM: The sweatshops of the world.

AD: The global sweatshops. And the challenge is to, as Marx argued long ago, to uncover the social relations that are both embodied and concealed by these commodities.

EM: Now, African American political thought, Black political thought in the United States, has been deeply influenced by Marxism and communism; there is a great tradition. But one way in which we sometimes talk about Black political thought is in terms of two figures in tension. John Brown versus Frederick Douglass; Booker T. Washington–W. E. B. Du Bois; Malcolm X–Martin Luther King. And this is as a way to talk about a tension between Black Nationalism and assimilation or integration. How do you see yourself in relationship to this tradition, these two tensions: nationalism–integration?

AD: Well, of course it is possible to think about Black history as it has been shaped by these debates in various eras. There was of course also W. E. B. Du Bois and Marcus Garvey. But I actually am interested in that which is foreclosed by the conceptualization of the major issues in terms of these debates between Black men. And I say men because of course we never take into consideration that women may have also participated in these conversations. But I am interested precisely in what gets foreclosed by this tension between nationalism and integration. Those aren't the only alternatives.

EM: Right. So you see your work as contesting this way of viewing the Black tradition of political thought . . .

AD: Yes.

EM: . . . that way of making sense of integration.

AD: Exactly, exactly.

EM: I'm thinking of your "Unfinished Lecture on Liberation—II," which begins with Hegel and goes to Douglass and then works that you were producing at the same time that you were producing works on women in slave communities. So you wanted to displace the focus and say there's another way in which Black political thought can proceed.

AD: Absolutely, and I think that the assumption today that Black political thought must either be nationalism or it must disavow Black formations and Black culture is, is very misleading.

EM: Yes, but one of the things—we are talking about globalization here—one of the things that is attributed to globalization is the end of nationalisms. Do you think that there is no role for Black Nationalism in the United States? Has it become entirely obsolete? Perhaps an anachronism?

AD: Well, in one sense it has, but in another sense one can argue that, of course, the nationalisms that have helped to shape Black consciousness will endure. Now, I've always liked to define myself in relation to this debate about nationalisms. First of all I should say that I don't think that nationalism is a homogeneous concept. There are many versions of nationalism. And I've always preferred to identify with the pan-Africanism of W. E. B. Du Bois, who argued that Black people, say Black people in the new world, do have a special responsibility to Africa and other parts of the world, Asia . . . not by virtue of any biological connection, not by virtue of any racial link, but by virtue of a political identification that is forged. So that it is not about Africa because Africa happens to be populated by Black people. It is about Africa because Africa has been the target of colonialism and imperialism. And what I also like about Du Bois's pan-Africanism is that it is open to notions of Afro-Asian struggles as well, and this is something, I think, that has been concealed in the conventional tellings of history at many historical gatherings that were designated as Afro-Asian solidarity. So I prefer to think about the kind of political approach that is open, that is not racially defined but that is poised against racism.

EM: You know that last year was the one hundredth anniversary of the publication of W. E. B. Du Bois's *The Souls of Black Folk*, thirty years of your autobiography, and also this year we are celebrating fifty years of *Brown v. Board of Education*. Do you think that the forces of Black integration, forces of civil rights—this agent that transformed so much of the United States and the life for Blacks in the United States—has been betrayed and somehow rolled back because of two decades . . . if we think of Rehnquist being made the chief justice by Reagan and what has happened.

AD: Well, absolutely, absolutely. But I don't think it is helpful to think about an agent that gets established at one point in history that is successful. I don't think it makes sense to assume that this success will be enduring and that it will weather all of the changes and mutations that happen in other areas of society. As a matter of fact, I think that the civil rights movement managed to bring about some enormous shifts that opened the doors for people previously excluded from institutions, from the government, from education, from housing, etc. However, a civil rights approach, as even Dr. King recognized before he died, does not have the potential for ending racism, does not have the potential for ending structural racism. And so, what the civil rights movement did, it seems to me, was to create a new terrain for asking new questions and moving in new directions. It's not a betrayal that people like Colin Powell and Condoleeza Rice and the Black conservatives who are the heart of government are where they are. As a matter of fact, the civil rights movement demanded access, right? But I don't think that we can assume that what was done in the 1950s and 1960s is going to do the work of the 1980s and 1990s.

EM: But don't you worry about the Rehnquist court? I mean, if we think about the role of the Warren court in advancing the racial justice agenda . . .

AD: Oh, absolutely!

EM: . . . and the Rehnquist court, which is avowedly conservative. People in it are very outspoken about their conservatism and in fact saying we are going to roll back the gains of the Warren court. What does this mean for racial justice in the future?

AD: Of course I'm worried about that. The only point I'm attempting to make is that past struggles cannot correct current injustices and that, as a matter of fact, many people who tend to sit back and bemoan the betrayal of the civil rights movement are not prepared to imagine what might be necessary at this moment to challenge the conservatism of the Supreme Court, the rollback of so many gains that were won before, the sort of retreat of racism into the structural recesses of the society. It's very difficult for people to recognize racism, especially when it is not explicitly attached to racialized bodies. So what I'm suggesting is that we need a new agenda. We can't depend on the old agenda. The old agenda facilitates assaults on affirmative action, as Ward Connerly pointed out in his campaign for Proposition 209 in California. It's civil rights, yes, but what's needed now, Connerly basically argued, is the protection of civil rights of white men.

EM: Right. But they are using a very smart strategy, which is to do a displacement from questions about racial justice towards multiculturalism. An example is last year's court decision, the Michigan decision—in *Grutter v. Bolinger*—that says we have to do some sort of affirmative action for the sake of preserving multiculturalism. What is the difference between multiculturalism and racial justice?

AD: Oh yes, there's a huge difference. Diversity is another one of those words in the contemporary lexicon on what presumes to be antiracism. Multiculturalism is one of those categories that can admit both progressive and deeply conservative interpretations. There's corporate multiculturalism because corporations have discovered that it is more profitable to create a diverse workplace.

EM: Benneton multiculturalism!

AD: Yes. They have discovered that Black people and Latinos and Asians are willing to work as hard, or even harder, than their white counterparts. But of course there are those who talk about a strong politically inflected multiculturalism which emphasizes cross-racial community. But cross-racial community not for the purpose of creating a beautiful bouquet of flowers or a beautiful salad bowl, as these are some of the metaphors that have been used with respect to multiculturalism, but as a way of fighting for equality, challenging structural inequalities. And I think that kind of multiculturalism makes sense.

EM: And along with this question of multiculturalism and racial justice, there's this question, which is actually a question that worries me personally—existentially—tremendously. That's, we keep talking about the "browning" of the United States; you know by 2050 a quarter of the American population will be of some sort of Latino-Hispanic descent. Do you think that this browning of America will entail an eclipse of the quest for racial justice?

AD: Why should it?

EM: Well, the conservatives see that this is a problem. I mean the multi-culturalism and racial integration of Hispanics is in conflict with questions about racial justice, for instance, affirmative action or reparations. They're saying, "well, these questions are Black questions. They are not questions of . . ."

AD: Well, you see. That's the problem.

EM: OK.

AD: That's the problem and we can look at histories of struggle that have brought together people of African, Indigenous, Latino, Asian descent. And you know, as a matter of fact, it seems to me that contemporary ideologies precisely encourage this assumption that there must be racial conflict particularly when communities of people of color are at question. If one looks at the labor movement, there are many historical examples of Black–Latino solidarity and alliances, and I think this is a new era. The postcolonial conditions that are not only evident here in the US but literally all over the world. Europe is not now what it used to be. Europe is not a white geopolitical site. And the same of course is true of the US. I think it is important for Black communities to acknowledge the mutations that occurred. There's often the assumption that Black people set the antiracist agenda for the United States of America and it will always be that way. No, it will not. And, as a matter of fact, those Black figures—oftentimes as part of popular discourse as well—who attempt to live on the laurels of the past on the assumption that what Black people do is always progressive should think more seriously about this question. As a matter of fact, what we've seen in recent years is a trend towards conservatism in Black communities. So I would suggest that the very simple racial connections of communities of color . . . that no longer works in this day and age. And, as a matter of fact, we have to imagine different kinds of communities, communities that arise out of common political aims and goals. And that, of course, is what we might call the strong multi-cultural approach.

EM: I'd like to shift our conversation to your contemporary work, more recent writing and also activism. We are going to talk about prisons. Now, you wrote your autobiography under the shadow of the State. The State considered you an enemy of the State. Nixon and Hoover called you an enemy of the State. They also called you a terrorist, yet you produced a major indictment of the prison at the time, and you have continued. Your work has gravitated for the last thirty years around questions of prisons. What are the differences between the work from 1970, 1971, 1972 to the work that you have recently published, for instance, *Are Prisons Obsolete?*

AD: Well, I guess you are right. This engagement with prisons has kind of defined my life. And it actually precedes my own imprisonment, since I was engaged in many campaigns to free political prisoners. I think what I've been trying to do recently is to think critically about the contributions that were made by people, myself and many others of course, during that period thirty years ago, and to take seriously the contributions of prison intellectuals. But also to think about the ways in which slavery continues to live on in contemporary institutions. We might say that, beginning with the various campaigns to free political prisoners when I was a teenager, that was my first sort of encounter with this institution. Moving then during my own imprisonment towards an analysis that shifts to the institution itself—and of course I was assisted on this a great deal by George Jackson—to think about the prisons as a repressive apparatus. But also the repressive role . . . the role in promoting racism that the institution actively produces. Now what I'm doing is trying to think about how this happens with the aid of those aspects of history that continue to be embedded in our contemporary institutions, the sort of sedimented slavery in the prison and the death penalty. And this of course shifts. It has the potential for shifting how we think about reparations. And it has the potential for enlarging the contemporary political demand for reparations in such a way that it embraces not only Black people but all people who've been touched by these essentially racist institutions, whether they be people of color or whether they be white.

EM: The prison in the United States has become a kind of hyper-ghetto. And if I hear you correctly, you're suggesting that there can be in the United States no nonracist prison system, that a nonracist prison system is an oxymoron.

AD: Yes, I suppose you may put it that way. As a matter of fact, the assumption that an institution of repression, if it does its work equitably, if it treats, say, white people in the same way it treats Black people, that this is then a sign of equality and justice. This should be somewhat suspect. Some years ago when the Black man in Texas, James Byrd, was lynched by a group of white supremacists . . . Do you remember that incident?

EM: Yes, and he was dragged as well.

AD: Two of the white men who participated in that were sentenced to death. And at the moment that was celebrated as a victory, as if the way to racial equality and racial justice is to mete out the same treatment, the same horrendous barbaric treatment to white people that Black people have historically suffered. And that doesn't make very much sense to me.

EM: Can you expand on that? That's fascinating. In other words, there's a continuum between the antebellum period, the Reconstruction, the ghettos, and today when we have this situation where the prison system is a hyper-ghetto, and the death penalty, which is equally racialized. Indeed, all of these institutions and spaces seem to have their roots in slavery. Are these links and continuities what you're alluding to?

AD: What's interesting is that slavery as an institution, during the end of the eighteenth century and the nineteenth century, for example, managed to become a receptacle for all of those forms of punishment that were considered to be barbaric by the developing democracy. So you know, rather than abolish the death penalty outright, it seeks refuge within slavery so that white people are only subject to the death penalty if they commit one crime, which is murder. Whereas Black people, slaves, are subject to the death penalty in some states as many as seventy different offenses. But there's a sense in which the institution of slavery acts as a receptacle for those forms of punishment that are considered to be too barbaric to be meted out to white citizens in a democratic society. But of course with the abolition of slavery, these clearly racialized forms of punishment become deracialized, and they persist under guise of color-blind justice. They continue to be meted out primarily to Black people, but the Black person approached the law as the abstract judicial subject, the individual, not as a member of the community, so that the racism becomes unrecognizable, it becomes invisible. And it seems to me that one can make that kind of argument, too, so that it becomes apparent that the racism of an institution, like the death penalty or the larger prison, is very much a consequence of the sedimented slavery that lives on.

EM: The structure and—if you allow me this word—the "grammar" of these institutions is thoroughly racialized. An example would be the way in which prisoners get their rights suspended. I mean, they enter a type of civil death. This is also part of this racism, right? You mention in your book *Are Prisons Obsolete?* that Bush would not have been elected if prisoners had been allowed to vote.

AD: Absolutely. What's interesting is that disenfranchisement of prisoners while they are in prison is a commonsense insight. Most people in this country do not question that people, when they go to prison, should be robbed of their right to vote. As a matter of fact, they might laugh when they discover that there are some states in which prisoners can vote while they are in prison. That they set up polling booths in the prison as they do in an educational institution like this. And why has this discourse of prisoner-felony disenfranchisement become so much a part of the commonsense thought structures of people in this country? It has a great deal to do with slavery, right? I mean, in the same way, of course slaves weren't supposed to vote. They weren't full citizens. Of course prisoners aren't supposed to vote. They aren't really citizens any more, regardless of the reasons why they may have been imprisoned.

EM: You also mention in your recent work, and make a claim that is quite fascinating, that there is a symbiotic relationship between the prison industrial complex and the military industrial complex. How are those relationships sustained? How are they interwoven?

AD: Well, first, I should indicate that the use of the term prison industrial complex by scholars, activists, and others has been very strategic, precisely to produce the resonance with the military industrial complex. And when one considers the extent to which both complexes produce the means with which to maim and kill and devour . . . and this whole process of producing death, of producing destruction, is rendered profitable. And at the same time, of course, we noticed during the Vietnam War that military production was becoming a more central element of the entire economy, one that began to colonize the economy, so to speak. One can see similar proclivities in the prison industrial complex. It's no longer this minor niche in the economy, but rather it has reverberations. As a matter of fact, one never knows whether one is sitting on a table that was produced by prisoners or wearing clothes that may have been produced by prisoners or buying commodities produced by a corporation that uses prison labor or that had dealings with . . . So it's very much entangled with everyday lives of people who are targeted by and participate in the political economy of this country.

EM: You have argued as well that there is no correlation between crime and imprisonment. That the "prisonization" of American society has transformed the racial landscape of the United Sates, augmenting the racial aspect of this landscape. What is this relationship, that crime doesn't correlate with imprisonment? I mean, we are under the assumption that we have so many prisoners because there's so many criminals, because they are committing so many crimes. But you argue the opposite.

AD: Well, the link that is usually assumed in popular discourse and scholarly discourse is that crime produces punishment. What I have tried to do, along with many other public intellectuals, activists, scholars, is to encourage people to think about the possibility that punishment may be a consequence of other kinds of forces and not primarily a consequence of the commission of crime. Which isn't to say that people in prisons have not committed crimes—I'm not making that argument at all—or what we call "crimes."

Punishment, to be brief, can be seen in connection with surveillance. Increased punishment is very often a consequence of increased surveillance. Those communities that are subject to police surveillance are much more likely to produce more bodies headed in the direction of prison. But even more importantly, the institution of the prison, it seems to me, has evolved over the centuries, but especially during this period over the last twenty years, into the punitive solution to a whole range of social problems that are not being addressed by the institutions that could make people's lives better. So instead of building housing, throw the homeless in prison. Instead of developing the educational system, throw people who are illiterate into prison. Throw people in prison who lost jobs as the result of the de-industrialization process connected with the globalization of capital and structural adjustment. You know, get rid of them. They are considered to be dispensable populations. So the prison becomes a way of disappearing people and disappearing the social problems associated with those people.

EM: Is this also, this process of disappearing people without resolving the social contradictions, related to the 1996 welfare reform act, which sent so many women into the prison industrial complex . . .

AD: Oh, absolutely.

EM: . . . and increased the women's population in prisons?

AD: Absolutely, yes. As a matter of fact, women still, I think, constitute the fastest-growing sector of the imprisoned population, not only here but in other parts of the world as well. And it has in part to do with this establishment of something like the welfare system, which did not provide the solution to the problems of single unemployed mothers or single low-skilled mothers. One visits a women's prison and looks at the women who are imprisoned for, say, drug charges, and one can often discover that involvement with drugs was produced precisely by the shutting down of all alternatives, including welfare.

EM: Do you think, in parallel to the symbiotic relationship that exists between the military and the prison industry complexes, there's a symbiotic relationship between the prison industry and the judiciary in the United States?

AD: Well, but they are part of the same system, basically law enforcement. If one looks at the connection between the judicial system and law enforcement . . . you cannot really desegregate them. And of course the sentencing practices that have developed over the last two decades are in part responsible for the huge number of people that are behind bars. That is to say, more than two million people are in the various prisons, including military prisons, and the so-called truth sentencing, mandatory sentences—in New York, the Rockefeller sentencing laws—have a great deal to do with that.

EM: There's a fascinating phenomenon, and you talk about this in your work, that building more prisons seems to make us safer, but at the same time there's a declining rate of crime since the 1970s. Why is that? Why do we feel safer having prisons?

AD: This is a question of what makes people feel safer. It's not a question about what makes people safer. It is, of course, as many people have pointed out, quite ironic that with the continued pandemic of domestic violence, violence in the home, the family is still considered to be a safe place, a haven. Now, the threat appears always to come from the exterior, from the outside. So the imagined enemy, who is of course the enemy, the two million people who are imprisoned, are embodiments of that imagined enemy. That makes people feel better and at the same time prevents them from recognizing the threats to security that come from the military, that come from the police, that come from sometime one's intimate partners.

EM: We are continually under the threat of a crime, and it seems to be instigated by the media. Is this a panic that is fabricated? Or is there some substance to it?

AD: Well, these moral panics have always erupted at particular conjectures. We can think about the moral panic about Black men rapists, particularly in the aftermath of slavery. Now that was not so much about any real threat; it was about the problem of managing newly free Black bodies in the aftermath of slavery. And so it seems to me that the moral panic around crime is not related at all to any rise in crime in a material sense, but rather related to a similar problem of managing large populations, particularly people of color who have been rendered dispensable by the system of global capitalism. It's a simplistic analogy, but I do think it works. One could pursue that and explore the complexities.

EM: In this complex web of relation between the fabricated criminal, punishment, and prisonization, you make a suggestion which is quite glaring to me, and very provocative.

You say that the criminalization of the youth because of the so-called war on drugs followed on the coattails or simultaneous use of psychotropic drugs. But there's a difference between crack and Prozac, isn't there?

AD: Well, yes. One provides enormous amount of profit for the pharmaceutical corporations, and the other doesn't. The other provides profit for underground economies on drugs. I would hesitate to talk about the chemical similarities or dissimilarities, but I would argue that there is a major contradiction when one looks at the extent to which psychotropic drugs are promoted as the answer to all kinds of problems that people have, not just psychological problems. And one looks at how Prozac and Haldol and all of these drugs are prescribed.

EM: Ritalin for the kids . . .

AD: Ritalin, that's right.

EM: . . . and Viagra, for instance.

AD: That's right. One of the points I always make is, what do you do if you are a poor person receiving this barrage of commercials about the advantages of psychotropic drugs? That seems to me to sustain the underground drug traffic as well. But, of course, we are talking about illicit drugs on the one hand and licit drugs on the other, and that, it seems to me, is the difference.

EM: You have also in your work talked about this continuum, which is highly problematic, the continuum of the "red scare," anticommunism, McCarthyism, then the war on drugs, narco-traffickers, terrorists, and now we have a war on terrorism. What are the continuums, the similarities? What are the differences?

AD: Well. It would be very complicated to explore all of the differences and similarities, but I would like to suggest that the terrain for the production of the terrorist as a figure in the American *imaginaire* has been significantly created by previous moral panics—if you will, the criminal. The criminal was the threatening figure if one considers the Willie Horton campaign and so forth. And then of course the communist has been at certain periods of US history the major figure threatening security. So now the terrorist, and of course the terrorist has been evoked in various periods as well. I was labeled a terrorist when I was on the FBI's Ten Most Wanted list. Nixon publicly referred to me as a terrorist. I'm saying that parenthetically. The point, however, is that these emotional responses to the allocation of the figure of the terrorist are overladen with these ideas of the criminal, the communist. It's always about the external enemy against which the nation mobilizes in order to save itself. Of course, this is one of the major problems I have with nationalism. Nationalism always requires a kind of external threat. It's not really new. The material consequences are of course horrendous, with the assaults on people by virtue of their Muslim or Arab ancestry both in the US and Iraq and Afghanistan. Horrible prison abuses.

EM: Why don't we bring the conversation around to this question which is so burning today, these disclosures about torture not only in Guantánamo but also in Iraq that we are now hearing about. And we also hear that the United States is shipping off prisoners to Middle Eastern prisons to be tortured. What is your take on this?

AD: Of course, as we talk, the revelations have continued to be published about the abuses, the torture, the sexual intimidation in what was the most notorious prison in Baghdad during the regime of Saddam Hussein, Abu Ghraib. As difficult as it is to view those photographs, as horrendous as they may appear, particularly to people in this country who find it hard to believe that a woman, a young woman from North Carolina, would participate in this (I'm referring of course to one of the reservists who's been captured on photograph). But I prefer to think about this not so much as an aberration, or not as an aberration, not as an exception, but as a part of regimes of punishment that are deeply embedded in the history of the institution of prison. And I know that it may be difficult for people to accept the fact that this has always gone on, it continues to go on, and it will go on in the future if we are not willing . . . not simply to say "let's get rid of this particular incident," but to think deeply about the impact that these institutions have on a world that is supposed to be striving for democracy. Is this the kind of democracy that is produced in and through and against these prisons? What is the opposite of democracy?

EM: I would like to ask you a last question, the parting question. *Prisons and Democracies* is the title of your forthcoming book, and this profiles itself as your political testament. What does this political testament say?

AD: Oh! I didn't know it was profiled as my political testament.

EM: I just did.

AD: OK. I think it's . . . hopefully it will be a small contribution. Hopefully it will encourage people to think not only about the institution of the prison but about this kind of democracy, the particular version of this democracy that can only invent itself and develop itself as the negation of the kinds of horrors that unfold on daily bases within prisons inside the country and all over the world. It's an extremely flawed democracy. I'll end with the example that I like to use because I think it challenges people's common sense. We acknowledge the fact that—and it kind of relates to the sexual intimidation that we recently witnessed in Iraq—women in prisons all over the world are forced, often daily, often several times daily, to go through strip searches and cavity searches. That is to say, their vaginas are searched, their rectums are searched. And this is represented as a normal routine. This is what happens when you go to prison. This is what happens to the citizen who is divested of her or his citizenship. It is right that the subject be subjected to sexual coercion. I want to urge people to think a little bit more deeply about the extent to which these kinds of regimes inform in very powerful and profound ways the kind of democracy we inhabit today. And I'd like to urge people to think about different versions of democracy: future democracies; democracies inflected with socialism. Democracies in which all of the social problems, or a good deal of the social problems, that have helped to construct the prison industrial complex will be directly, if not solved, at least encountered and acknowledged.

EM: Thank you so much for those wonderful prophetic words. Thank you for our conversation.

AD: Thank you for your wonderful comments and questions as well.

Law and Resistance in the Prisons of Empire: An Interview with Angela Y. Davis

Chad Kautzer and Eduardo Mendieta / 2004

From *Peace Review*, vol. 16, no. 3, 2004, pp. 339–47. doi: 10.1080/1040265042000278586.
Reprinted by permission of the publisher Taylor & Francis, Ltd. http://www.tandfonline.com

Angela Davis's political activism began when she was a youngster in Birmingham, Alabama, and continued through her high school years in New York. But it was not until 1969 that she came to national attention, after being removed from her teaching position in the Philosophy Department at the University of California Los Angeles (UCLA) because of her social activism and her membership in the Communist Party, USA. In 1970 she was placed on the FBI's Ten Most Wanted List on false charges and was the subject of an intense police search that drove her underground and culminated in one of the most famous trials in recent US history. During her sixteen-month incarceration, a massive international "Free Angela Davis" campaign was organized, leading to her acquittal in 1972.

Professor Davis's long-standing commitment to prisoners' rights dates back to her involvement in the campaign to free the Soledad Brothers, which led to her own arrest and imprisonment. Today she remains an advocate of prison abolition and has developed a powerful critique of racism in the criminal justice system. She is a member of the advisory board of the Prison Activist Resource Center and currently is working on a comparative study of women's imprisonment in the US, The Netherlands, and Cuba.

Former California governor Ronald Reagan once vowed that Angela Davis would never again teach in the University of California system. Today she is a tenured professor in the History of Consciousness Department at the University of California, Santa Cruz. In 1994 she received the distinguished honor of an appointment to the University of California Presidential Chair in African American and Feminist Studies (http://huwww.usc.edu: 16080/HistCon/fac ulty_davis.htm).

Kautzer: You have been a longtime prison activist and were yourself once imprisoned. Could you tell me about your experiences in prison and how they shaped your view of the prison system itself?

Davis: My imprisonment did have an impact on the way I eventually began to think about the role of prison in relation to racism and generalized repression. I went to jail as a result of my involvement in a case involving political prisoners, so prior to my own arrest I had been intensely active in many campaigns to free political prisoners—from Nelson Mandela to Huey Newton and Ericka Huggins, to the Puerto Rican nationalist Lolita Lebron—and this particular case involved George Jackson and the Soledad Brothers. During the time I spent in jail in New York and later in California—two different facilities in California—I corresponded with George Jackson, and I would say that George, more than anyone else, more than any other influence, urged me to think about the general function of the prison, not only in terms of political imprisonment but about the relationship between the institution of the prison and racism, that is to say, the relationship between criminalization and racism and racialization. So I do think that the time I spent in jail had a lasting impact on my ideas.

Kautzer: We're talking about the early 1970s, with racist trials and political repression across the country, yet you were eventually acquitted [in June 1972]. What role do you think activism of local and even international groups played in your eventual acquittal?

Davis: That activism was the determining factor. There is no doubt in mind [*sic*] that I would never have been released had it not been for the organizing that took place both within this country and all over the world. There is no question. As a matter of fact, I often imagine what might have happened, particularly since I've gotten even more involved in prison activism and doing research around prisons over the last ten years or so. I often imagine what my own particular trajectory might have been had not that movement intervened.

Kautzer: In addition to these schisms and borders, there was of course that shadow of the Vietnam War. In what ways do you think the ongoing war was linked to legal and extralegal repression of domestic political activism and liberation struggles?

Davis: I might talk about that in two different ways. First, yes, there was repression that was directly linked to the war and in very material ways.

For example, the attack on the Black Panther Party in Los Angeles that announced a whole series of attacks essentially organized by the FBI [Federal Bureau of Investigation], participated in by local police forces. The participants in that attack were former Green Berets and former Vietnam soldiers, who had been given some special dispensation to join what was then a very new formation: the Special Weapons and Tactical Squad [SWAT]. Of course, SWAT is now a common name, but its very first public appearance was the attack on the Black Panther Party office. We knew at the time that these were policemen trained in Vietnam, trained in counterinsurgency. As a matter of fact, we could even see very visibly the ways in which they launched this attack, conducted this attack, and in my autobiography I think I described them as "slinking along the ground" and then of course there was the helicopter above. So there are very material ways in which the military repression was domesticated in order to be unleashed against the internal enemies. We also had the direct assaults against the Vietnam War protesters: the Kent State and Jackson State assaults.

Kautzer: Now we have the USA Patriot Act and the Department of Homeland Security as part of a rising security state. What do you think about the continuity between the forms of repression you just described during the Vietnam War and this new security state? Do you see continuity here, or are we experiencing a new logic at work?

Davis: I think there is an historical continuity, but there are also some ruptures. As a matter of fact, I would also talk about the Cold War. I would also talk about the McCarthy era. When I first learned about the Patriot Act and all of the measures that were being used to silence people who were defending immigrants who were under attack, when I learned about academics who were under attack for their resistance to the Bush administration especially, I immediately thought about the McCarthy period. I immediately felt those historical resonances, and what struck me most, I think, was the extent to which the very similar process of self-censorship seemed to be happening. It would seem to me that, particularly now, it would make sense to revisit the McCarthy era and think about the extent to which people who considered themselves progressive and on the side of justice played a major role in the success of McCarthyism. So rather than awaiting the repression to come down from above, guaranteeing they would not become targets of this repression, they were doing the work of the House on Un-American Activities before the hearing took place. By not hiring communists, by kicking communists out of unions . . . and it seemed to me that there was a period in the aftermath of September 11 when something very similar was happening. Particularly considering that during that first vote Barbara Lee as the only congressperson in the entire country who dared to vote against [a resolution authorizing President Bush to use military force in retaliation]. That was very scary, particularly given the fact that some in the Congress, particularly in the Black Caucus, indicated afterwards that they were really opposed to the resolution, that they didn't want to be viewed as being soft on terrorism, so they voted in favor of it. Those are the makings of fascism, I'm sorry to say.

But you were asking about continuity. I do think that there is some continuity, but this is an unprecedented historical moment in so many ways, it seems to me. We're ruled by a president who was not elected and an administration that is composed of people who, long before September 11, 2001, already decided that they were going to invade Iraq—the whole Project for a New American Century. There is something qualitatively different about the extent to which those who sit in government are willing to ignore public opinion, ignore demonstrations—the demonstrations that took place on February 15, 2003: there were millions of people. This was unprecedented. Never before had so many people simultaneously gathered in so many parts of the world, and Bush had no response to it, or he said something like, of course this isn't going to affect foreign policy, I don't listen to—what did he call them—"focus groups." There is something remarkably different. I have spoken to many people who directly experienced the McCarthy era, and their sense is that this is a far more dangerous moment than was that period—during which many of them actually spent time in prison.

Kautzer: In this moment, we have the globalization of the so-called war on terror and, in turn, of US detention centers and prisons, which are, practically speaking, beyond the reach of US and international law. This week [April 2004], for example, we witnessed the release of photographs documenting the torture of Iraqi detainees carried out by US soldiers in Saddam Hussein's infamous Abu Ghraib prison. What connections, if any, do you see between the globalization of these outlaw prisons and the domestic prison industrial complex?

Davis: I think they are related. It is important to understand the growth of domestic imprisonment, the globalization of the prison industrial complex, and the way in which immigrant detention centers, facilities in which prisoners of war are incarcerated, are very much entangled in that whole process. First of all, I would argue that this phenomenon we call the prison industrial complex is a global phenomenon. It can't really be understood as a specifically US development. What has been enabled in the US—the rapid proliferation of prison facilities and prison populations; the rapid degree to which capital has moved into the punishment industry in such a way that it is a small niche—it is a major element of the US economy. That is why people choose to use this term "prison industrial complex," precisely because of the ways in which it recapitulates the development of the military industrial complex . . .

I think it is important to think about all of the different layers and levels and aspects of this. The prison in Guantánamo, for example, or the Abu Ghraib prison just outside Baghdad, and the normalization of torture. As horrendous as it is, it is not qualitatively different from what happens in US prisons, when one thinks about the sexual violence that many women have suffered, the lawsuits that women in Michigan filed against the state, arguing that they were sexually assaulted by guards. Human Rights Watch produced this report, *All Too Familiar*, that documented abundantly the pervasiveness of sexual abuse . . . So when I read an article about the sexual assaults that happened in the Abu Ghraib prison outside Baghdad, it confirms my sense that this is part of a process of discipline and power. It is really easy to traffic between the various systems. What seems absolutely barbaric and awful when *60 Minutes* reports it and there are photographs, is what happens here on a daily basis.

Kautzer: Your focus on this disciplinary continuity makes me rethink the assumptions of my question, one of which concerned the importance of a legal discontinuity. The fact that these US-run prisons and detention centers were beyond the reach of the US law, of US legislators, of the US media.

Davis: But you could say the same thing about domestic prisons.

Kautzer: Which then raises the question of the role of law itself. Does law really make a significant difference in this case? What about the potential for challenging these abuses? Is the existence of law in the case of the domestic prison system a potential lever, or ground, by which we can act?

Davis: I think so. It is important to stress the continuum on which these institutions stand but also at the same time indicate the differences. There have been similar revelations—I can remember the private prison in Texas that was shut down because a video was released of guards conducting practice cell extractions. They created the simulated conditions of a response to a riot, and all of this was taped, including dogs biting prisoners, prisoners being forced to run the gauntlet. I can actually think of similar images . . . but there was protest. People did rise up, people did insist on the rule of law, if you will. But I don't know if we should assume that this is not also possible with respect to Abu Ghraib, for example. Because it is in a far-flung place doesn't mean we don't also have a stake in challenging it.

Kautzer: I would agree that we have a stake, but do we have the means of challenging the actions if we don't have the law?

Davis: I don't know. I'm a little ambivalent here, because I don't know that I would give the law that much power. It seems that in instances where there have been major victories, in the cases of US prisoners, those victories have in many, if not most, instances been produced by mass movements, so I don't see the law operating within a vacuum. Certainly, yes, we rely on it when it can be used to accomplish what we call progressive goals, but by itself it is pretty powerless. As someone who has been involved in this work against the prison industrial complex for quite a number of years, I think that it is important for us to mobilize people who have already committed themselves to doing the work in their communities, in their states, in the country, to get involved in campaigns against these prisons in Guantánamo, Afghanistan, and Iraq.

Kautzer: Going back to your own acquittal: it seemed to be more a result of political organizing and the subsequent changes in the national discourse than a result of deliberations on legal grounds.

Davis: Yes, and the impact that had on the proceeding in the courtroom. So I would really emphasize the dynamic, that dialectic.

Mendieta: Listening to you, it dawns on me that what you're describing is just another aspect of state terrorism. Would you accept this kind of reflection that the prison industrial complex is one of the mechanisms by means of which the state carries out a form of state terrorism, the kind of terrorism that Chomsky has been talking about, and how does that differ from Islamic terrorism, narco-terrorism, etc. Chomsky says that the primary agent of terrorism is the state.

Davis: Yes, it is true. I agree with him.

Kautzer: As with the "communist" and the "criminal," when we talk about the "terrorist," talk about their incarceration is not far behind. We've seen that Guantánamo Bay, in particular, has become a powerful symbol of incarceration. What ideological work do you think Camp X-Ray in Guantánamo Bay performs?

Davis: You mean in this particular moment?

Kautzer: Yes.

Davis: Because of course historically we can think of Guantánamo Bay in connection with Haitians and in other contexts, but today, of course, it is the outlaw military prison to which you were referring, where anything can happen because it is not a part of the territory of the US, and therefore, US law does not necessarily apply. I think that I'd like to use this question to talk briefly about the notions of democracy that circulate today. About ways in which activists, public intellectuals, scholars, artists, cultural producers, need to take very seriously what are very clear signs of an impending fascist threat. And I use that term advisedly. It is not a term that I have ever thrown around. But if you consider what happens in a place like Guantánamo, where people were picked up for no other reasons than they happened to be in the wrong place at the wrong time, where children were imprisoned for years without any contact with their families, and where the highest governing officials argue that they have no right to a lawyer because they're not on the actual soil of the US. When one takes into consideration the increasing erosions of democratic rights and liberties under the auspices of the Patriot Act, for example, it ought to be a sign that some kind of movement is needed. It should frighten people. Fortunately, because of the British citizens who were recently released and had press conferences, we've been able to acquire a great deal more information about what goes on there than we might have had there not been British citizens, which disturbs me, because what about people from Afghanistan who don't have that British passport, or the people from Iraq who are treated the way the pictures from the Abu Ghraib prison have shown? I can only say that they are very frightening signposts of what may portend horrible things that I do not even want to think about, but we must if we feel we have any stake in the creation—and I would not even say preservation—I would say the creation of a democracy in this country.

Kautzer: Your observation about the release of British citizens from Guantánamo seems to illustrate yet again the power of an organized public in pressuring both the US and British governments, in the absence of legal mechanisms and jurisdiction, to gain their release.

Davis: Absolutely.

Kautzer: Before leaving the question of Guantánamo, do you think Camp X-Ray has displaced the supermax prison as the ultimate carceral threat in the social imaginary?

Davis: Guantánamo exists in the imaginary of those who have already been labeled as the enemy, and it is wielded as a weapon against them. Actually, I would say that the military, Guantánamo, Camp X-Ray—that these facilities have been enabled by the rapid development of new technologies within domestic prison sites, and at the same time these supermax facilities have been enabled by the military tortures and technologies that are used. I like to think of them together as opposed to standing as competitors with each other, and I don't think therefore that the specter of this military facility displaces the specter of the supermax. In many ways, you might argue that the threat of the supermax even surpasses that of . . . I don't like to create hierarchies in general, so I'm not even certain whether I should formulate it in that way, but I'm thinking about the normalization of torture, the everydayness of torture that is characteristic of the supermax. There is sensory deprivation, there is no human contact at all, the fact that prisoners are often driven to the point that the only way they can exercise agency is to do something with their own feces. I would tend to think that this regularization, this normalization, is even more threatening, and yet it never receives the kind of attention . . . it is never even represented as an aberration as Camp X-Ray is represented as an aberration, or Abu Ghraib in Iraq. This is represented not as normal or a normalizing practice, but rather as something exceptional, individual; these six soldiers are responsible for it. But there can't be any attempt to describe the supermax in that way, as an aberration. It is now the highest level of security classification within the system. It used to be that a minimum implied a maximum, and of course a medium, but now this surpasses that. Now the minimum implies the supermaximum, and who knows what is to come after that. It was seemingly generated on its own, seemingly self-generated from this classificatory process, so its staying power is something . . . which is not to [in] any way underestimate the horrors that are happening in these outlaw prisons.

Kautzer: How do you think these horrors link up with the reemergence of national discourses in the US advocating torture and political assassination? From Harvard lawyer Alan Dershowitz's discussion of torture to Bush's wink and nod to Sharon and his use of assassinations, why is such talk arising now?

Davis: First of all, I think the Bush administration has worked hard to lower the level of political discourse, because I don't think the extent to which the discourse has become so simplistic happens unintentionally. It is very difficult to even engage any kind of interesting debate . . . The debasing of political discourse, it seems to me, gives rise to what we think of as extreme expressions. You're either for terrorism, or if you're not for terrorism, then you have to be against terrorism, and if you are against terrorism, then you have to embrace all of the ideas that are put forth by the administration. This simplification of the rhetoric, of the discourse, is, I think, in part responsible for the ease with which these extreme positions are expressed. I think that the challenge is to complicate it; to complicate the discourse, and to make it very clear that it is not an either/or, for-and-against situation. One can be against the Saddam Hussein regime but at the same time opposed to the US military, but the way they represent it, it is either one or the other.

Mendieta: Do you think that this lowering of the standards of political discourse is related to a president saying that we will get Osama bin Laden dead or alive, basically issuing a death sentence? Do you think that this contributes to turning the American public, and even the US military, even more lawless, more violent?

Davis: Absolutely. As a matter of fact, when Bush first began to talk about the hunt for Osama bin Laden, wanted dead or alive, people in some places began to use his photograph for target practice, and, because of the extent to which people live inside their representations, it is very easy to move from target practice to shooting down a Seik [*sic*] person, who becomes that representational symbol of the enemy. There were so many examples of that, especially in the period after 9/11.

Kautzer: Going back to Bush's initial "wanted dead or alive" remarks about bin Laden after 9/11, I found it noteworthy that he avoided direct speech, invoking instead the analogy of old western films and their imagery of "wanted dead or alive" posters. This calls forth resonances of the frontier, outlaw country, and the colonization of Native Americans.

Davis: What is interesting is that he may have been urging people to travel within their fantasies, because there is a disjuncture between what people think they are supposed to express regarding racism, regarding Native Americans, and the pleasure that they experience when they watch a western, with John Wayne, or whoever it is, killing all the bad Indians. After all there are still cowboy and Indian customs that kids . . . It is still very much a part of the collective fantasy, the collective psyche. It invites people to engage in a certain kind of regression, a certain kind of infantilization, so that political positions are based more on the kind of pleasure that people get from different representational practices and fantasies. We know that there is this major disjuncture, so this simplistic discourse would play an important role. It wouldn't be just a sign of Bush's lack of intelligence, it would be strategically very important.

Kautzer: It lowers the gate, unleashing a flood of fantasy.

Davis: What it does is disarm people. It removes their critical capacities. It invites them to forget about their criticism. I think this is one of the reasons why so many people, including progressive and radical people, in the aftermath of the attacks could not speak out against Bush. I talked to people in New York for whom I've had a lot of respect, and we have these racial histories . . . but when this happened, all of that flew out the window. So people were already disarmed when Bush talked about "hunting down" or wanting bin Laden dead or alive.

Kautzer: I'd like to return to the topic of activism, if I may, and the kind of role it can play in strengthening democratic and critical practices, which might prevent this kind of politics of fantasy. What lessons might we learn from movements of resistance in the past and apply to contemporary struggles?

Davis: This is a very difficult question, because the terrain on which organizing happens is so different today from what it was thirty years ago. We began the interview by talking about the organizing that took place around my case, while I was in jail. There are, as I said before, some lessons that may persist, although I do not like to appear to evoke nostalgia about those good old days when it was possible to build radical and revolutionary movements—not at all. But I do think, as I've said on a number of occasions, there is a sense today in which movements are supposed to be self-generating. There is a lack of patience. It is difficult to encourage people to think about protracted struggles, protracted movements that require very careful strategic organizing interventions that don't necessarily depend on the ability to mobilize. It seems to me that mobilization has displaced organization, so that in the contemporary moment, when we think about organizing movements, we think about bringing out masses of people. Of course, it is important to bring out masses of people to give expression with their bodies and their voices, to give expression to their goals, whether it is ending the war in Iraq or in defense of women's reproductive rights. I have always thought that demonstrations were supposed to demonstrate the power of the movement, right, that that was their purpose. There was supposed to be an ongoing movement that at certain strategic moments needed to bring everybody out who was somehow touched by that movement to be seen. I think now that we think of that making visible as the movement itself, so that when the millions leave they don't go back into formations that continue to do the work. They go back into their private spaces and express their relationship to this movement only in private discourse. I think there has to be a way to organize movements now . . . We rely on the internet, and it is an incredible tool, but it may encourage us to produce instantaneous movements, fast-food movements. The organizing is around the mobilizing, and then the mobilization happens, and what do you do next? You organize to mobilize again . . . We need to figure out a way so that when the people do go back into their homes after a mobilization, they have a sense of community; they bring with them a sense of community that does not involve this disjuncture from the private movement to the monumental public moment of the demonstration.

Kautzer: What factors do you think are mitigating that kind of organizing today? I completely agree with need for day-to-day organizing and community building, but not having an experiential sense of what it was like on the ground thirty-five years ago, I would like to hear your reflections.

Davis: Well, you see, everything has changed, so I don't think we can have that kind of a discussion and really have it work. Everything has changed. The funding of basic movements has changed. The professionalization of social movements has changed. The mode of politicization has changed. The role of culture and the globalization of cultural production have changed. I don't know how else to talk about this other than to encourage people to experiment. That is actually what I would gather from that period, the lesson I would draw from the period when I was involved in what were essentially experimental modes of organizing that challenged the conventional civil rights organizing. Nobody knew whether it was going to work. Nobody knew where we were going. I often think that young people today have too much deference toward the older organizers, the veterans, and are much too careful in the sense of having to have a model. Everyone wants a role model. Everyone wants some guarantee that it is going to work. I think the best way to figure out what might work is just to do it, regardless of the mistakes. Be willing to make the mistakes. As a matter of fact, I think the mistakes help to produce these new modes of organizing.

Chad Kautzer is a political organizer and cofounder of the Social Justice Alliance in Stony Brook, New York, where he is also a PhD candidate in philosophy at Stony Brook University. Currently, a DAAD scholar at the Insitut für Sozialforschung in Frankfurt, he is the author most recently of "Rorty's Country, Rorty's Empire," forthcoming in *Radical Philosophy Review* (2004). *Correspondence*: ckaurzter.id.sunysb.edu

Eduardo Mendieta is a professor of philosophy at the State University of New York at Stony Brook. *Correspondence*: Philosophy Department, 213 Harriman Hall, State University of New York at Stony Brook, Stony Brook, NY 11794, USA

Angela Davis on *Free Angela & All Political Prisoners*

Livia Bloom Ingram / 2012

From *Filmmaker Magazine*. September 15, 2012. Reprinted by permission of Livia Bloom Ingram.

"When the doors slid open, furious flashes of light jolted me out of my reflections. That's why they had cuffed my hands in front. As far as I could see, reporters and photographers were crowded into the lobby. Trying hard not to look surprised, I lifted my head, straightened my back and between the two agents, made the long walk through the light flashes and staccato questions toward the caravan waiting outside."

These lines from Angela Davis's 1974 autobiography, written at the age of twenty-nine and edited by Toni Morrison, describe the way she remembers a humiliating perp walk four years before. At the time, Davis was among the FBI's Most Wanted. She had been fired from her UCLA professorship for being a Communist. She had spent the last three months living underground. She faced charges of murder, kidnapping, and conspiracy. Yet Davis's instinct, in this situation, was not to assume the traditional position of a fugitive in handcuffs, cowering, hiding her face. Instead, she *tried hard not to look surprised. Lifted her head. Straightened her back.* She stood tall.

Remarkable poise and dignity are among the characteristics that *Free Angela & All Political Prisoners*, the new documentary by Shola Lynch (*Chisholm '72*), conveys most strongly about the professor, activist, icon and force of nature at its center. The subject of songs by musicians including the Rolling Stones and John Lennon and Yoko Ono, at the age of sixty-eight, Davis still glows with the charisma, warmth, and fierce intellect that brings the film's extensive archival material—from personal letters to lectures to her extensive FBI files—to life. Lynch's film, whose producers include Jay-Z, Will Smith, and Jada Pinkett Smith, is a valuable complement to studies of Davis's books and speeches, which remain all too resonant and relevant today. When *Free Angela & All Political Prisoners* premiered at the Toronto International Film Festival, Angela Davis was once again thronged by reporters and photographers, flashbulbs, and staccato questions. Once again, she lifted her head, straightened her back, and stood tall.

In this conversation Davis discusses the filmmaking process, explains what it means to be a "political prisoner," and contextualizes her work for a new generation.

Filmmaker: How did you become involved in the documentary *Free Angela & All Political Prisoners*?

Angela Davis: The director, Shola Lynch, is a friend of my niece [performer Eisa Davis, who portrays Angela Davis in the film's reenacted scenes]. Shola approached me with the idea, and I thought about it . . . It took a while before she persuaded me. [laughs] We had a number of conversations, and finally I decided it might be a good thing. Sometimes it is important for a younger person to have a fresh new perspective on historical events. But from the beginning, I said to Shola, "This is your film; this your perspective on that era." I did lots of interviews and had lots of discussions with her, but in the end, it's her work.

I am not interested in people learning more about my life. However, I am interested in people recognizing the power of the campaign that developed around my case. Large numbers became involved, and many of them came to feel as if it was their story as well. It's important to convey to new generations that it is possible to join together and feel solidarity and togetherness across racial, ethnic, economic, gender, and national borders. We could use some of that today.

Filmmaker: What do you think of our current political moment?

Davis: It's a difficult moment, given the economic crises all over the world, but at the same time there have been sparks of hope. The revolutions in the Middle East gave some hope to people around the world; so did the Occupy movement. We need some staying power. We need to feel that it is possible to pursue things in the US such as free health care, which we still don't have . . . even though Barack Obama is quite right when he boasts that he was responsible for the first major legislation on health care in the history of the country since the New Deal.

We still have a long way to go. We may be powerless as individuals—and even someone like Obama may be relatively powerless as an individual—to do things that will be bring us a better world. But if we come together, we can build movements and put pressure on the major political figures. This is what we need to be doing in the coming months before the election. The first time around, we elected Obama for what this election *meant*: the historical election of an African American to the presidency. We were doing it for him. This time, we need to think about ourselves. We need to do it for us. Then we need to continue that movement after the election.

Filmmaker: The title of the film is *Free Angela & All Political Prisoners*; what does the phrase "political prisoner" mean to you?

Davis: A political prisoner is someone who is imprisoned for his or her political beliefs or affiliations. Mumia Abu-Jamal, for example, is still in prison. But at the same time, we can argue that there is a broader definition of "political prisoner": those imprisoned because of the overall political situation. In the United States, of course, there are more people incarcerated than anywhere else in the world. Prison has become the default solution for problems that should really be solved by educational institutions, health care, housing, etc. The concept of a political prisoner cannot remain static.

I'm glad that Shola used the title *Free Angela & All Political Prisoners*, because that was an issue around which we had major arguments as the case was unfolding. There were many people who were willing to support me, but they didn't necessarily want to get involved in the bigger issues. When the campaign around my case began to develop, I and other comrades argued that it had to be a campaign not only focused on me as an individual but on the larger question of political repression. At first, the organization was called "National United Committee to Free Angela Davis," but it came to be called "National United Committee to Free Angela Davis *& All Political Prisoners*." As soon as I was freed, we began to work on other cases. We created another organization called the National Alliance Against Racism and Political Repression, and I guess you might say that since then I've been working consistently on prisoners' rights, political incarceration, and the racist implications of the prison system.

Filmmaker: In what way were you a political prisoner?

Davis: I was involved in a number of political organizations: I had been active in the Black Panther Party, I had been active in the Student Nonviolent Coordinating Committee (SNCC), and I joined the Communist Party. When I was first singled out and I lost my job teaching at UCLA, it was for my membership in the Communist Party.

When I was charged with murder, kidnapping, and conspiracy, my Communist affiliation and my background in the Black Panther Party made me an easy target. And, as a matter of fact, the attorney general asked potential jurors whether they thought I was a "political prisoner," as part of his jury selection. He did not want to take those who thought I was a political prisoner; instead, he argued, I was in jail only on criminal charges. Of course, the US doesn't have a category for political prisoners, so people who are incarcerated for their political beliefs are *always* charged with criminal charges.

To this day, in the US it is still said there are no political prisoners. Unlike South Africa, for example, which acknowledged Nelson Mandela as a political prisoner, here we have the guise of democracy. We're supposed to be inhabiting a country in which people have the right to free speech and political affiliation. When I was fired simply for being a member of the Communist Party, I discovered that was not the case.

Filmmaker: In retrospect, your firing seems much clearer than the court case, which has many shades of gray.

Davis: Well, the second time I was fired from UCLA, it was because of my activity in support of the Soledad Brothers [George Jackson, Fleeta Drumgo, and John Clutchette, who had been incarcerated in Soledad prison]. So that was, again, a question of political activities and issues.

Filmmaker: Was the administration up front about your political activity as the reason for your second firing, too?

Davis: Oh yeah. "Activity unbecoming of a professor": I wasn't supposed to be speaking at rallies or involved politically off campus. Which is, of course, ridiculous.

Filmmaker: Today, with everyone's public persona so easy to access, it can be very hard to know where your professional responsibilities end and your private beliefs and rights as a civilian and a citizen begin.

Davis: Yes, that's true. When I was teaching at UCLA, there were those who argued that because I was a Communist, I would be indoctrinating my students rather than teaching them. But I've always made a practice of telling my students what my political affiliations and principles are and then asking them to choose their own. Rather than assume that I could be objective and my political ideas would not insinuate themselves into what I was teaching, I would say to my students, "This is what I believe. I am not asking you to join me, but you need to know what I believe in order to judge for yourselves my remarks on any particular subject."

Filmmaker: I can't think of a single one of my history teachers making clear their political opinions.

Davis: Well, I was teaching Marxism so . . . [laughs] I was hired to teach a subject that I had been involved with on a practical level for a very long time.

Filmmaker: Today, Marxism remains relevant; in fact, it seems to be referenced more frequently than ever.

Davis: Capitalism is still with us, and Marx developed the most compelling analysis of capitalism. I never saw Marx as a philosopher who informed us about what the revolution was going to be like or what would come after capitalism. He provided a way to understand the world we inhabit and the extent to which political economies insinuate themselves into all aspects of our lives. That was true fifty years ago when I first encountered Marx, but today, with the impact of global capitalism, it's even more true. I could never have imagined the degree to which capitalism would develop.

To use an academic term, capitalism has overdetermined everything. You might say that even people's dreams are capitalist dreams. As a professor, I see students who are professionalizing themselves even before they even learn what they need to know in order to go on the market; the assumption is that the market is everything.

This is capitalism. We used to be able to distinguish more clearly between capitalism and democracy. But now people all over the world assume that democracy is just a synonym for capitalism. In the countries of the southern region, like in Africa, economies have been completely transformed into capitalist economies—even though the majority of people live in abject poverty, and it doesn't make sense to have an economy rooted in profit when you are trying to satisfy the needs of such vast numbers of people.

We have to work through this issue. This is why the Occupy movement erupted as it did: it was an indication that we need to find a new vocabulary to talk about capitalism publicly. It is now possible to talk about, to criticize capitalism in a way that may not have been possible even five years ago.

Filmmaker: Where does feminism fit into this?

Davis: I see feminism not so much as emphasizing the rights of women— although it does—but as a way of understanding the interconnectedness of gender, race, class, sexuality, the economy and transnationalism. Feminism is one of the most important strategies for helping us to understand these issues and the ways they are tied together. More than ever, what we need is a Marxist-inflected feminism—that's the best strategy at this particular moment in history.

Livia Bloom Ingram is a film curator and the director of Exhibition and Broadcast at Icarus Films. Special thanks to Brian Geldin, GAT.

Angela Davis

Frank Barat / 2013

From Frank Barat, "Angela Davis." *New Internationalist*, March 2013, p. 46. Reprinted by permission of New Internationalist/newint.org

Once on the FBI's "Most Wanted" list, the radical political activist, author, and scholar has been making waves in the civil rights movement since 1961. She talks to Frank Barat about her past, her present, and her hopes for the future.

Frank Barat: What's your earliest memory?

Angela Davis: I grew up in the Jim Crow South [of the US] at a time when spectacular manifestations of racist violence were the major interruptions of our daily routines. When I was quite young, my parents moved to a neighborhood that was repeatedly attacked by the Ku Klux Klan. The earliest event I can remember was a bombing across the street from our new home. Black people were allowed to move in on the side of the street where we lived, but they were not allowed to purchase property or live on the other side of the street that divided the white zone from the black zone. On several occasions, committed white allies purchased homes in the forbidden zone as surrogates for Black people who were determined to resist the racist zoning laws. One Saturday night when I was close to three years old, I was washing out my white shoelaces that I would need for Sunday school the next day. Suddenly the entire house shook violently. It would have felt like the end of the world, but there was no such conception in my young consciousness. I remember being more frightened than I had ever been and ran screaming to my mother. To this day, whenever I hear loud, explosive noises, I am brought back to that moment.

Barat: What does ageing mean to you?

Davis: As I grow older, I try my best to hold on to the courage, enthusiasm, and willingness to venture into new territory that is most often characteristic of young people. But at the same time I try to draw appropriate lessons from the experiences I have accumulated. For example, I really do understand now the importance of physical, mental, and spiritual self-care. As an older person, I find that a great proportion of the new knowledge I encounter comes from young people. Intergenerational contact is good for us all.

Barat: What are you politically passionate about?

Davis: I could name a number of political issues that are close to my heart—violence against women, the global prison-industrial complex, immigration rights. Palestine solidarity. I am passionate about all of these issues and many others. However, what concerns me today are the connections between these issues. Especially in relation to Palestine. I am especially happy that increasing numbers of African Americans are speaking out against Israeli apartheid.

Barat: Who or what inspires you?

Davis: I have been active around Palestine for most of my life and thought I knew what I needed to know about the subject, until my visit to the West Bank last year. I did not expect to be both shocked by the brazen character of Israeli state repression and immensely inspired by the people who refused to give up, even after many decades of occupations. I was inspired by women activists, former prisoners, educators, and especially by the children, who have learned how to combine a sense of struggling for a better life with an ability to find joy in every day.

Barat: What's your biggest fear?

Davis: My fear right now, as Barack Obama's second term in office begins, is that we will forget that the real victory was not the election of an individual but rather an indication that people in this country really want a change. During Obama's second term, we will have to accelerate our mass mobilizations and our movement building, so that what we considered by itself to be a historic victory will indeed have made a difference in the lives of people who continue to suffer as a result of policies that have led to poverty, mass imprisonment, and war.

Barat: Where do you feel most feel at home?

Davis: I feel at home where there are people who have dedicated their lives to struggling for a world beyond capitalism, racism, and heteropatriarchy.

Interview with Angela Davis

Tony Platt / 2014

From *Social Justice*, vol. 40, no. 1–2, pp. 37–53. Reprinted by permission of Social Justice.

Tony Platt (TP): First of all, I want to thank you, and I appreciate the fact that you made the time to be here. I think you know this is a group of people from several different countries. We have people from graduate programs in law, sociology, social work, and justice studies. We have people coming together for the first time, with state college students and UC students taking the same class and having conversations. So we welcome you to this conversation.

And also on a personal note, I want to thank you for setting a model of being an academic, an intellectual, and an activist, which is not an easy thing to do. You set that model for many, many people, and we appreciate it.

To begin, I noticed that you were fired in 1970 from UCLA for what they called "inflammatory language."

Angela Davis (AD): That was the second time, I think.

TP: But then you came back.

AD: The first time I was fired for being a Communist.

TP: Then they rehired you.

AD: Then I took the case up through the California Supreme Court, and the case was overturned. The second time was "inflammatory language" and conduct unbecoming of a professor.

TP: All I can say is, congratulations. But here you are, a respectable emerita professor from UC Santa Cruz invited back to the university.

AD: I don't know how respectable. I try not to be too respectable.

TP: But you've always been someone who has strived to bring together intellectual work and writing and research with your activism. That has always been an important part of your life.

AD: Yes.

TP: I'd like to start off by asking you something about the earlier part of your life. You grew up in the segregated South, in Birmingham, Alabama, as a young child and a young teen. But you came from an unusual family in that they were politically active. You grew up in that atmosphere. Would you say that obviously race was important to you in that political time and in your family? Was also class and economics an important part of your political training, so to speak, as a teenager?

AD: Absolutely. Because I grew up in what was at that time the most segregated city in the South—Birmingham, Alabama—I couldn't avoid thinking about race. Race was literally everywhere. My mother had become involved before I was born in an organization called the Southern Negro Youth Congress (SNYC). It was an organization created by Black communists who had come down from the Northeast, primarily from New York to organize in the South. Have any of you seen that film called *The Great Debaters* (2007)? Do you remember the scene when Melvin Tolson, the character played by Denzel Washington, is organizing Black and white tenant farmers? Apparently that was based on the work of the SNYC. I found this out because Dorothy Burnham, my mother's best friend (whose daughter is my closest friend), was one of the people who came down to the South. She saw that film and asked me if I knew the history behind it. I said, "Well, not really." She said, "That was our organization. That was the SNYC. That is the work that we did." So class was always involved as well.

TP: So was that unusual among the other young people and teenagers who you knew, to take class and economic issues, as well as racial issues, as seriously as you did? We're talking about the 1950s in the South, in Alabama.

AD: Probably, but you know, when I think about it, I don't think about a discrete position on class and race. I think about them as being connected in a way that makes it impossible to talk about them separately. Of course, years later, when we began to talk, write, and organize around the intersectionality of these various categories, I remembered that this is actually what was being done then. But, of course, not having the same categories with which to work at that time, I did not think about it in the same way.

TP: Did you think of yourself as doing political organizing when you were a teenager?

AD: The first organization I can remember being involved in was an interracial discussion group that took place at the church I attended. I didn't think of myself as an organizer, but I knew there was something very different about doing that work, because the church got burned as a result of our meetings.

TP: What year was that?

AD: I was eleven, so . . .

TP: Was it 1955?

AD: I guess it was. So you know my age! It was probably in the year before the conclusion of the Montgomery bus boycott.

TP: So not just class and race, not just economics and race, but also an interracial politics early on in your life is something you were used to.

AD: Oh, absolutely, yes. I was fortunate because my mother stayed in touch with the Burnham family and other people who had come from New York to Birmingham to organize. Because a number of them were Communists, at some point, they were forced to leave the city by police commissioner Bull Connor, who is most notorious for violently confronting civil rights activists. My mother actually did her graduate work at NYU during the summers. So she would take all us children to New York, and we would stay with the Burnhams, who had an equal number of children in the family. Now when I try to imagine her studying with six and then eight children in the house, it seems impossible. But she got her master's degree in that way. She also made friends, white friends, who sometimes came to visit us in the South. I remember those as being particularly tense times, because it was literally illegal to engage in any kind of interracial intercourse that was not economic in nature. That is to say, a Black person could work for a white person, but a Black person could not be friends with a white person. I can remember very tense moments when her friends would visit us. She would drive them somewhere, and they had to lie down in the back of the car so nobody saw a Black woman driving a white woman.

TP: In your junior year, when you got a scholarship from the American Friends Service Committee and you had some choices of places to go, you had already been to New York with your mother. Is that why you chose New York as the place to go?

AD: Yes, I really fell in love with New York when I was six years old.

TP: The Village, right?

AD: Well, it just so happened that Greenwich Village was the location of the Little Red School House/Elisabeth Irwin High School (LREI). This school was a cooperative run by teachers, many of whom had been kicked out of the public school system because of their politics during the McCarthy era. I very much looked forward to going to New York, although I was tempted to go to Fisk. I had it all worked out. At that time I wanted to be a doctor and received early admittance to Fisk University. I'd graduate from Fisk at nineteen, because I was fifteen at the time. Then I would attend medical school, do my specialties, and be a doctor by the time I was twenty-three [laughter]. But I decided instead to finish high school in New York.

TP: So then, instead of ending up at Fisk, a historically black college, you ended up at a predominantly Jewish college like Brandeis? You must have been one of a handful of African American students on campus when you were there.

AD: Yes. The high school I attended was also predominantly white, with a few Black students here and there. I was interested in a school in the Northeast and thought about Mt. Holyoke. The choice was between Skidmore, Mt. Holyoke, and Brandeis. Brandeis gave me a really nice scholarship, so that helped.

TP: Then began an extraordinary intellectual period in your life. You were at Brandeis, then studied in Paris and Germany, and eventually received a PhD in philosophy in Germany. There you came to know Herbert Marcuse and became one of his graduate students. While this was happening, the movement was erupting and diversifying in the United States. Without going into the long, interesting history of your education, when you finally returned to live in the United States and joined the political movement here, did the Black movement view your education and training, as well as the exposure to French, German, and other colleges, as an asset or a deficit? What kind of situation did it create for you?

AD: No one has ever asked me that question before. It's complicated, because I was seen as an anomaly, I guess. When I first attempted to get involved in Black movements in San Diego, people thought I was an agent. It took me a while to figure out why no one was responding. They said, "Well, she just came from Europe and she did this and she did that, so she must be an agent."

TP: There was a lot of that in those days.

AD: Yes, I went to the World Youth Festival in Helsinki in 1961, just after my first year in college. Gloria Steinem was there, and other people. It turned out that Gloria Steinem was working for a student organization that had ties to the CIA. So it wasn't unusual. Now I totally understand why people assumed that.

TP: Have you seen your FBI record?

AD: Yes, some of it. It's too long.

TP: Do you know what year they started observing and reporting on you? Was it that trip to Helskinki that they are reporting on?

AD: Well, that, but actually I think it begins before that, because when I was very young and a number of my parents' friends were underground during the McCarthy era, we would sometimes be followed by the FBI.

TP: Could you explain the McCarthy period and what it meant to be underground?

AD: I am referring to people who were fleeing the consequences of the Smith-McCarran Act. According to the McCarran Act (or Subversive Activities Control Act of 1950), a communist is defined as someone who wants to violently overthrow the government. The Smith Act required communists to register. So if you registered under the Smith Act, then immediately you would be charged under the McCarran Act. Quite a number of people went to prison during that period. Some people decided that instead of turning themselves in, they would work underground. A number of my parents' friends were underground—James Jackson, for example. We were often followed by the FBI, which apparently believed that we might be in touch with him. One of the most important lessons I learned as a child was never talk to the FBI. You didn't talk to them, because you had no idea what kind of information they were actually seeking. They often lured you into a conversation that you assumed was about one thing, but as a matter of fact, you ended up giving them precisely the information that they wanted. So when I was arrested in 1970, I did not say a single word to the FBI. I am very proud of that.

TP: So, talking about communism, you were an active member of the Communist Party from the 1970s?

AD: Actually, from the late 1960s. I had been involved in a number of organizations, including the Los Angeles Student Nonviolent Coordinating Committee (SNCC) and the Black Panther Party (BPP). It's very complicated. But for reasons you can research if you want, there were major problems within SNCC, especially around the role of women. The same thing happened with the BPP. It was in that context that I joined the Communist Party, precisely at that time.

TP: Because of gender and sexism and other internal problems going on in these organizations?

AD: Yes, but also because I felt the need to be a part of an organization that addressed class as well as race and gender.

TP: You were a public member of that organization, ran for national office on the vice presidential ticket—twice I think—and left the party in 1991. So a big part of your life was as an active organizer in the Communist Party and in communist circles. Reflecting back on that training, history, and participation, how do you talk about it now, given the collapse of the communist world and the debates going on about what we were fighting for then and how we understand that today?

AD: My relationship is still good with what remains of the Communist Party (CP). In fact, last Friday I spoke at election rally in Detroit that was organized by the Communist Party, the Democratic Socialists, and a number of church people. When I think back on that era, what I treasure most about my involvement in the Communist Party was the sense of collectivity and the arena the party provided for engaging in discussions about a range of issues. I never belonged solely to the CP, and was never a functionary. I was always involved in other organizations: for example, the National Alliance Against Racism and Political Repression and the Black Women's Political Caucus, when Shirley Chisholm was in Congress, as well as a number of organizations like that. I've always done my political work primarily in broader organizations.

TP: At that time, a variety of communist and socialist nations existed around the world. We could point to them and ask whether they fit our model or aspirations, what we agreed or disagreed with, and so on. Now we live in a very different world, one lacking real places where such experiments are occurring. Has this profoundly changed your life, as it has those of many other people on the Left? Are you a "recovering communist"?

AD: I don't want to throw the baby out with the bathwater. I want to be critical of communist parties while holding on to what was good and important. I look at Cuba now, and am still very much a supporter. Look at the health-care system there. In the United States, we cannot even begin to meet the challenge that a health-care system poses. So, I don't simply assume that because a particular version of communism or socialism did not work because of the failure to incorporate economic and political democracy, then we must completely let go of the prospect of socialism or communism.

TP: Perhaps we can now shift the conversation to criminology and prisons and the work that has occupied you for a long time. First, you were held in detention. While you were awaiting trial and during your trial, for about eighteen months, you were held in a women's detention center in Marin and then in Palo Alto. Is that right?

AD: The first jail was in New York.

TP: When you were arrested for the first time?

AD: I was there from October until December 1970. Then I was extradited to Marin County and spent about a year in the Marin County Jail.

TP: Were you held in Palo Alto during your trial?

AD: Yes. We obtained a change in venue to San Jose, in Santa Clara County. I was held in a very, very bizarre detention center in Palo Alto. It was a jail that was meant to hold people for a few days, but I was there the entire time.

TP: Did the eighteen months you spent in those three different institutions change your views in any way about the justice system? Did that give you an impetus to start doing political work later on around justice issues and prison issues?

AD: Actually, I was already doing that work. One reason I was arrested was because of the work I was doing to free political prisoners. Among a number of cases were the political prisoners within the Black Panther Party, and especially the Soledad Brothers—George Jackson and the Soledad Brothers. Through my involvement with the Soledad Brothers and George Jackson, I began to think about prison repression in a much broader context. Initially I was thinking only about political prisoners. I was familiar with political prisoners both here in the United States and around the world. As I grew up, people were talking about the Rosenbergs and Sacco and Vanzetti. During high school, I will never forget that Carl Braden and Anne Braden were two of the most courageous white civil rights activists in the South. Carl Braden was sentenced to five years in a federal penitentiary because he and his wife Anne had bought a house for a Black couple in a white neighborhood. He was convicted of having instigated a riot or something like that. I talked with him just before he entered prison, so I had a sense of political imprisonment, but not yet that the prison institution constitutes a mode of racist repression.

TP: During your incarceration, were you able to have conversations with imprisoned people who were not political prisoners?

AD: In New York I was in solitary confinement almost the entire time. People from the outside could visit me, but I did not have much contact with prisoners. The National Conference of Black Lawyers, W. Hayward Burns, and many others came and filed a suit to get me out of solitary confinement. I managed to live in the main population for three weeks, perhaps a little bit longer.

TP: That experience must make you very knowledgeable about what prisoners in Pelican Bay and other similar places are going through in terms of solitary confinement. Did being in solitary affect you?

AD: It did. Normally I wouldn't joke about something like this, but it occurred to me that having been a graduate student for so long really prepared me [laughter]. Because you spend a lot of time reading and writing, often in a solitary situation, and that is basically what I did. I did a lot of reading and writing. I also exercised. I taught myself how to do yoga, and since I had already learned karate, I practiced my katas. I had a way of dealing with solitary confinement that people in other situations probably did not. But I do not mean to minimize the importance of political campaigns against long-term solitary confinement.

TP: So you could get the books you wanted as long as they were sent to you in the right way?

AD: I was my own cocounsel. This is one of the things that law students might be interested in. At the time I wanted to represent myself but had not studied the law. Thus, I needed to have lawyers. Apparently, no one had ever claimed the right to represent oneself and the right to counsel simultaneously. So we had to file a special brief that I wrote with the assistance of Margaret Burnham—the daughter of Dorothy Burnham, the woman I mentioned who went down to the South in the 1930s as a communist organizer. Judge Richard Arneson agreed that it didn't have to be either/or. That was the issue. You could either represent yourself, or you had the right to counsel, but not both. So I said, "I want to represent myself, and I want counsel with me." We successfully made that argument, so I could get whatever books I wanted, since the jail authorities had no right to tell me what would or would not be useful for my case. Interestingly, some of the guards considered paperback books to be storybooks. The rule they wanted to impose was that I could get hardback books, but not paperbacks.

TP: Graduate or law students looking for a paper topic, a research topic, or master's thesis might look at your experience as a counsel. It would be very interesting, don't you think? Has it been done?

AD: The problem is that it took place at the trial level. So it is not in any of the books. I think perhaps something has been done on it. Margaret Burnham, my attorney from the beginning and now a professor at Northeastern School of Law, should know.

TP: In 1975 when I conducted the interview with you that this class read, you said that the movement had a tendency to forget the sisters in prison, and that the prison movement focused mainly on men. Not that their struggle was unimportant, but women tended to be neglected. When did your political work begin to emphasize women's issues, gender, and sexuality? Was this from the beginning? When did you first seriously take this on as a political project?

AD: Interestingly, I hadn't really thought about the fact that there might be differences that one could attribute to gender. It hadn't occurred to me.

TP: Are we talking about 1975 or 1970?

AD: I'm talking about 1970, which marks the beginning of the women's liberation movement. At that time, we didn't even use the term "gender." It was a process. After I had been in jail a few days, it occurred to me that we were missing so much by focusing on only or primarily on political prisoners, and then primarily on *male* political prisoners. Ericka Huggins was one of the few women political prisoners of that era.

During the few weeks that I was in jail in New York, I was in the main population. We actually did some organizing that corresponded to the work that was being done on the outside—a bail fund for women in prison. At that time many women, if they had access to a hundred dollars, would not have to spend so many months behind bars. People were on the outside raising money, and on the inside we would decide who would benefit from those funds. Women released on bail in this way had to make a commitment to work with the organization to raise more money so that more women could get out on bail. Most likely, that is the first organizing around prisons I did that specifically focused on women.

TP: For the last thirty years, this has been a central part of what you write about, do research on, and talk about: issues of sexuality, sexism, and gender differences. This been a central concern for a large part of your life.

AD: Yes. And here we are today addressing what Michelle Alexander has called mass incarceration and what many of us have called the consequences of the prison industrial complex. Because of the number of people behind bars, almost 2.5 million, we tend to assume that given the relatively small percentage of women in prison, it is a male issue. Beyond this question of forgetting those who don't correspond to the male gender, a feminist approach offers a deeper and more productive understanding of the system as a whole. Many of us have argued that if we look very specifically at the situation of women in jails and prisons, we understand the workings of the system in a much more complicated way. We must address issues that otherwise might come up, such as the link between intimate violence and institutional violence. Of course, we can see that connection with respect to men, but if we look at the relationship between the kind of violence women suffer from in the world, we get a deeper sense of how the punishment system works and of the connections—or what I often call the circuits of violence—that move from intimate settings to institutional settings. For me, that is the question, rather than simply a focus on women. It is important to focus on women, but it goes beyond that.

Student: Could you elaborate on the connection between violence against women and institutional violence in the prison industrial complex and how the feminist movement relates to those two issues?

AD: An organization emerged out of the work Critical Resistance and others were doing. It is called Incite!

TP: They have read the dialogue with Critical Resistance.

AD: If you look at Incite!'s website, you see how their work attempts to address intimate violence without relying on law enforcement and imprisonment. If we are serious about prison abolition, we have to ask what criminalization of the perpetration of violence against women has accomplished. It is very interesting that vast numbers of men and others who have engaged in violence against women over the last thirty years or so have been arrested. It used to be that domestic violence was not a matter for law enforcement. Invariably, their response was, "This is a domestic matter." I take that to mean that the state delegated the authority to punish women to the men in their lives, whether their husbands or fathers. But what I want to emphasize now is that with all the work that has been dedicated to the ending of violence against women over the last three decades, the incidence of violence against women has remained the same. All the people arrested, all the organizations and crisis lines around the world have not had an impact on the pandemic of violence that is suffered by women. That means we must think beyond imprisonment as the solution to violence against women. I am trying to restrain myself, because I could speak about these topics for several hours.

Student: Does the institutional violence people experience in prison affect the way they treat women when they leave prison?

AD: Are you referring to male prisoners?

TP: Prisoners are victimized or learn how to victimize others in prison, then in a sense come out and revictimize women they have relationships with.

AD: Yes, I think so. It is a question of how we might eventually eradicate violence against women and children. Where do people who engage in that conduct learn that women can be targeted in that way? For those of you who are law students, it is important to learn the law well. Simultaneously, you must be critical of the law and recognize that it compels us to think about these issues as individualized. The subject of the law is an individual, a rights-bearing individual. How do we move beyond the notions of individual culpability and individual responsibility? Where do people learn this conduct? Where does it come from? Certainly, since we live in a violence-saturated society; there is a connection between violence occurring in intimate relationships and violence in the military, in war, on the street, and by police and vigilantes. In this context last year's discussion about Trayvon Martin was really instructive. For a few months, newspaper articles, television programs, and talked about him so long as George Zimmerman remained at large. As soon as Zimmerman was arrested, it all died down as if the arrest of one individual were sufficient to address an issue that affects individuals but has an historical dimension and certainly concerns communities, not just individuals.

Student: I am taking a constitutional litigation class and would like to add what you are saying. To have standing in front of the court, you must show injury in a way that is highly individualized. For example, third parties cannot bring a suit simply because they have seen injury, the issue really touches home for them, or affects their neighborhoods. Causality must be very direct, and the injury must be to the plaintiff. It is all about the individual. Barriers exist in cases where plaintiffs are trying to change larger schemes, of the way the law is applied, as being unlawful. We cannot even make those cases in front of the court. This I find to be incredibly frustrating. As you are saying, it is a man-made phenomenon, but that is how we are allowed to litigate, and only in that way.

TP: Now that we are discussing more recent issues around prisons and violence, I want to note that in the 1970s you were very active in the National Alliance Against Racist and Political Repression and were focused on political prisoners. About eleven or twelve years ago, you were among the founders of Critical Resistance and started being very active, talking and writing about as well as organizing around issues concerning the long-range abolition—or hopefully the short-range abolition—of prisons, making prison abolition an important part of your political life and being. I will ask Jonathan Simon for specific questions on this.

Jonathan Simon (JS): One theme that has engaged us here is the relationship between grassroots movements and elite opportunities for change, such as Supreme Court decisions or the recent national crisis. I would like to call on your remarkable experiences and observations to consider two moments in time. The first is the relationship between the radical prison movement of the late 1960s and early 1970s, which failed in some ways, and what some have called the mass incarceration that followed. The second seems to be perhaps the line of success between reopening a grassroots struggle in the mid-1990s around this and what seems to be a gradual turn away from mass incarceration at the elite and popular levels today.

Among the letters George Jackson wrote to the *New York Review of Books* in 1970 before the publication of *Soledad Brothers*, one dated June 10, 1970, stated that "black men born in the US and fortunate enough to live past the age of eighteen are conditioned to accept the inevitability of prison." It is remarkable to read that now, knowing that according to Bruce Western's research in *Punishment and Inequality in America*, of the Black men of

George Jackson's generation who did not finish high school, approximately 18 percent went to prison, or nearly one out of five, which nobody is talking about. For that same cohort in 1975, two-thirds of them went to prison, representing a shocking escalation. This represents a remarkable regression in racial justice during these years. Michelle Alexander and others have written about this.

Against that background, I would like you to reflect on two things as an activist, as one of our most observant scholars of social change and social movements. First, from a critical perspective, do you see flaws in the direction of the movement around prisoner rights in the early 1970s? Did a combination of the demonization of George Jackson after his death and the state-produced imagery after Attica help to persuade white America that lockdown was necessary to bring peace to the country? In rethinking the strategies of that period, would another approach have been more effective? Second, by 1996 why did you believe it was an opportune time to start a grassroots movement again centered around prisons?

AD: First of all, whenever we attempt to organize radical movements, we must recognize that all in a sense we can never predict the outcome of our work. As Stuart Hall has said, "There are never any guarantees." At the same time, you have *to act as if it were possible to change the world*; I am rewriting the Kantian categorical imperative here. I don't know whether I would say that the radical prison movement of the late 1960s and 1970s was a failure. New conditions had emerged. For example, we were involved in the campaign against indeterminate sentencing—George Jackson was sentenced to from one year to life for his involvement in a gas station robbery, in which $70 was taken. He was eighteen. We thought that by organizing against indeterminate sentencing we could arrive at something more just. We all assumed that. We could not imagine mandatory minimums. We could not imagine three strikes. That was not the fault of the activists. Perhaps we as activists could have recognized more rapidly what was going on. Often, when we are involved in movements, we have a goal, and we assume that we will know when we get there, right? Often, the changes we make are not necessarily the changes we thought we were going to make. So how do we recognize that fact and that we have also reconfigured the whole terrain of struggle? The way in which the movement brought about unexpected changes became very helpful, because it made it possible to think about issues today in a way that would have been previously impossible.

Over the last few years, I have thought extensively about past union organizing among prisoners and the legal efforts to legitimize union organizing among prisoners. In an amazing 1977 case, *Jones v. North Carolina Prisoners Union*, what was at issue was the right of the prisoners union to organize. The warden of one of the main institutions refused to allow recruiting and organizing to take place and was ordered by a lower court to allow the organizing to proceed. Then the North Carolina department of corrections appealed to the Supreme Court, which overturned the lower court decision. One of the most interesting dissents was by Thurgood Marshall, who strongly favored the right of prisoners to organize unions. In California the United Prisoners Union called for all of the rights union members enjoy, including vacation pay. If you look up the United Prisoners Bill of Rights online, a manifesto outlines all the rights for which they fought. So, here we are, forty years later, and the labor movement writ large has suffered enormous assaults within the context of the globalization of capital. Today, it would be very interesting if some of the major unions were to take up the demand to organize prisoners and prisons. Prisoners continue to do work, are paid practically nothing, and have no rights. This situation seems analogous to the position of labor unions toward Black people early in the 1920s and 1930s, when white labor unions refused to allow Black people to join, while treating them as if they were all potential scabs. A similar situation exits with prison labor. The labor movement totally opposes prison labor, but only because of its effect on labor in the free world. If they were to take up the call to organize—and I have held discussions with some unions on this—it would be amazing. It could begin to address some problems the labor movement faces given the erosion of the unions in context of deindustrialization.

Questions and Comments

JS: Looking back on the history of Critical Resistance, 1996 does not look like a promising moment to start a movement for prisoners who are in some ways at a high-water mark, the high noon of the arc of penal severity that began in the 1970s. This is the moment of Three Strikes, the Prison Litigation Reform Act of 1995 (Eastern District of Pennsylvania), with the state and federal governments becoming just as comfortable as they can be with severely punishing people. It does not look like a promising moment for a grassroots movement about prisons.

AD: Why wouldn't it be promising?

JS: The whole country appears to be mobilized to think about the war on crime as a patriotic duty. Perhaps the best thing the Left could do would be to forget prisons or that we ever talked about prisons. A cynical perspective on that moment would be to move on to a different topic.

AD: Yes. Precisely because of what you articulated, we decided to attempt to bring together people who were doing this work. In 1996 it was very difficult to talk about prison issues. We did not have a public discourse that allowed us to talk about anything except crime in relation to prisoners. Those of us who tried find ourselves to be constantly under attack. So a number of us decided to see what we could do to create a new discursive framework. We thought that a few hundred people were doing the work across the country. In Santa Cruz and in the Bay Area, we formed an organizing committee of about twenty-five to thirty people. We decided to hold a conference in the fall of 1998 on the UC Berkeley campus. Since Mike Davis had written an article in *The Nation* on the California prison industrial complex, on the transformation of agribusiness into prison business, we thought we should try to popularize the term "prison industrial complex." That would at least help people think about the soaring numbers of people being imprisoned in a context that is different from crime. You know, "Do the crime, do the time." We consciously took up the term to transform popular thinking about prisons. We have no idea that we would succeed, relatively speaking—that it would catch on.

JS: Is it accurate to say that five thousand people showed up to that conference? It was much bigger than you expected.

AD: Yes, we were expecting about five hundred people. That was going to be an amazing conference. We had no paid staff; it was volunteer work. We did it all, including typesetting the program. We initially hoped that three hundred would show up. When more interest was shown, we revised the number to five hundred people. Yes, some 3,500 people registered, and many more people came. It was an eye-opener that people from all across the country and other parts of the world wanted to experience community in doing this work. Many people were working in their own communities, in their towns. People from Europe and Australia came.

TP: A lot of ex-prisoners came to the conference?

AD: A lot of ex-prisoners came. It was an amazing organizing experience. We wanted to undo the hierarchy that normally asserts itself when prisoners work together with people in the so-called free world.

TP: Could you explain that further?

AD: We wanted prisoners to play an equal role. We wanted to attempt to create an egalitarian relationship between people who were doing the work in the "free world" and people who were imprisoned, so as to address the "missionary problem"—e.g., we're going to help these poor, poor prisoners. So at the conference we set up telephone numbers that prisoners could use to make collect calls. We amplified that system so that prisoners could talk in the sessions we held. We also looked very carefully at each of the nearly 250 panels and workshops. We sought to avoid all academic journals or all lawyers panels, instead attempting to assure that we had a mix and diversity that could create conversations. We especially encouraged people to move beyond their own language boundaries. Some said that academics like to use big words and so forth, but we pointed out that even organizers often speak a specialized language. If you have never been involved in the movement and hear the word "struggle," what does it mean to you? We therefore asked everybody to be self-reflexive about their manner of expressing themselves. As a result, there were quite amazing cross-talks in the panels.

TP: Did you take on homophobia from the early days of Critical Resistance or was that later?

AD: It began in the early days.

TP: So that was a remarkable change for the movement around prison issues.

AD: Yes, and later transgender issues were addressed, beyond homophobia and issues of gender within a binary framework. Trans people have a greater likelihood of going to jail or prison than is the case for any other group in the country. You must look at the reflections in the institutional framework. How does the prison system itself consolidate a binary notion of gender? How does the prison system contribute to all of the prejudices that people have about those who do not correspond to this binary construction of gender?

Student: You are the first person to speak to us from the perspective of a self-identified abolitionist. What does an abolitionist vision look like today? Would prisons vanish completely or have a greatly reduced role? Also, what is an appropriate response to crime, even if its definition were to change dramatically?

AD: I first encountered the possibility of prison abolition in the 1970s, or perhaps it was in the late 1960s. During the Attica rebellion, which you have discussed, the prisoners in the leadership self-identified as abolitionists. Not long afterwards, a book, *Instead of Prisons: An Abolitionist Handbook*, appears (Critical Resistance republished it, so it is available today). That book was largely produced by Quakers, who, interestingly, were partly responsible for the emergence of the prison in the United States. The move from capital punishment to imprisonment was supposed to be a more humane alternative.

TP: Next week, we are reading *Struggle for Justice: A Report on Crime and Punishment in America*, which was also published by the Friends.

AD: Good. It is interesting that the Quakers introduced this new mode of punishment, which was supposed to allow people to engage in reflection on themselves and establish a relationship with God. Imprisonment and solitary confinement were based on that concept. When it became clear that it did not work, they introduced the notion of the abolition of imprisonment.

There are several ways to talk about this. First, it is helpful to acknowledge the degree to which imprisonment has become naturalized in and through ideological processes. We assume that punishment can only be addressed by imprisonment, forgetting that other forms, such as transportation and the various corporal punishments, preceded it. The history of this institution has been characterized by pendulum swings in terms of reforms. Michel Foucault's *Discipline and Punish*, of which you have read excerpts, points out that reform is at the heart of the history of the prison. We think about calls for reform once the prison had emerged, but actually the prison itself was a call for reform. Throughout its history, calls for prison reform have helped to consolidate the prison, which is not conceivable outside the context of these reforms and calls for reform. Unfortunately, over the years many people assumed that reforms would make the prisons better. In actuality, attempts to improve prisons have so thoroughly entrenched them in our institutions and our ways of thinking that they become the only possible approach to addressing crime. Boundaries are erected and you cannot go beyond the boundaries of the prison. For instance, it does not matter whether rehabilitation works or not within the context of prison. You must still observe those boundaries and talk about rehabilitation. Rehabilitation may be perceived to work in one moment, but then there are calls for more repressive modes of punishment. The pendulum swings back and forth from rehabilitation to repression. In the past few years, we have seen this pendulum effect in California. Nothing changes; it just becomes worse. So how do you imagine ways of addressing harm that do not rely on imprisonment and, in the United States, on the death penalty—for the two are inexorably linked here?

We must imagine solutions that do not respect the boundaries of the prison. If we think that crime or harm should be eradicated, how do we go about doing that? We can't just throw people in prison, since that often reproduces the very problem that you think you are solving. I believe the prison serves as a material institution that hides the real problems, while allowing us to conceptually render those problems invisible. With respect to violence against women, by imprisoning those who commit such violence, you don't have to deal with the problem anymore. In the meantime, it reproduces itself. After being released, as was noted earlier in this conversation, a person will probably be even more inclined to commit violence against others.

How do we find solutions that are not prison based? In Critical Resistance we often talk about moving beyond the footprint of the prison. That institution is so powerful that even the alternatives we propose arise within a context created by the prison itself. Thus, we try to talk about education or health care as alternatives—especially those services should be available to people but have been removed during the era of the dismantling of the welfare state and the rise of the carceral state.

The value of abolitionist approaches are [sic] most clearly visible in the global South, which has suffered structural adjustment. Have you seen that amazing film *Bamako*, directed by Abderrahmane Sissako? The International Monetary Fund [IMF] and the World Bank are placed on trial in a compound in Mali. The film reveals the costs to people's lives when press from the IMF and the World Bank led to the forcible removal of capital from human services and redirected it into profitable arenas. More prisons are being built to catch the lives disrupted by this movement of capital. People who cannot find a place for themselves in this new society governed by capital end up going to prison. In many countries, such as South Africa and Columbia (which I visited last year), demeritorialization is under way to allow agribusiness to expand, thus producing surplus populations. In Colombia people have been removed from their land to make way for sugar cane production for the biofuel consumed by us in the West who wish to minimize our carbon footprint. All the people ejected from that land, who had protected its biodiversity, are being pushed into slums. It is most intense near Cali, in the western part of Colombia, where they are building the largest prison in South America—in part to catch those people who have been deprived of their land and have no source of cash. Thus, the value of abolition is clear in places now acquiring US-style prisons due to shifts in the economy.

Student: At a personal level, I have a political soul fueled by outrage, which often prevents me from living the life I want to and seeing the humanity in everyone—the brotherhood and sisterhood of everyone. Has your political self ever taken over your life, making it difficult to balance the two? That is, to be the person who sees the connection and is hopeful for a difference or change in our society versus the person who is outraged and propelled by that outrage?

AD: Outrage is not the only emotion that political people should experience. Joy is a political emotion as well. Because I grew up the way I did—and I'm just realizing this now—I have never felt that I could engage in the process of severing the political person from whatever is left of the self. Of course, I have different desires at different times. I also become exhausted, but I think that imagination is a political process. I don't express my political aspirations through rage. Perhaps sometimes it is important. For instance, the general elections tomorrow [laughter]. Make sure you vote for the right candidate!

If one is going to engage in this collective struggle over a period of years and decades, one must find ways to imagine a much more capacious political self—in which you experience rage as well as profound community and connections with other people. The humanity you mentioned is something we often lack because we have been persuaded that we are first and foremost individuals. We are in community, and we are, I hope, connected with people across various racial, gender, or natural boundaries. I don't have that problem. Sometimes I have to do other things; for instance, before coming to speak to you, I had to figure out a way to meditate and breathe in my yoga class as well.

JS: Is hope one of those political emotions? How hopeful are you? You talked about the elections tomorrow. A proposition on the ballot to repeal the death penalty has been leading in some polls. Another proposition would reform Three Strikes, though it's inadequate. For the first time in decades, populist movements may be moving the other way. Is this a time of hope for you, either in terms of prisons or more broadly?

AD: I think it is a time of hope. But I keep having a nightmare. You might be too young to remember when Al Gore was running against George W. Bush. We went to bed thinking that Gore had won the presidency and discovered the next morning that he hadn't. So, I'm not going to go to sleep tonight [laughter].

It is a hopeful period, but we should be wary of why some people are coming toward the antiprison movement. We must always be prepared to move one step further. In April 2011 the NAACP released a remarkable report, *Misplaced Priorities: Over Incarcerate, Under Educate*. It draws upon Michelle Alexander's book, which shows that more Black men are in prison, on parole, and under the control of correction agencies today than there were enslaved in 1850. Newt Gingrich and Grover Norquist supported the report. Their belated opposition to mass incarceration is based on their opposition to big government and, by extension, its big prisons. You have to stop and think: Do you really want them as allies?

If we wish to address the crisis of mass incarceration, the government will have to play a much larger role in creating programs and helping to develop the educational system, recreation, and mental health care. This is definitely not what conservative opponents of mass incarceration are seeking.

TP: That's why you chose the name Critical Resistance, which is a fairly unusual name, right? Resistance, we understand; but it is critically minded and wary of different kinds of coalitions and political traps.

AD: We mean critical in two senses: it is critical that we resist; we must be engaged and understand the implications of our resistance. We must be critical in our resistance.

TP: We very much appreciate your critical resistance [applause].

Angela Davis is a well-known author activist, professor emerita at Santa Cruz, and proponent of prison abolition. Tony Platt is the author of *Grave Matters: Excavating California's Buried Past* and a member of the *Social Justice* editorial board. This interview was conducted on the UC Berkeley campus on November 5, 2012, as part of a joint class between the Department of Justice Studies at San José State University and the UC Berkeley Law School. We thank Judy Rosenfeld for transcribing this interview, which has been edited for length and clarity.

Angela Y. Davis on What's Radical in the 21st Century

Patt Morrison / 2014

From *LA Times*. May 6, 2014. © 2014. *Los Angeles Times*. Used with permission.

Forty-five years after her first UCLA teaching gig attracted the wrath of Gov. Ronald Reagan, Angela Y. Davis is back on campus this semester, as regents' lecturer in the gender studies department. Her Thursday address in Royce Hall, about feminism and prison abolition, sums up some but not all of her work—a long academic career paralleled by radical activism. President Nixon called her a "dangerous terrorist" when she was charged with murder and conspiracy after a deadly 1970 courthouse shootout. She was acquitted, and since then, the woman born in the Jim Crow minefield of Birmingham, Ala., has written, taught and lectured around the world. Her iconic afro has morphed from its 1970s silhouette; her intensity has not.

Patt Morrison: Congress is working on prison-sentence reform. Many states have banned capital punishment. Isn't this encouraging?

Angela Davis: I've associated myself with the prison abolition movement; that does not mean I refuse to endorse reforms. There is a very important campaign against solitary confinement, a reform that is absolutely necessary. The difference resides in whether the reforms help to make life more habitable for people in prison, or whether they further entrench the prison-industrial complex itself. So it's not an either-or situation.

Morrison: What would a just prison system look like to you?

Davis: It's complicated. Most of us in the twenty-first-century abolitionist movement look to W. E. B. Du Bois's critique about the abolition of slavery—that it was not enough simply to throw away the chains. The real goal was to re-create a democratic society that would allow for the incorporation of former slaves. [Prison abolition] would be about building a new democracy: substantive rights to economic sustenance, to healthcare; more emphasis on education than incarceration; creating new institutions that would tend to make prisons obsolete.

Morrison: You think prisons won't be necessary one day?

Davis: It is possible, but even [if it doesn't happen], we can move to a very different kind of justice that does not require a retributive impulse when someone does something terrible.

Morrison: Do you watch the prison-themed comedy-drama *Orange Is the New Black*?

Davis: I not only saw the series but I read [Piper Kerman's] memoir. She has a much deeper analysis than one sees in the series, but as a person who has looked at the role of women's prisons in visual culture, primarily films, I think [the series] isn't bad. There are so many aspects that often don't [appear in] depictions of people in those oppressive circumstances. "12 Years a Slave," for example—one thing I missed in that film was some sense of joy, some sense of pleasure, some sense of humanity.

Morrison: You are back this semester at UCLA, the campus from which Gov. Ronald Reagan had you fired.

Davis: This was an offer that I could not refuse. The students are very different from the students of 1969, 1970. They're so much more sophisticated, in the sense of having more complicated questions.

Morrison: When you consider feminism today, do you think women have retreated, except maybe when it comes to boardroom feminism?

Davis: One can talk about multiple feminisms; it is not a unitary phenomenon. There are those who assume feminism is about moving up the hierarchy into positions of power, and that's OK, but that's not what feminism does best. If the women at the bottom move up, the whole structure moves up.

The kind of feminism I identify with is a method of research but also for activism.

Morrison: Stokely Carmichael sort of joked that the position for women in the civil rights movement's Student Nonviolent Coordinating Committee was "prone." Are women full partners in politics today?

Davis: Perhaps not completely, but we have made a lot of progress. In the way we think about past movements, I encourage people to look beyond heroic male figures. While Martin Luther King is someone I revere, I don't like to allow his representation to erase the contributions of ordinary people. The 1955 Montgomery bus boycott was successful because Black women, domestic workers, refused to ride the bus. Had they not, where would we be today?

Morrison: You support free birth control and abortion, which is denounced in some quarters as genocidal.

Davis: Sometimes [in] what might appear to be outlandish statements, we discover there may be a kernel of truth. While I would never argue that birth control or abortion rights constitute genocide, I have to take into consideration how sterilization has been imposed on poor people, especially people of color, and that someone like Margaret Sanger argued [birth control] was a privilege of affluent women but a duty for poorer women.

Morrison: What do you think of the nation's first Black president?

Davis: There are moments of enormous possibility, and the election was such a moment. People all over the world felt as if we were moving toward a new world. However brief that sense of euphoria was, we should not forget that. That allows us to understand what possibilities might reside in the future. [But] many people tended to deposit so many aspirations in this single individual that they failed—we failed—to do the work [to take] better advantage of that moment. People went to the polls and said, "We've done our job," and left it up to Obama.

Morrison: Is democracy a good chassis on which to build a political system?

Davis: I believe profoundly in the possibilities of democracy, but democracy needs to be emancipated from capitalism. As long as we inhabit a capitalist democracy, a future of racial equality, gender equality, economic equality will elude us.

Morrison: You ran for vice president on the Communist Party ticket in 1980 and 1984; was that about faith in the democratic process?

Davis: It was about suggesting that there are alternatives. No one believed it was possible to win, but the eighties [saw] the rise of globalization of capital, the prison industrial complex, and it was important to provide some alternative political analysis.

Morrison: What's your thinking on communism now?

Davis: I still have a relationship, [but] I'm not a member. I left the party because I didn't feel it was open to the kind of democratization that we needed. I still believe that capitalism is the most dangerous kind of future we can imagine.

Morrison: Why did communism fail where it did?

Davis: That would require a long conversation. There may have been economic democracy, which we lack in the West, but without political and social democracy, it just doesn't work. I don't think we should throw the baby out with the bathwater; it would be important to look at what really worked and what didn't.

Morrison: Like free speech?

Davis: Yes.

Morrison: 2016 will be the fiftieth anniversary of the Black Panther Party; you were a member for a time.

Davis: The civil rights movement tended to be focused on integration, but there were those who said, "We don't want to assimilate into a sinking ship, so let's change the ship altogether." The emergence of the Black Panther Party marked a moment of rupture, and we are still in that moment.

The party had two different kinds of activism: grass-roots activism that helped to create institutions that are still working—for example, the Agriculture Department now runs free breakfast programs. On the other hand, the posture of self-defense and monitoring the police.

If one looks at the party ten-point program, every single point is as relevant or more relevant fifty years later. The tenth point includes community control of technology. That was very prescient. It's about using technologies rather than allowing them to use us.

Morrison: Some people must still see in you the young woman who endorsed violence against police, violence in political movements.

Davis: It's important to understand the differences between that era and this era. Our relationship with guns was very different, largely revolving around self-defense. Today, when there's something like 300 million guns in the country, and we've experienced these horrendous shootings, we can't take the same position. I am totally in favor of gun control, of removing guns not only from civilians but also from police.

Morrison: Guns you owned were used in the 1970 kidnapping and shootout at the Marin County Civic Center. You were acquitted of all charges. I read you purchased the guns for self-defense.

Davis: Yes, and I talked about the fact that my father had guns when I was growing up; our families needed to protect themselves from the Ku Klux Klan. We have laws against hate crimes [now]; I am ambivalent about [them], because oftentimes they end up being used against people who were initially the victims. Anti-lynching legislation is issued more against Black kids and so-called gangs. Oftentimes the tools against racism are being used in the service of a kind of structural racism.

Morrison: The documentary *Free Angela and All Political Prisoners* makes much of your relationship with George Jackson, the prison activist killed in Soledad Prison. Too much?

Davis: I would have placed the emphasis elsewhere. If you talk to [director Shola Lynch], you'll see she was working with conventional genres; she sees the film as a political drama, a crime thriller, and a love story. Even so, the research she did was quite amazing. She found archival material I had never seen before. She interviewed one of the FBI agents who arrested me, and in that interview, I discovered how they caught me. I'm impressed by the way the film has affected young people. It can help intergenerational conversations that help teach me something and teach younger people something.

Morrison: What became of the radical, personal, confrontational writing of the 1960s and seventies?

Davis: It's an interesting question. In many ways we were on our own. We were experimenting. Those experiments are important, because without moving into realms about which one knows nothing, there will never be any change.

Morrison: I expect people to say to you, "If you don't like America, why are you here?"

Davis: I have lived in other places, but this is my home, and I feel committed to transforming this country. I have felt that way since I was a child. My mother was an activist believing in the possibilities of transforming the world. I still have not given that up.

This interview was edited and excerpted from a transcription.

Angela Davis: "There Is an Unbroken Line of Police Violence in the US That Takes Us All the Way Back to the Days of Slavery"

Stuart Jeffries / 2014

From *The Guardian*. December 14, 2014. Copyright Guardian News & Media Ltd 2019. Reprinted by permission.

The activist, feminist, and revolutionary explains how the "prison industrial complex" profits from Black people, that Barack Obama can't be blamed for the lack of progress on race, and why Beyoncé is not a terrorist.

"There is an unbroken line of police violence in the United States that takes us all the way back to the days of slavery, the development of the Ku Klux Klan," says Angela Davis. "There is so much history of this racist violence that simply to bring one person to justice is not going to disturb the whole racist edifice."

I had asked the professor, activist, feminist, and revolutionary, the woman whom Nixon called a terrorist and whom Ronald Reagan tried to fire as a professor, if she was angered by the failure of a grand jury to indict a white police officer for shooting dead an unarmed Black man, Michael Brown, in Ferguson, Missouri, earlier this year. "The problem with always pursuing the individual perpetrator in all of the many cases that involve police violence," the seventy-year-old replies, "is that one reinvents the wheel each time, and it cannot possibly begin to reduce racist police violence. Which is not to say that individual perpetrators should not be held accountable—they should."

We're talking at the Friends Meeting House in London before a memorial service to her friend and colleague Stuart Hall, the Black British cultural studies theorist and sociologist, who died in February. It was Hall, she tells me, as much as her mentor, the German Jewish philosopher Herbert Marcuse, who made her think about the structure issues in any given political struggle.

Not that Davis is insensitive to the outrage over specific cases of police violence against Black men, be it the riots in Ferguson, the worldwide protests over the death of Eric Garner in police custody, or Trayvon Martin. Davis focuses on the latter to make an incendiary point about the racism endemic in Obama's America. In 2012, she reminds me, Martin, a Black high school student, was fatally shot at a gated estate in Florida by George Zimmerman, a white neighborhood watch coordinator. Zimmerman, who was later acquitted of Martin's killing, reminds her of "those who were part of the slave patrols during that slave era."

Surely, the lives of African Americans in 2014 are better than during the days of slavery? Yet Davis isn't the only Black American intellectual to be less than sanguine.

Professor Cornel West recently said that the US still has in effect a "Jim Crow criminal justice system" that "does not deliver justice for Black and brown people." Davis agrees, "You have this huge population of people who come up against the same restrictions that the Jim Crow South created," she says. The segregation laws that existed until 1965 in the American South, where she grew up, might have gone, but, as Davis points out, racist oppression remains.

One key feature of the racist oppression, Davis says, is what she and other leftist intellectuals call the "prison industrial complex," the tawdry if tacit alliance between capitalism and a structurally racist state.

"The massive overincarceration of people of color in general in the US leads to lack of access to democratic practices and liberties. Because prisoners are not able to vote, former prisoners in so many states are not able to vote, people are barred from jobs if they have a history of prison."

But, lest Britons get complacent, Davis tells me, "the proportion of Black people in prison in Britain is larger than the proportion of Black people in prison in the United States."

In Davis's philosophy, this should come as no surprise; for her, the prison industrial complex is not just a racist American money-making machine, but a means to criminalize, demonize, and profit from the world's most powerless people. "I think it is important to realize that this is not just a US phenomenon, it's a global phenomenon. The increasing shift of capital from human services from housing, jobs, education, to profitable arenas has meant there are huge numbers of people everywhere in the world who are not able to sustain themselves. They are made surplus, and as a result they are often forced to engage in practices that are deemed criminal. And so prisons pop up all over the world, often with the assistance or private corporations who profit from these populations."

If structural racism and state violence against African Americans, aided and abetted by global capitalism, are as rampant as Davis says, isn't she disappointed in the failure of the US's first African American president to speak out when a case comes up that seems to dramatize what she is indicting? Davis smiles and recalls a conversation she had with Hall two months before his death. "We talked about the fact that people like to point to Obama as an individual and hold him responsible for the madness that has happened.

Of course there are things that Obama as an individual might have done better—he might have insisted more on the closing of Guantánamo—but people who invested their hopes in him were approaching the issue of political futures in the wrong way to begin with. This was something Stuart Hall always insisted on—it's always a collective process to change the world."

Isn't she letting Obama off the hook? "Perhaps we should always blame ourselves," she says. "Why have we not created the kind of movement that would put more pressure on Obama and force the Obama administration to deal with these issues? We might have arrived at a much better health-care plan if those of us who believe health care is a human right were out on the streets, as opposed to the Tea Party."

This is classic Davis—offering bracing analysis that, instead of blaming someone else, puts responsibility for changing the world in our hands. For all that Davis was the late-sixties/early-seventies radical who stuck it to the man, for all that her indomitable spirit and iconic hairdo made her a poster girl for African Americans, feminists, and anyone with a radical consciousness, this is perhaps Davis's key significance now—a woman who comes at the hottest political issues from unexpected and inspiring angles. For instance, the day before we met, at a keynote lecture titled "Policing the Crisis Today," at a conference honoring Hall at Goldsmith's, she spoke about racist violence but focused on the case of Marissa Alexander, jailed for twenty years for firing a warning shot over the head of her estranged, unharmed husband, who attacked and threatened to kill her.

"Let us ask ourselves what is so threatening about a Black woman in the southern United States who attempts to defend herself against so-called domestic violence," said Davis, as she finished her speech to rapturous applause.

Why, I ask Davis, the day after, did you focus on the Alexander case? "We rarely hear about the women," she replies. "Just because the majority of the prison population is male doesn't mean we need to start with their experience."

Davis has long campaigned against prisons, regarding them as brutalizing racist institutions from which, latterly, big bucks are to be made. After her speech, when she is asked why the white cops who shoot Black men shouldn't face jail, Davis stands her ground arguing that the institution of prison "only reproduces the problem it putatively solves." Not that she has any answers about what the alternative to this prison industrial complex might be. "I don't think there's a predetermined answer, but I want us to think."

Someone else asks Davis if Beyoncé is a terrorist. The audience giggles, but the question is serious. During a panel discussion on liberating the Black female body earlier this year, feminist activist bell hooks described Beyoncé as a terrorist and antifeminist who was "colluding in the construction of herself as a slave." In an emollient reply, Davis said that she liked the fact that Beyoncé had sampled Nigerian novelist Chimamanda Ngozi Adichie's speech on feminism on her album.

The following day, I ask Davis more about it. "Whatever problems I have with Beyoncé, I think it is so misleading and irresponsible to use that word in connection with her. It has been used to criminalize struggles for liberation. But we don't use the words terror and terrorism to describe US history and the racism of the pre–civil rights era."

Certainly the terror, if that's the word, that was perpetrated on African Americans when Davis was a girl in pre–civil rights Birmingham, Alabama, is burned into her consciousness. She was born in 1944 in a city that was notorious during the civil rights struggles for setting dogs and turning hoses on African Americans seeking the vote—and much, much worse. "I grew up at a time when, as a response to an interracial discussion group I was involved in, the church where we were having discussions was burned. I grew up at a time where Black people would move into the white neighborhood right across the street from where we lived, and bombs would be set in those houses. I've never heard the word terrorism used in that context, but on the other hand it is used to evoke this sense of danger coming from the outside without ever recognizing the extent to which the history of the United States has been a history of terror against indigenous people, a history of terror against people of African descent."

Davis looks at me and laughs: "So, to call Beyoncé a terrorist just does not work!"

The word terrorist has a deeper personal resonance. That is what President Nixon called Davis when, forty-four years ago, she was one of the FBI's top 10 most wanted, a furtive from so-called justice. She was finally arrested and faced charges of conspiracy to kidnap and murder, charges for which she could have been executed. At her trial in 1972 she was acquitted, while other codefendants, former Black Panthers who she insists are political prisoners, were less fortunate: "My former codefendant Ruchell Magee has been in prison for fifty-one years now." There are many other such political prisoners from that Black Panther era still languishing unjustly in jail, she says. George Jackson, whom she once called her "lifetime" husband (even though the pair never married), is not among them: he was shot dead in 1971 during an attempted prison breakout, three days before he was due to stand trial for the murder of a white prison guard. Davis has not married since.

I ask her about another Black Panther, Albert Woodfox, jailed for armed robbery and later convicted with two other men for the murder of a prison guard at Louisiana State Penitentiary (also known as Angola prison); last month, Woodfox had his conviction overturned after enduring forty-two years in solitary confinement. "Of course, I'm so happy, having been involved in the campaign to free the Angola Three for many, many years, but why has it taken so long?"

If the Black Panthers were active in 2014, Davis believes, "they'd be on the receiving end of the war on terror." She cites Assata Shakur, the activist and Black Panther supporter who was convicted as an accomplice to the murder of a New Jersey state trooper and was put on the FBI's Most Wanted list earlier this year. "I think that the move to designate Assata a terrorist and to post a $2 million reward for her capture, which means that any of the mercenaries from the new privatized security firms might try to travel to Cuba [where Shakur has been living for thirty-five years], capture her, and bring her back for the $2 million reward, that is not so much an attack on Assata, which it is—but it sends out a message to vast numbers of young people who identify with her. Her autobiography is very popular, and it seems to me that there is the message to young people today: "Watch out! If you get involved in progressive struggles, radical movements, this is how you will be treated—you will be treated as a terrorist.""

Still, Davis thinks young people are made of sterner stuff than to be browbeaten by a terrorizing state. "I'm very, very hopeful. I hear people repeatedly referring to the apathy of young people, but there are probably more people who are actively involved in radical political projects in the US today than there were in the 1960s."

She takes particular succor from the Occupy movement, at whose encampments she spoke repeatedly in 2011. "They didn't know necessarily where they were going, but they did know they were standing up to capitalism." For a veteran communist (Davis stood twice as vice-presidential candidate for the Communist Party USA in the 1980s), that anticapitalism is especially heartening. "I think the influence of Occupy will continue even though the encampment could only exist for a very defined period of time. One can see the influence of Occupy in the Ferguson demonstrations now, in the sense that they recognize that it's not only about demanding that this one individual cop be convicted, but it's also about recognizing the connection between racist violence and the profit machine. That's what we're fighting against."

The Radical Work of Healing: Fania and Angela Davis on a New Kind of Civil Rights Activism

Sarah van Gelder / 2016

This article was originally published by YES! Media. February 18, 2016. © YES! Media 2016. www.yesmagazine.org. https://www.yesmagazine.org/issues/life-after-oil/the-radical-work -of-healing-fania-and-angela-davis-on-a-new-kind-of-civil-rights-activism-20160218. Sarah van Gelder is a cofounder and editor at large of *YES!*

Sarah van Gelder wrote this article for Life after Oil, the Spring 2016 issue of *Yes!* magazine. Sarah is cofounder and editor at large of *Yes!* Follow her on Twitter @sarahvangelder.

Angela Davis and her sister Fania Davis were working for social justice before many of today's activists were born. From their childhood in segregated Birmingham, Alabama, where their friends were victim of the 16th Street Baptist Church bombing, to their association with the Black Panther Party and the Communist Party, to their work countering the prison-industrial complex, their lives have centered on lifting up the rights of African Americans.

In 1969 Angela Davis was fired from her teaching position at UCLA because of her membership in the Communist Party. She was later accused of playing a supporting role in a courtroom kidnapping that resulted in four deaths. The international campaign to secure her release from prison was led by, among others, her sister Fania. Angela was eventually acquitted and continues to advocate for criminal justice reform.

Inspired by Angela's defense attorneys, Fania became a civil rights lawyer in the late 1970s and practiced into the mid-1990s, when she enrolled in an indigenous studies program at the California Institute of Integral Studies and studied with a Zulu healer in South Africa. Upon her return, she founded Restorative Justice for Oakland Youth. Today she is calling for a truth-and-reconciliation process focused on the historic racial trauma that continues to haunt the United States.

Sarah van Gelder: You were both activists from a very young age. I'm wondering how your activism grew out of your family life, and how you talked about it between the two of you.

Fania Davis: When I was still a toddler, our family moved into a neighborhood that had been all white. That neighborhood came to be known as Dynamite Hill, because Black families moving in were harassed by the Ku Klux Klan. Our home was never bombed, but homes around us were.

Angela Davis: Fania is probably too young to remember this, but I remember that strange sounds would be heard outside, and my father would go up to the bedroom and get his gun out of the drawer, and go outside and check to see whether the Ku Klux Klan had planted a bomb in the bushes. That was part of our daily lives.

Many people assume that the bombing of the 16th Street Baptist Church was a singular event, but actually there were bombings and burnings all the time. When I was eleven and Fania was seven, the church we attended, the First Congregational Church, was burned. I was a member of an interracial discussion group there, and the church was burned as a result of that group.

We grew up in an atmosphere of terror. And today, with all the discussion about terror, I think it's important to recognize that there were reigns of terror throughout the twentieth century.

Sarah: So where were you when you heard the 16th Street Baptist Church bombing that happened?

Fania: I was attending high school in Glen Ridge, New Jersey. And I didn't take no stuff from nobody. I was always talking about James Baldwin or Malcolm X, and always bringing up issues of racial equity and justice.

I heard about the bombing when my mother told me that one of the girls' mother had called her up—because they were close friends—and said, "There's been a bombing at the church. Come ride down with me so we can get Carole, because Carole's at church today." And they drive down together, and she finds that there is no Carole, she's been . . . there's no body even. I think it fueled this fire, the fire of anger, and just made me determined to fight injustice with all of the energy and strength that I could muster.

Sarah: Can you say more about what everyday life was like for you growing up?

Angela: We went to segregated schools, libraries, churches. We went to segregated everything!

Fania: Of course, in some ways it was a good thing that we were very tight as a Black community.

When we went outside of our homes and communities, the social messaging was that you're inferior: You don't deserve to go to this amusement park because of your color or to eat when you go downtown shopping. You must sit in the back of the bus.

At the same time, at home, our mother always told us, "Don't listen to what they say! Don't let anybody ever tell you that you're less than they are."

And so I found myself—even as a ten-year-old—just going into the white bathrooms and drinking out of the white water fountains, because from a very early age I had a fierce sense of right and wrong. My mother would be shopping somewhere else in the store, and before she knew it, the police were called.

Sarah: Let's skip ahead to when it became clear that you, Angela, were going to need a whole movement in your defense. And Fania, you ended up spending years defending her.

Fania: Yeah, about two years.

Angela: In 1969 I was fired from a position in the philosophy department at UCLA. That's when all the problems started, and I would get threats, like, every single day. I was under attack only because of my membership in the Communist Party.

Fania: Angela had been very involved with prison-rights activism at the time, leading demonstrations up and down the state. And then she was all over the news: "Communist Fired from Teaching at UCLA," you know, "Black Power Radical."

Angela: Then in August 1970, I was charged with murder, kidnapping, and conspiracy. And so I had to go underground. I found my way to Chicago, then to New York and Florida, and finally I was arrested in New York in October. It was during the time that I was underground that the campaign really began to develop.

Sarah: So, Fania, when did you turn your focus to supporting your sister's cause?

Fania: The night before I left Cuba, I found out that she had been captured. So instead of going home to California, I immediately went to where Angela was in the Women's House of Detention in Greenwich Village.

Angela: All of my friends and comrades began to build the campaign. Once I was arrested and extradited, they all moved up to the Bay Area.

We were active in the Communist Party, and, you know, whatever criticism one might have of the Communist Party, we could go anywhere in the world and find people with whom we had some kinship, and people opened their homes.

It was the party that was the core of the organizing for my release, and the movement was taken up by students on campus and church people.

This happened all over the world. Every time I visit a place for the first time, I always find myself having to thank people who come up to me and say, "We were involved in your case."

Sarah: Did you know that there was that kind of support happening?

Angela: I knew, and I didn't know. I knew abstractly, but Fania was the one who traveled and actually got to witness it.

Fania: Yeah, I was speaking to sixty thousand people in France and twenty thousand in Rome, London, and East and West Germany, all over the world, and seeing this massive movement to free her.

Angela: It was an exciting era, because people really did believe that revolutionary change was possible. Countries were getting their independence, and the liberation movements were going on, and there was this hope all over the world that we would bring an end to capitalism. And I think that I was fortunate to have been singled out at a moment of conjuncture of a whole number of things.

Sarah: Your work since that time has centered on the criminal justice system. Are you both prison abolitionists?

Angela: Oh, absolutely! And it's exciting to see that the notion of abolition is being broadly embraced not only as a way to address overincarceration, but as a way to imagine a different society that no longer relies on repressive efforts of violence and incarceration.

Abolition has its origin in the work of W. E. B. Du Bois and the idea that slavery itself was dismantled but the means of addressing the consequences of that institution were never developed. In the late 1800s, there was a brief period of racial reconstruction that shows up the promise of what might have been. Black people were able to generate some economic power, start newspapers and all kinds of businesses. But all of this was destroyed with the reversal of Reconstruction and the rise of the Ku Klux Klan in the 1880s.

Fania: Yeah, we abolished the institution of slavery, but then it was replaced by sharecropping, Jim Crow, lynching, convict leasing. The essence of the racial violence and trauma that we saw in the institution of slavery and in those successive institutions continues today in the forms of mass incarceration and deadly police practices.

Angela: We're taking up struggles that link us to the antislavery abolitionists, and the institutions of the prison and the death penalty are the most obvious examples of the ways in which slavery has continued to haunt our society. So it's not only about getting rid of mass incarceration, although that's important. It's about transforming the entire society.

Sarah: How might restorative justice help with this transformation?

Fania: A lot of people think that restorative justice can only address interpersonal harm—and it's very successful in that. But the truth and reconciliation model is one that's supposed to address mass harm to heal the wounds of structural violence. We've seen that at work in about forty different nations; the most well-known is, of course, the South African Truth and Reconciliation Commission.

In South Africa, the commission invited victims of apartheid to testify, and, for the first time ever, they told their stories publicly. It was on all the radio stations, in all the newspapers, it was all over the television, so people would come home and tune in and learn things about apartheid that they had never known before. There was an intense national discussion going on, and people who were harmed felt vindicated in some way.

That kind of thing can happen here, also, through a truth and reconciliation process. In addition to that sort of hearing commission structure, there could be circles happening on the local levels—circles between, say, persons who were victims of violence and the person who caused them harm.

Angela: How does one imagine accountability for someone representing the state who has committed unspeakable acts of violence? If we simply rely on the old form of sending them to prison or the death penalty, I think we end up reproducing the very process that we're trying to challenge.

So maybe we can talk about restorative justice more broadly? Many of the campaigns initially called for the prosecution of the police officer, and it seems to me that we can learn from restorative justice and think about alternatives.

Sarah: Fania, you told me when we talked last year that your work on restorative justice actually came about after you went through a personal transition period in the mid-1990s, when you decided to shift gears.

Fania: I reached a point where I felt out of balance from all of the anger, the fighting, from a kind of hypermasculine way of being that I had to adopt to be a successful trial lawyer. And also from around thirty years of the hyperaggressive stance that I was compelled to take as an activist—from being against this and against that, and fighting this and fighting that.

Intuitively, I realized that I needed an infusing of more feminine and spiritual and creative and healing energies to come back into balance.

Sarah: How did that affect your relationship as sisters?

Fania: My sister and I had a period—right in the middle of that—when our relations were strained for about a year, due in part to this transformation. It was very painful. At the same time, I finally understood that it needed to happen because I was forging my own identity separate from her. I had always been a little sister who followed right in her footsteps.

Yeah, and so now we are coming close again. And she's becoming more spiritual.

Angela: I think our notions of what counts as radical have changed over time. Self-care and healing and attention to the body and the spiritual dimension—all of this is now a part of radical social justice struggles. That wasn't the case before.

And I think that now we're thinking deeply about the connection between interior life and what happens in the social world. Even those who are fighting against state violence often incorporate impulses that are based on state violence in their relations with other people.

Fania: When I learned about restorative justice, it was a real epiphany, because it integrated for the first time the lawyer, the warrior, and the healer in me.

The question now is how we craft a process that brings the healing piece together with the social and racial justice piece—how we heal the racial traumas that keep reenacting.

Angela: I think that restorative justice is a really important dimension of the process of living the way we want to live in the future. Embodying it.

We have to imagine the kind of society we want to inhabit. We can't simply assume that somehow, magically, we're going to create a new society in which there will be new human beings. No, we have to begin that process of creating the society we want to inhabit right now.

Sarah van Gelder wrote this article for Life After Oil, the Spring 2016 issue of Yes! Magazine. Sarah is cofounder and editor at large of Yes! Follow her on Twitter.@sarahvangelder.

Additional Resources

Anthology of Angela Davis's Writings

James, Joy, ed. *The Angela Y. Davis Reader*. Blackwell, 1998.

Additional Interviews of Angela Davis

Abolition Democracy: Beyond Empire, Prisons, and Torture. Interviews with Angela Davis. Seven Stories Press, 2005.

"Angela Davis Talks about Her Future and Her Freedom." *Jet*, July 27, 1972, vol. 42, no. 18, pp. 54–57, Angela Y. Davis Collection, Stuart A. Rose Manuscript, Archives, and Rare Book Library, Emory University.

"Angela Davis Works to Bring Change in Prison System," by Robert A. DeLeon. *Jet*, May 16, 1974, vol. 46, no. 8, pp. 12–18, Angela Y. Davis Collection, Stuart A. Rose Manuscript, Archives, and Rare Book Library, Emory University.

Barat, Frank. "Ferguson Reminds Us of the Importance of Global Context." In *Freedom Is a Constant Struggle: Ferguson, Palestine, and the Foundations of a Movement*, edited by Frank Barat. Haymarket Books, 2016, pp. 13–30.

Barat, Frank. "Progressive Struggles against Insidious Capitalist Individualism." *Freedom Is a Constant Struggle: Ferguson, Palestine, and the Foundations of a Movement*, edited by Frank Barat. Haymarket Books, 2016, pp. 1–11.

Barat, Frank. "We Have to Talk about Systemic Change." *Freedom Is a Constant Struggle: Ferguson, Palestine, and the Foundations of a Movement*, edited by Frank Barat. Haymarket Books, 2016, pp. 31–49.

"Coalition Building among People of Color: A Discussion with Angela Y. Davis and Elizabeth Martinez." *The Angela Y. Davis Reader*, edited by Joy James, 297–306. Blackwell, 1998.

"Interview Angela Davis." *Frontline*. PBS. https://www.pbs.org/wgbh/pages/frontline/shows/race/interviews/davis.html.

"A Look at Angela Davis from Another Angle: Her Jail Cell," by Robert DeLeon." *Jet*, February 24, 1972, vol. 41, no. 22, pp. 8–14. Angela Y. Davis Collection, Stuart A. Rose Manuscript, Archives, and Rare Book Library, Emory University.

Lowe, Lisa. "Reflections on Race, Class, and Gender in the USA." *The Angela Y. Davis Reader*, edited by Joy James, 307–25. Blackwell, 1998.

"Prison Interviews." *If They Come in the Morning: Voice of Resistance*, edited by Angela Y. Davis et al., 177–88. Third Press, 1971.

White, Dan. "Toni Morrison and Angela Davis on Friendship and Creativity." UC Santa Cruz Newscenter. October 29, 2014. https://news.ucsc.edu/2014/10/morrison-davis-q-a.html.

Yancy, George. "Angela Y. Davis." *African American Philosophers: 17 Conversations*, edited by George Yancy, 13–30. Routledge, 1998.

Books/Articles about Angela Davis and/or Her Writings

Aptheker, Bettina. *The Morning Breaks: The Trial of Angela Davis*. 2nd ed. Cornell University Press, 1999.

Ards, Angela A. *Words of Witness: Black Women's Autobiography in the Post-Brown Era*. University of Wisconsin Press, 2015.

Bosničová, Nina. "Transgressive Black Female Selfhood." *Brno Studies in English* 37, no. 2 (2011): 31–40. *MLA International Bibliography*, doi: 10.5817/BSE2011–2–3.

Braxton, Joanne M. "Autobiography and African American Women's Literature." In *The Cambridge Companion to African American Women's Literature*, edited by Angelyn Mitchell and Danille K. Taylor, 128–49. Cambridge University Press, 2009.

Brown, Kimberly Nichelle. *Writing the Black Revolutionary Diva: Women's Subjectivity and the Decolonizing Text*. Indiana University Press, 2010.

Bruzek, Alison, and Deborah Becker. "Angela Davis' Archive Finds a New Home at Harvard." Radcliffe Institute for Advanced Study, Harvard University. Radio Boston WBUR.org. February 20, 2018. https://www.radcliffe.harvard.edu/news/in-news /angela-davis-archive-finds-new-home-harvard.

Crane, Lisa L. "Guide to Angela Davis Materials, 1970–1972." Online Archives of California. oac.cdlib.org/findaid/ark:/13030/c8br8vch/entire_text/.

Danielle, Britni. "Angela Davis to Receive the Birmingham Civil Rights Institute's Highest Honor." *Essence*, October 22, 2018. https://www.essence.com/news/angela-davis -to-receive-the-birmingham-civil-rights-institutes-highest-honor/.

Hampton, Dina. *Little Red: Three Passionate Lives through the Sixties and Beyond*. Public Affairs, 2013.

"Honorary Co-Chairs." Women's March. https://www.womensmarch.squarespace.com /honorary-cochairs.

James, Robin. "On Popular Music in Postcolonial Theory." *Philosophia Africana* 8, no. 2 (August 2005), pp. 171–187. *MLA International Bibliography*, http://ezproxy.libraries .wright.edu/login?url=https://search.ebscohost.com/login.aspx?direct=true&db=mzh &AN=2008397289&site=ehost-live&scope=site On Popular Music in Postcolonial Theory.

Kaplan, Alice. "Dreaming in French." *The Nation*. April 2, 2012, pp. 35–45, *Academic Search Complete*, http://ezproxy.libraries.wright.edu/login?url=https://search.ebsco host.com/login.aspx?direct=true&db=a9h&AN=73500346&site=ehost-live&scope =site.

Kaplan, Alice. *Dreaming in French: The Paris Years of Jacqueline Bouvier Kennedy, Susan Sontag, and Angela Davis*. University of Chicago Press, 2012.

Locke, Angela. "Angela Davis: Not Just a Fair-Weather Activist." *Off Our Backs* 37, no. 1, (2007): 66–68. *MLA International Bibliography*, http://ezproxy.libraries.wright.edu /login?url=https://search.ebscohost.com/login.aspx?direct=true&db=mzh&AN=2009 651529&site=ehost-live&scope=site Angela Davis: Not Just a Fair-Weather Activist.

Lowe, Lisa. "Reflections on Race, Class, and Gender in the USA." In *The Angela Y. Davis Reader*, edited by Joy James, 307–25. Blackwell, 1998.

Marquez, Letisia. "Angela Davis Returns to UCLA Classroom 45 Years after Controversy." UCLA Newsroom. May 5, 2014. http://newsroom.ucla.edu/stories/angela -davis-returns-to-ucla-classroom-45-years-after-controversy.

Mostern, Kenneth. *Autobiography and Black Identity Politics: Racialization in Twentieth-Century America*. Cambridge University Press, 1999.

Neumann, Caryn E. "Angela Davis." Encyclopedia of Alabama. http://www.encyclopedia ofalabama.org/article/h-1427.

"The Ones We Have Been Waiting For." *Bryn Mawr Alumnae Bulletin*. Summer 2018, p. 14.

Perkins, Margo V. *Autobiography as Activism: Three Black Women of the Sixties*. University Press of Mississippi, 2000.

"Presidential Lecture Series." Wright State University. https://www.wright.edu/event /presidential-lecture-series/profile/angela-davis-phd.

"Speakers." Women's March. https://www.womensmarch.squarespace.com/speakers.

Films/Movies with Interviews of Angela Davis

American Revolutionary: The Evolution of Grace Lee Boggs. Directed by Grace Lee. 2013. *YouTube*, uploaded by YouTube Movies, January 13, 2015. https://www .youtube.com/watch?v=w2-e8eERg_c.

"Angela Davis." Alternative Radio. https://www.alternativeradio.org/ speakers/angela -davis/.

The Black Power Mix Tape, 1967–1975. Directed by Göran Hugo Olsson. *YouTube,* uploaded by YouTube Movies. November 26, 2012. https://www.youtube.com/watch ?v=FWb5HVAAQz0&t=22s

Free Angela & All Political Prisoners. Directed by Shola Lynch. Lionsgate. 2013. DVD. WSU Library Catalog.

"From the Vault." Pacifica Radio Archives. fromthevaultradio.org/home/ftv-459-angela -davis-a-lifetime-of-revolution/.

Mountains That Take Wing. Women Make Movies. Dir. C.A. Griffith and H. L. T. Quan. QUAD Productions. 2009. https://www.filmsforaction.org/watch/mountains-that -take-wing-angela-davis-and-yuri-kochiyama-trailer/.

A Place of Rage. Women Make Movies. 200?/ 1991. Dir. Pratibha Parmar. WSU Library Catalog.

13th. Directed by Ava Du Vernay. Netflix Studios. 2016. https://www.netflix.com/watch /80091741?trackid=142777281&tctx=97%2C-97%2C%2C%2C%2C.

Index

About the Editor

Photo courtesy of Wright State University, William Jones

Sharon Lynette Jones is professor of English language and literatures at Wright State University in Dayton, Ohio. She earned a bachelor's degree from Clemson University, a master's degree from Clemson University, and a PhD from the University of Georgia. She is the author of *Rereading the Harlem Renaissance: Race, Class, and Gender in the Fiction of Jessie Fauset, Zora Neale Hurston, and Dorothy West* and *Critical Companion to Zora Neale Hurston: A Literary Reference to Her Life and Work*. She is coeditor with Rochelle Smith of *The Prentice Hall Anthology of African American Literature*, and she is editor of *Critical Insights: Zora Neale Hurston*.

Printed in the United States
by Baker & Taylor Publisher Services